From The Highlands To The Himalayas

Jim Wilson

To MAUREEN

Publish & Print
www.publishandprint.co.uk

ISBN: 9798728454687

Acknowledgements

Thanks to my wife Margaret for her support and assistance in compiling these stories - and she is in one!

To Marguerite Robertson who took part in all these adventures

To my son Alastair for creating my website where more colour photographs reside of all my trips

To Maggie McGeary for her help in editing this book

Contents

Introduction

This first trip had been planned for ages, after listening to a guy in the Crown Hotel in Carluke, close to my hometown of Lanark. He had walked in the Annapurna Region in Nepal and raved about it. Our club had just finished a meeting in the hotel, and this guy asked if we had been to Nepal. None of us had. In the following months, half a dozen members of my club, the Upperward Mountaineering Club - we are really a hill-walking club - were enthused and going later that year. We had been talking to KE Adventure in Kendal about joining them for a trek to Everest Base Camp and we planned to go in October 2002. Then there was the Maoist insurrection and KE Adventure who we had planned going with couldn't run it, as the Foreign Office advised against all travel and so we would not get insurance. That meant waiting another year but gave me plenty of time to worry more about altitude sickness and the dreadful illnesses it is possible to pick up in Nepal. I read as much as I could, I got the pretty poor maps that there were then and we searched for someone to guide us. We also decided that since this would be an once-in-a-lifetime experience, we should not just trek but climb a Himalayan mountain as we were mountaineers! We were all in our early fifties and we didn't want to leave it too late either.

However the Maoist threat didn't go away, but it did diminish to the extent the Foreign Office relaxed restrictions. In our club at that time was a chap called Hamish. He had been a Gurkha officer and still had good contacts in Nepal. He 'obtained' confidential army reports about expected guerrilla activity including bombing of bridges and police stations. That put people off again, understandably. However, that year, three of us were determined to go but with White Peak Expeditions this time. Despite the Foreign Office cautions. And we would climb a mountain, Island Peak - at just over 20,000 feet! None of the three of us had been higher than Ben Nevis at 4,400 feet so it would be a challenge. John, the MD of the expedition company arranged a meeting of the expedition group in North Wales over a week-end in late summer and we climbed Snowdon for John to assess our fitness.

We got to meet the team and had a discussion about the trip, which I thought was really useful. We also bought some new equipment that John had recommended. The team were: Neil,

Derek, Diane and us three, Davy, Marguerite and myself, and led by John. Now the three of us were pretty fit and my two companions were, arguably the fittest two people in our club at the time and had climbed all the Munros, but we had no experience of altitude or climbing anywhere outside the UK. We would need immunisations for Typhoid, Hepatitis A and Diphtheria. My doctor checked my blood pressure and suchlike and my dentist X-rayed my fillings - if air is trapped in them it will expand at altitude and be very painful. John will bring a medical bag with medicine for altitude sickness. I decided I will take my old manual Pentax ME with slide film as well as my new Fuji digital camera, as there is a risk the digital camera's IBM Microdrive won't spin in thin air. Oh, and you can't risk drinking the water so I needed iodine tablets too.

Most of the climbing equipment we needed, we already had, such as harnesses, slings, karabiners, ice-axe and crampons. Although we had figure of eight descenders, John said we would need ascenders - or jumars - too, so they were bought at our weekend in Wales. We would need some practice with these. They clip onto a fixed rope and by a ratchet can only be pushed up the rope by squeezing the handle for you to pull yourself up, then release it to secure you on the rope. We were fit and experienced at climbing in Scotland but as our Visas arrived, increasingly I thought we had signed up for something that was maybe just beyond at least my capability. With our new ascenders, we practised that winter on Tinto, our local hill, on the steeper slopes with ropes and ice-axes. I was also aware that most expeditions to the Himalayas fail to get to the summit and we were neither heroes nor experts and, of course, illness and bad weather are factors we couldn't control.

Book One

Expedition to Climb Island Peak (Imja Tse) Nepal 2003

Sunday 5th October.

We left Edinburgh early Sunday afternoon to fly to Heathrow. At check-in, the guy turns out to be Nepalese and has spotted the labels on our bags. He was delighted we are going there and recommends a few pubs, writing them down for us. At Heathrow, we transferred ourselves to Terminal 3 with two trolleys for our bags and got checked in for our evening Gulf - Air flight to Abu Dhabi. I didn't sleep on the flight despite a couple of glasses of wine. We had a four-hour wait there for our next flight to Kathmandu and I got a seat on the right hand side - as our man in Edinburgh said to us we would get a view of the Himalayas that way. Our bags are booked straight through and I realised my eight slide films are in Davy's expedition bag. Need to sort that at the hotel in Kathmandu. The flight to Kathmandu must have been 90% Nepalese workers going home and the rest, trekkers like us. I had great views of the Himalayas as we descended through mist into Kathmandu. We arrived ahead of schedule but it was a bumpy landing though and some big scary, white mountains in the distance.

John was at the airport to meet us. Thank goodness! Getting our luggage took ages and everything looks disorganised. Chaotic in fact! We had a driver and helper who took the luggage and put a garland of celebratory marigolds - a 'mallas' - around each of our necks to welcome us. Our bags were slung up onto the roof bars. The minibus is ancient and the roads poor but crowded with traffic - cars, motorbikes and pedestrians all on some very narrow streets.

Monday 6th October.

It was Monday night and I hadn't slept much since Saturday night. Although I'm looking forward to getting to the hotel, John says we have all been invited to the Sherpa Society for welcome drinks as John sources his guide and porters through the Society. I don't relish the prospect of a late night, but we can't pass on their invitation. As we arrive at the hotel, my spirit sinks. It has shuttered-up shops outside it and it's all very gloomy - until we turn into the rear that is, where a uniformed guard opens the gate with a salute and it all looks pretty good! I have a room on my own with private facilities and I have a quick shower and change. I have to get my gear into two bags - one for clothes and one kit-bag for the climbing gear. My large bag will remain at the hotel with a change of clothes for my return.

We meet down in the lobby and have some tea before leaving - good to meet the full team again. They have all had an extra day in Kathmandu and seem quite relaxed. We are in the minibus and into the warm Kathmandu night. Everyone looks better than they did in Wales! I realise that the slide films are still in Davy's bag and decide I'll get them in the morning. Everyone is very polite at the Sherpa Society and we meet John's Nepali organiser. We have some drinks and then she announces that she would like to take us for supper to a Newari family - hers - for more hospitality but she is worried we might not like the food. We go anyway. Only a short drive and our driver is already waiting on us. At the house, we take our shoes off and go in to be welcomed by six or seven of the family. There are not enough seats and some of us sit on the floor. We are introduced to rakshi, poured from an ornate pot, like a teapot into small metal bowls. I think it's a bit like grappa and it certainly tastes home-made. Then the food arrives - small portions but umpteen courses and none of the family are eating while we are. They don't eat with non-Hindus. We all get a blob of red dye on our foreheads, from the grandmother. It is made from a sort of paste with vermillion to colour it and called a 'Tika' I think. The red dye mark would still be there the next day. John reminds us to accept food and eat with only our right hand!

Other family members come and go and we have beer now as well. The banter is good and some of them speak good English. They are glad to tell us about their customs and their beliefs. It's hard to believe that most of them stay in this relatively small apartment. With some flourish, we finish the rakshi, the local firewater and it's time for us to go. Their hospitality - to strangers - and their desire to share their food and drink is wonderful and gives all of us a good feeling to be in Nepal. On the way back, some of the streets look apocalyptic, with fires burning in the dark streets and scraggy cows, which are of course sacred, wandering about. No street lights here at all.

Back at the hotel I re-pack the bags. I will take one kit bag, which John bought for me here for a fiver - it's a fake North Face - and the climbing gear will now go into his gear bag. My rucksack still feels too heavy for the plane but I don't want to overload my kit bag, as a porter will have to carry it for a few weeks. There is water, apparently drinkable, in a jug in the room, but I give it the iodine treatment anyway before drinking almost all of it. All of the water here is treated as suspect and even some of the bottled water can be contaminated. I set the alarm as we are away at eight but then can't get to sleep for ages! Adrenaline!

Tuesday 7th October.

After a quick shower I was down for breakfast and it was surprisingly good, with a varied buffet. We all ate well and completed documents for the British Embassy confirming we were in the country for three weeks. John ran out of forms and my details went on the back of someone else's. Not reassuring at this early stage! I also changed some British money for rupees as you can't buy Nepalese currency at home. We re-packed some of the climbing gear into John's gear bag to reduce the individual weight. I was still sure my bag was too heavy. The boys are already in the hotel lobby and we get our bags up onto the minibus roof. Our passports are left at the hotel in individual safe deposit boxes, but we all carry photocopies. I leave my mobile, as there is no signal anywhere as well as some British money. My large, travelling kit-bag is left with the porter with a set of clean clothes for my return. The Sherpa Society is looking after our flight tickets to re-confirm our flights home. I have my cash in a money belt for safety, but actually never wear it again on the trip after today.

The journey to the airport is the first I have seen of Kathmandu in the daylight. We go through very crowded and often very narrow streets. At the approach to the domestic airport there is some army presence and a Scout armoured car, which must be a collector's item. I had a Corgi model of one at primary school just like it! The airport is total chaos, and packed, and I'm glad John and the porters know their way about. All of our bags are weighed together on a giant Avery scale, like old railway scales, although bigger. The biggest scale I've seen. The bags are piled to about six feet, so no worries that any individual bag is too heavy! We get our 'Yeti Airlines' boarding passes and go through security. The guard takes a box of matches out of my rucksack but otherwise the search is pretty basic.

After about twenty minutes there is a shout for us to board and we get on an ancient bus and drive out onto the runway. There are lots of ex-Russian Air Force planes and helicopters still in Russian colours and sporting red stars. The helicopters are huge but are only used now to transport goods (after many crashes apparently!). We notice as we get out that there is no plane, but there is a refuelling tanker waiting beside us. It is pleasantly warm even at this early hour. We can see a plane in the distance come into land and then taxi up to stop beside us. Passengers and bags are out within minutes and it's our turn to board. I take some photos on my Pentax and I realise my slide films are back at the hotel in Davy's bag but it's too late now! I never got them back at all.

Neil poses in a white top, being photographed by Diane, Davy is kneeling and Marguerite is just behind Diane. To the right, behind her, is Derek in shorts. I am third to board with Davy and Marguerite and all of us are up front in the Twin Otter. There is no door on the cockpit and we can see all the controls. We are re-fuelled and with our pilot and co-pilot and the engines started and the whole turn-around has been less than fifteen minutes. We are offered cotton wool for our ears from a tray, which the cabin steward passes round. I thought we were getting sweets! It is very noisy and reminds me of the old Short 360 planes that I used to get to Belfast. The flight is quite smooth but, disconcertingly, we seem to clear each ridge of hills by only a few feet. We fly over ridges and valleys and the rivers are almost white, like alpine rivers. We can see some white peaks in the far distance and then the engine note changes as we descend into Lukla. The runway, built in 1964, looks very small, carved into the mountainside and is angled downwards towards us, making the landing quite interesting. There are probably longer aircraft carriers than this!

The plane taxis to the terminal building and we exit the plane, get our bags and head inside as the return load of passengers get on. One of the engines is still running and a few minutes later our plane is charging down the runway to fly back to Kathmandu. We meet Norbu, our Sherpa guide and our porters and cooks. They will each carry two kit-bags weighing almost thirty kilos. They look very young but as always, smiling. Instead of a taxi rank there are Yaks waiting to be loaded up, as well as porters with huge loads. Lukla translates in Nepalese as 'sheep corral' apparently. From here on there are no roads, only tracks, and no motor vehicles at all. Yaks carry all the big loads. There are no sheep. We walk up to the optimistically named Shangri-la Lodge. It is pretty basic and facing the sloping runway. Here we have some tea. It is warm and quite nice to just hang about and watch the planes in the sunshine. John decides we will have an early lunch here and we learn that we will stay in this lodge for our last night on the trek. At least it will be handy for the airport, in another three weeks. Hard to believe!

After lunch, we walk out of Lukla and onto the trail, which will take us to Ghat, at just over 9,000 feet. The trail is very up and down, but this afternoon we will mainly descend, giving us an easy day to start us off. Apparently, villagers hereabouts sleep outside on platforms in their fields so they can chase away bears from the crops. Not particularly reassuring! At Ghat, we are actually sleeping in Norbu's house and lodge. As the lodge is quiet, I have my own room, quite a luxury - well, just plywood walls. We have tea on arrival. The big mountain we can see at the head of the valley is Kyshar, one of the hardest of all the 20,000-foot trekking peaks apparently. I quickly film our plane leaving Lukla. Only one shot at this for the pilot! There is a sheer drop at the end of this runway. We passed a wrecked plane at the side of the runway and a crashed helicopter! The crashes are mainly under-carriages collapsing I'm told.

The lodge building is basic - I can see down into the kitchen through gaps in the floor of my room and also through gaps in the wooden, planked walls into adjacent rooms. The room is basic with a small bunk on either side. We will be using our own sleeping mats and bags. I have a silk liner for mine for when it gets colder. The shower is also basic and the toilet a hole through boards, high up over the garden rubbish pit. The human waste is used as fertiliser in the gardens. The separation of human waste from the human food chain is a real issue here and apparently why 90% of the population have intestinal worms. However, it is better than camping - although that is coming too as we prepare for the climb. This is the easy bit. Both toilets and showers are outside in separate wooden buildings. I remember now about the bears! The shower is facilitated by standing in a basin in a wooden shed with a primitive piped water supply, but at least it's warm. We will not often have electricity from here on. John is getting us sorted out with Tache, Norbu's son, who will come with us some of the way. Once I am changed, it's down into the dining room, and by now it's pretty cold and the ubiquitous cast iron Chinese wood-burning stove is being lit. We get invited through into the kitchen, which is warmer, and we are offered 'chang', a homemade beer made from fermented rice. As it's not polite to refuse, we all try it.

It is thick and grey/white and not a taste I will ever come to like. Apparently, it's also not polite to refuse a top-up and we get the next two refills. In fact, the glasses are continually topped up. Eventually it doesn't taste that bad as numbness sets into the taste buds. Back in the dining room I start with chicken soup. Packet soup is popular because the packets are light to transport and it's easy to make. It's also a good way of helping to keep hydrated. My main course is omelette with noodles and for a sweet I have freshly made pancakes with marmalade. John says jokingly that I need carbohydrate not eggs! At one point an American comes in looking for a room and says that near Jiri, on his trek from Kathmandu, he was held up by the Maoists and relieved of some cash. We have more tea before heading up to our rooms for an early night at eight fifteen. Our porters are Nima and Kami and our cook for the trip is Nawang. Nima is a relative of Norbu and his father is dead and Nima is the sole breadwinner. His family are apparently very poor, even by Nepal standards.

Wednesday 8th October.

Breakfast is really good - porridge with apple flakes and lemon tea. Lemon tea is my secret for keeping hydrated without ingesting vast amounts of caffeine. All our bags are packed and we leave at seven thirty five - an early start for a longish day. We are heading for Namche, which involves a steep pull. Norbu's son, Tache will come with us as he is off school for a few weeks. He's fourteen, just a year older than my youngest son, Cameron, and walks a couple of miles to school and back each day. He is very fit and speaks very good English. And he has a great personality too. Although he will trek with us to Everest Base Camp, he will not climb the mountain but will stay in a lodge and wait for us. Last night his sisters did their homework in the dining room throughout our meal, at a table close to us. Learning is the route out of poverty for these people and their dedication to schoolwork is quite impressive. Or, is it just the girls beating the boys here as well at this age?!

We walk mainly downhill to get to the riverside, which we follow until we cross over on the first of many bridges. I am getting used to the Sherpa greeting of 'Namaste' after thinking people were saying 'have a nice day'. We are all using it to greet people along the way. There were prayer flags tied to all of the bridges, which should be re-assuring and we stopped once across a large one at Phadking, a collection of about twenty-five lodge houses and just over 8,000 feet. A relation of Norbu has a teahouse here and we rest for half an hour. I am now sticking to black tea if I don't go for the lemon drink (which isn't tea at all), as the milk could be suspect. I know the butter is certainly from Yak's milk and it tastes awful. Like a cup of liquid gorgonzola I think Chris Bonington described it as.

The toilets are a mess. Like most countries of the world, no toilet paper is used and the system, such as it is, can't cope with it, so everywhere there is a box for used paper which is collected and burned. Nice. The smell is awful. We trek on to Monjo where

15

at mid-morning we stop again for tea. This is the entry point into the Sagarmatha - Everest - National Park. We are now at just over 8,000 feet and it's a nice morning with blue skies and super views. We stop here for well over an hour - more tea - then press on to Jorsale where the entrance to the National Park is. We have lunch here and wait for Norbu who has our passes. At this point, most of us are experiencing some mild altitude issues. This is a weird feeling for me and like a headache although not really that sore. We cross the river a few times and the final time we cross high over the Dudh Kosi on the spectacular high rope-bridge at the confluence of the Bhote Kosi, from the west, and then the steep pull up to Namche Bazaar. It is a Lord-of-the-Rings-type bridge and looks quite dodgy. Especially dodgy with a yak team coming the other way!

In 1997 an avalanche on Ama Dablam sent a thirty-foot tidal wave down the Dudh Kosi and washed away seven bridges and most of the village of Jorsale. As we walk through the entrance portal to the Sherpa capital, my head is definitely sore. It has also started to rain a bit. We have climbed over 3,000 feet today and have gone from a 'safe' altitude to one where altitude sickness could be a real issue. A big help to combat this is to prevent exhaustion, which is hard after the pull up from the valley floor. There are great views of Thamserku, another big 20,000 footer. If we had been earlier on the way up we might have seen Everest and Nuptse in the far distance, but they are in cloud. The lodge is quite busy and John and I are sharing a room. This will now be the pattern for the rest of the trek. The room is ultra basic, but OK and there is a real WC with a real shower on the same floor. This will become a novelty as we progress from here. We arrange to have dinner at seven and some of us wander down into town, but it's still drizzly. We have a game of cards before dinner, which reserves our seats. I hear someone say that there has been an avalanche at Island Peak but it didn't reach base camp. I wish I hadn't heard it! Apparently, it is common for avalanches to reach base camp. At dinner, Diane has bought two bottles of red wine and I have a glass. I've taken some ibuprofen and feel OK and sleep well. We are now above 11,000 feet.

Thursday 9th October.

Today is rest and acclimatisation day. Even at this altitude, John says three trekkers die each year from Acute Mountain Sickness (AMS), so we need to be careful. It's still raining. At breakfast I have porridge again. John suggests that those of us with a headache take Diamox - acetazolamide - to aid acclimatisation. The drug works by improving the respiratory rate and depth, thereby mirroring the breathing of a good acclimatiser. So if you feel better, you are better! Derek has gone off apparently walking on his own and when John asks where, someone says he mentioned Pokalde. John is raging at this, as you need a permit and we might all be in trouble for our trip, but it turns out it was just a wee walk towards that mountain.

We plan an easy walk over to the village of Khumjung, which gives us some height as well as keeping our legs moving. It's raining harder as we climb out of the town up to the head of the pass at around 11,500 feet. Everyone has their waterproofs on. We stop in a hovel of a building for tea - someone Norbu knows, no doubt. The highlight of the walk is a trip to the Everest Bakery in Khumjung for apple pie and milky coffee - with cow's milk. I think it's run by Germans. On our return the rain is all but off and we wander around the town. Namche is the 'Sherpa Capital' and in the past was an important trading area. Sherpa simply means someone from the east. Herders and traders still come here from Tibet over the very high pass of Nangpa La. John introduces me to Tenzing, a lovely looking Sherpa girl with long straight brown hair, who runs one of the stores that seems to sell everything. I buy some postcards to send home to each of my four sons. I am introduced to another delicacy in a coffee shop owned by the Everest Bakery here - marble cake, and lovely too! We all meet in the pub for a couple of cans of Bud and I write the cards and give them to Tenzing to post, which she kindly offered to do. There is apparently a postal dispute and the cards won't be put into the box by her until it's over in a few days. They will actually take two months to arrive and not all together. It's maybe a surprise they arrived at all.

Friday 10th October.

This morning, the rain is off and the sun is coming up over the mountains, which are quite spectacular. Had my best sleep yet last night and no headaches due to two Diamox a day - this will last for five days when they will have done their job, hopefully. We climb out of Namche by another route and the main route to Base Camp and at the top of this pass we get our first view of Everest in the distance. We can also see Lhotse. Ama Dablam is ahead to our right and is absolutely stunning in brilliant white. Arguably the most beautiful mountain in the world I am told and I think I agree. John says it's not too difficult to climb but it seems awfully vertical from here. "No, no" he says, "snow will only stick where the slope is less than 40%". Aye, right, I think. The walk is pretty easy going here and we stop for tea to admire the views. It's so warm that most of us have shorts and T-shirts on. This, I feel, is what we came for.

At Phunki Thanga, a small village, we stop for lunch after crossing the Imja river. There are prayer wheels everywhere, but here, they are water driven. Always to be passed on the left. Lemon tea and noodle soup are offered. Nice to sit in the sun and watch the yak trains go past, some with really big loads, some going down without a load to Lukla to meet planes from Kathmandu. We cross over the Dudh Kosi again before the hard pull up to Tengboche. We could see the trail up through the trees from the river, and it proves to be as hard as it looked. Neil and I take up the rear and take it easy. There is no rush after all, but it still takes us three hours. It's quite a pull and I walk up here talking to Neil about our adventure. Tengboche is the site of a big and

18

important monastery and some young looking monks, with shaven heads and dressed in their maroon robes, are playing a type of volleyball as we pass. There are about fifty monks based here, some look like young boys. It's starting to get cold now as the sun goes down and the clouds roll up the valley. Our accommodation is not impressive. The whole place is very busy and there are some big camping groups, which will put a strain on the teahouses' cooking facilities. We are three to a very small room in a terraced, plywood shack. No lights. No room between the beds.

I went down to have a look in the monastery while it's still light. There was a ceremony going on and, after taking off my shoes, I sat quietly on the floor with many others. At some points, cymbals are clashed and huge horns are blown. Hope there isn't an early morning ceremony! I could only manage ten minutes then I got cold. A bit of a headache as well, which is a nuisance. Leaving my shoes outside means my feet are cold now too. In keeping with the accommodation, the food is poor. I have noodle soup and mixed fried rice, but it's really dried up and probably re-heated. We all try to order the same food otherwise it can take an hour to get all different meals cooked. The dining room is full and there is no heat from the stove, mainly because people have surrounded it. We will learn later it is usually the guides who hog the fire! The toilets are a walk away and just a hole in the floor. And they stink. Cold and miserable, but got to sleep.

Saturday 11th October.

Davy gets up in what seems like the middle of the night to photograph sunrise over Everest. Frost on the ground this morning but a perfectly clear sky. Porridge again and we set off early at eight. Although the morning was cold it soon heats up and the shorts are on again. Superb views of Everest, Nuptse, Lhotse, Ama Dablam, Kangtega and Thamserku. We go downhill through woods to meet the Dudh Kosi and then cross into the sunshine. We stop for tea this morning at the small Sherpa hamlet of Shomare and then lunch at Pangboche. The hillsides are full of Edelweiss, but we keep quiet, in case it prompts a song from Marguerite from her "the Hills are Alive" repertoire. Super views all around us with new peaks coming into view all the time. We are really close to Ama Dablam. After lunch we climbed up the valley and then dropped down to where the Dudh Kosi splits. I found the climb from here hard going and have to take two ibuprofen pills for my head. Again the pattern of late afternoon developed, with clouds coming up the valley and the sun dropping into it and making it cold quickly.

The lodge at Dingboche is good with quite big rooms. We are at just over 14,000' here. We are all upstairs and John says they have showers but you have to pay. I am first to order a shower and soon I am shouted on to come down. The shower room is a little shack with a concrete floor. Inside, there is a small hosepipe with a tap. As I go in, a boy carrying a big basin of steaming water climbs a precarious homemade wooden ladder to the roof and pours the hot water into a wee barrel. This is the hot shower supply. No health and safety here! After the shower, I do some washing then join some others for tea. The washing will dry by morning I hope and it's safe to leave the socks out overnight. We make a plan to walk up to a place called Bibre tomorrow as it's another rest and acclimatisation day. It seems an easy walk but again it will give us more height, though we will come back down to sleep here again. "Walk high, sleep low" says our leader.

My head is sore and I down a couple of aspirin. So I will take more Diamox tonight as well. I don't feel good at all and over dinner I really struggle to eat. I am getting stomach cramps as well. Everyone is warned to be careful about hygiene and I have been but have now come down with the runs. The fear is of course that it's dysentery or more serious! I realise I have Imodium in my medical kit and take one to allow me to get a sleep without running to the toilet - another hole in the floor type on our floor so a long drop. John comes up after dinner and I tell him about the runs and the Imodium. He is not happy that I've taken Imodium and promises to give me a broad-spectrum antibiotic in the morning if I'm not better. I read my guidebook for a bit about illness and now note that it says aspirin should never be taken with Diamox. Going to sleep with my drug cocktail doing goodness knows what to my guts. Hope to wake up. I sleep badly. Worried about being ill, thousands of miles from home.

Sunday 12th October.

Still feel lousy this morning so John gives me one 500mg capsule of Ciprofloxacin. Struggle with my porridge but have three cups of black tea. We take our Sunday morning stroll up to Bibre in the sunshine and after an hour I start to feel OK. It only takes an hour and a half to get to Bibre and we are all walking very slowly, not just me. We stop for tea here at a shack in the middle of nowhere, but with great views. We will be up past here in a few days when we head further up this valley to Island Peak, which we can clearly see. It looks big and quite steep from here. It's the dark coloured, twisted peak to the right in the distance. Jeez, I thought it looked like the Matterhorn!

I took a picture of the view from the teahouse at Bibre looking towards Island Peak. We get back early in the afternoon and I sit in the sun and read - and have some tea of course. There is a ritual about tea and sugary biscuits at four o'clock.

As the cloud comes up the valley, we go inside to book our spaces for dinner. This is now an established pattern as well. We will sit here and read or write up our diaries until we order dinner. After dinner, and sometimes before, we play cards. Sometimes Tache will join us when we play switch. He's picked the game up really quickly. Or he's a Nepalese card sharp and has taught the rest how to play. Usually our 'boys' alert us with the cry of 'black tea' when we sit down. Today they are not here and have taken some loads (not ours) up to Island Peak base camp - our rest day means they are not working (or earning) and they have taken on a day's work from some other party. They are doing this and coming back tonight. We learn later it's for a group of climbers from the German Alpine Club. Just one way will be a day's walk for us.

Dinner tonight for me is chicken soup followed by a big, homemade spring roll, washed down with lemon tea. The dining room is quite warm, heated with wood and dried yak's dung, the smoke from which is eye watering but aromatic! It's also a bit disconcerting to see the cook load the stove with yak dung before he prepares dinner. Hmm! Apparently, drying the dung is quite an art. The dung is first made into a paste with water, then kneaded by hand and thrown onto rocks or a wall to dry in the sun. Tonight again, young American doctor volunteers have come up from Pheriche to check if anyone has symptoms of acute mountain sickness. They are also conducting a study of trekkers who have been on a Diamox programme from back in Namche. I almost put my hand up last night as I felt ill, but last night's illness had causes other than AMS.

After dinner, the teahouse owner gave an impromptu slideshow of some local peaks and of some of the views around the area. He even invited the audience - and there were all nationalities in - to guess where the views were from. As is now the pattern, we turned in at eight thirty for an early rise in the morning. As always, we have pre-ordered our breakfasts for the next day. John gives me another antibiotic but seems to have caught a cold and is coughing and sneezing all over the place. As we are sharing relatively small rooms, I am a bit concerned that I'm going to come down with it too. I really don't want to be ill again. What happens if you are too ill to continue?

Monday 13th October.

I am up at five o'clock thanks to a side effect of Diamox - it's diuretic and makes me pee regularly, even at night. The other side-effect is a tingling in the extremities! Apart from that, I slept well and the dodgy stomach seems to have been cured. It is very cold this morning, but the usual, pristine, blue sky. John is worse this morning and Davy is feeling ill as well and has the runs. Breakfast today is just toast and red jam (jam it seems is ordered by colour, not flavour), washed down with black tea and hot chocolate. Today, we are heading for Lobuche and it's good to be on the move again. We will climb Kala Pattar from here, near Everest base camp, which will be another aid to acclimatisation as it's the highest we will be before Island Peak. We leave at eight to climb up from the village, past a Chorten, a memorial, and then over a flat tundra for a few miles. As usual, the porters are away before us. This is snow leopard country and also the habitat of Yetis. I see neither.

The sun is incredibly strong on our backs as we walk towards Duglha, where we stop for the inevitable tea. As a precaution, this morning I have taken two ibuprofen tablets, as I want to enjoy today's walk. Also, John has said this will be a hard day. It takes two and a half hours to reach Duglha and I have seen Davy disappear a few times behind boulders with the runs. It's still mid-morning but we hang about and have an early lunch. There is no other habitation after here until we reach Lobuche. The HRA (Himalayan Rescue Association) doctors at Pheriche urge everyone to stay a night at Lobuche to aid acclimatisation. The height gain today has been twice the recommended ascent for one day. There are, however, not many places to stay on this part of the route.

I have good homemade hash browns and get talking to a tall Canadian guy. He is heading towards Everest base camp but has been working in a volunteer programme in China, teaching English, and has been in the south of Nepal working as well. He is a big fit guy, who reminds me of another son, Alastair. From here, the path rises very steeply to a ridge where there are many memorials to Sherpas killed on Everest, as well as some others including a party of Japanese climbers who were killed in an avalanche. There is also a memorial, or Chorten, to Scott Fischer, an American who died in the 1996 Everest disaster and to Jangbu Sherpa, who was killed a year later. We stop here for half an hour. John has built a memorial for a friend who died a few years back. The area is called Chukpilhara I think. The views are absolutely stunning but it makes you think as well. From here we follow the Khumbu glacier, on our right, and on the opposite side the towering white pyramids of Nuptse and Lhotse until we reach Lobuche. It is quite cool due to the wind, but has still clear skies.

The glacier isn't the pristine gleaming white thing I'd

23

imagined but grey and covered in stones and debris. Our lodge is really basic but OK, the usual plywood construction and the toilet is a distance from the lodge. Marguerite, Davy and I sit outside in the sun with tea until it's too cold. The draughts in the dining room are fierce and the stove pretty useless. This is really only a 'summer' village and will shut down in winter. Everything here is, naturally, more expensive. The rooms are tiny and as John is now really struggling, I am alarmed to be only a couple of feet from him when we're sleeping. I need a mask! To catch a cold now would probably rule out being able to climb Island Peak and maybe not even get over the Cho La pass if we head to Goyko? There is no electricity here and the only source of communal light is a single bulb powered from a small, single Chinese solar panel. We will be here two nights. And the door in the lodge dining room won't keep closed.

Some of us have struggled today and a few of us have sore heads, despite being on Diamox. There are a lot of Japanese trekkers here - come to get to Everest base camp. We are now over 15,000 feet and it is really cold outside and not much better in the dining room. There is a rumour that to get to Kala Pattar and back on the same day we will need to leave at five am. A couple come in looking for a room saying all the accommodation is full in the village. It would be as warm sleeping outside anyway. None of the doors fit and the draughts make it uncomfortable. It doesn't help that people sometimes leave the door open. The stove seems to be running on cardboard and wood shavings, but, of course, there is no wood to burn at this height, or any fuel unless it's carried on someone's back from Namche probably. We are glad to get to bed after dinner. Had to use the toilet at midnight and I was really taken aback at the star-studded sky, really an amazing sight. I haven't ever seen so many stars in my life.

I am quite pleased with my new digital camera. Still using it on micro drive despite dire warnings that it won't work at altitude, but I'll shove in a card to make sure of photos on Island Peak and probably replace the batteries as well. Whether the thing is actually recording shots properly is another matter. The single Pentax roll of film, I'm keeping for the mountain.

Tuesday 14th October.

I am up at 5:00am to get ready for the off. No breakfast at this hour. The cold, dry wind has everyone coughing, not just John, who has decided to have a day's rest. In the dark this morning I brush my teeth with Germolene, having taken the wrong tube out of my toilet bag! Germolene is now safely in my medical kit bag and it gives everyone a laugh later. It is a hard pull up over moraine as we follow the Khumbu glacier towards Gorak Shep. The boys are with us today to carry just our tea-making stuff, as there are no bags to carry. Davy is not 100% and has a sore head. Last night, we had the usual visit from the American doctors, only this time there was a casualty, a Korean walker who has become ill, but spoke no English. It looked like serious AMS. The Canadian I had talked to earlier was able to translate using his knowledge of Chinese and the Korean had to leave right away to get lower quickly and to get to the first aid post at Pheriche - in the dark and with an oxygen cylinder on his back - a good three hours walk down the valley. A guide goes with him. That is still a precarious journey and dodgy river crossings too and in pitch blackness.

It took a couple of hours to get to Gorak Shep, once a summer yak-herding valley, using our head torches for some of the way. The boys made our tea at this point and from here we could look across a dried-up lake to Kala Pattar - it didn't look too bad. The going was tough enough, and it was a really hard pull up but the views of Everest were just amazing! Tilman was first to climb here in 1956 and Kala Pattar just means black rock. Norbu realised we were struggling and made us walk at a very slow pace. Despite this Marguerite was suddenly physically sick. However, hard going as it was, this is my second day with no altitude symptoms. Diane had already stopped before this and would go no further. But to see Everest so close is, I think, all she wanted. And that's no bad thing. She has also decided not to attempt to climb Island Peak and that's probably wise. I have amazing views of Everest and Nuptse.

We reached the summit of Kala Pattar, over 18,000 feet in just over an hour and it was very cold and very windy. Strange to think that from Lukla we have ascended almost 16,000 feet and descended 8,000 feet. We stopped for shelter looking back to dark Kala Pattar with the impressive bulk of pure white Pumori behind. I wouldn't want to be on a ridge with this blustery wind but we found some shelter down a bit from the summit and took some photographs. I get Kala Pattar in some and of course, Everest as well, before plodding down to Gorak Shep for lunch at a cold tea house. The boys were now carrying some of the rucksacks, but I felt OK to carry mine. The walk back to Lobouche felt hard and never-ending and the sun was strong in our eyes all the way back. The air felt really dry and everyone has a dry cough - the Khumbu cough as it's called.

The only washing facility was the river, but I gave that a miss as the water is straight from the glacier. When the sun goes down it is worrying that there is absolutely no source of heat except the cardboard and sawdust stove and apart from our head torches, only one light bulb in the building powered by a small Chinese solar panel. We ordered dinner for half past six and I was glad to get into my sleeping bag to get warm not long after that.

Wednesday 15th October.

After breakfast we are heading back to Dingboche, which is an easier day as it's mostly downhill, but then we will trek up to Chukhung, closer to Island Peak base camp. A bit disappointed that we won't be staying in Dingboche, as we quite liked that lodge and we know it has a hot shower of sorts. When we got up at seven thirty, it was still very cold and it stayed that way until the sun came over the mountains. John gets one of the boys to fetch water from the river and then using his filter pump, we get our bottles refilled. I ask how long the filter lasts and he says thousands of times. Because of this I am still putting an iodine tablet and a vitamin C tablet into every litre. The Vitamin C hides the iodine taste. Unlike the porridge with Yaks milk and had to add sugar to make that go down. You just hope it stays that way!

The ritual sun cream is on every morning; we will head firstly for Dingboche for lunch and hang around for the Yak team bringing up the climbing gear and tents from Namche. John and Norbu have great faith that this will happen. When we meet the Yak team, we will head off as a caravan to Chukhung where we will stay in a lodge which I'm sure isn't even booked yet. Need to get a shower, cut my nails and sort out my cameras and change the head torch batteries. The wee important expedition things like drinking enough and checking the colour of your pee. Amazingly, the Yaks arrive, three of them and two boys, with our climbing gear from Ghat and Namche, where two of the party and John, had hired climbing boots, crampons and ice axes. We all set off after lunch, three porters, three yaks, two Yak boys, our cook and Norbu, the boys and then the rest of us. We climb up past the tea house at Bibre, pulling upwards all the time to arrive in Chukhung. We at least look like an expedition now. The lodge is good with a warm dining area, although fired with dried Yak's dung as well as wood. This has been the only warm dining room since Ghat, but it cools quickly when the windows have to be opened to let out the Yak dung smoke. I had some stomach pain on the way up today, but I slept OK.

Thursday 16th October.

After breakfast, I had a shower and got ready to roll. The base camp isn't far but our porters want to get there early to clear a good spot for the tents. We will sleep two to each tent, which is usual practice at high altitude, I think. I don't get to choose who to be with so I just hope John has a miracle cure in his medical kit as he is worse again and can hardly talk. We walk from the lodge and cross, rather precariously on icy rocks, the Imja river, which is a raging torrent. After a couple of hours of easy walking we come down into a very broad plain, which is really alpine in character. From here we follow the river before heading over moraine to a dried-out lakebed that is very dusty. That doesn't help our throats. By now we are quite stretched out with the porters probably at the camp by now and the yak team ahead of us in the distance, all in single file. We came up the final rise into the base camp and it's pretty bleak here at just over 16,000 feet. The wind is cold coming up the valley and the camp is covered in rocks and boulders. Not what I expected. There are strings of prayer flags across the site, many of them in tatters from the wind. There are no good spots to pitch a tent, only rocky areas. There are half a dozen blue German Alpine Club tents and a huge Mountain Equipment dome tent, which is full of their climbing gear. In charge of all this is Norbu's brother, Pasang Sherpa, who also knows John. It turns out he has been to the top of Everest and he seems to be really switched-on. All the German stuff looks new and shiny. Ours doesn't. The porters have cleared space for our tents, but they seem exposed, although everything up here is. The cook has made the inevitable tea before we have lunch. We take this huddled behind a wall of rocks. This is definitely colder than before and it's still early afternoon. No stove tonight so there is no heat, just a cold tent to eat in.

Pasang has set up some fixed ropes on the mountainside for us to practise using our ascenders, which few of us have used before. We will then abseil down, again to sharpen up our technique for the real thing in two day's time. The angle isn't too steep, and we are all OK about using the equipment and it's good to gain some confidence. Glad I brought all my own gear though as Neil is suffering with his hired plastic boots. The Germans arrive, dressed in identical, expensive looking gear. They plan to climb the peak directly from base camp, leaving at 2:00am the next morning. Amazingly, Pasang comes over to us as we sort out our tents, to say the Germans have no descenders, effectively meaning they could not easily abseil off unless they used double karabiners. We agree to loan them our figure of eights and Pasang will hand them back tomorrow. By then we will be at advanced base camp as they come down. In return we can use the fixed ropes, which Pasang has already put in place on the final steep sections of the climb. And there must be hundreds of feet of fixed ropes, which would have taken us ages to fix.

There are huge snow cocks everywhere, like big partridges. They are really tame and will eat from your hand. Bet they taste good too. We have not had a lot of meat so far. We eat in the dining tent at six thirty, using our head torches to see, and avoid the yak dung now all over the place. The yaks are right outside the dining tent but seem very placid. We eat sitting on rugs and I find a comfortable backrest in a corner, only to discover later that it's the blankets off the yaks but no itching though that night. The boys are really showing off now that cooking and serving the food is down to them. We head off to our tents. By now it's freezing and the only source of heat is the hot water the boys have put in all our drinking bottles. These go into the bottom of the sleeping bags to keep us warm and provide a drink the next morning. Slept well and kept warm, using a pee bottle to prevent me from having to trek outside. Need to be sure not to mix the bottles up! Especially in the dark!

Friday 17th October.

We are awakened by the cry of 'bed tea!' and one of the boys hands in two mugs, black tea for me, tea with milk for John (or milik, as the boys say). There is frost on the tents. Inside as well! I've never seen this before - wee floating flakes of frost particles. We have breakfast in the dining tent. It's still cold as the sun takes longer to get over the mountains and reach us. Today will be a short day, with us arriving at high camp by lunchtime. I have a look at the map and Neil and I agree it looks like a reasonable route. Both of us assumed we would walk around the base of the mountain, but John says no, we are to climb almost directly up. This is shown on our map as the 'Attack Camp' and is a shorter, but steeper, way than what we thought. After about an hour walking we start to trek relentlessly upwards and we need frequent rests and go really slowly. We are all exhausted when we arrive and the mountainside is so bleak there seems no clear, flat area for our tents. The boys are talking to some other porters who are taking down some tents. We huddle in a stone shelter to try and keep out of the freezing wind and the cook brings us tea. It's great to get your hands heated by the cup. It is not very hospitable here. I wonder how Marguerite will handle the cold, and then I wonder how I will handle it. Below us is the vast Lhotse Shar glacier.

Eventually the porters have a site cleared for the tents and it is only us at this camp. Although we are well above 18,000 feet, I don't feel the altitude sickness at all. We are camping tonight at a higher level than the highest mountain in Europe! Across from here spectacular views of Baruntse and the Amphu Labtsa pass. Later, an American party of four shouted a greeting and passed us to camp higher, about a mile away, to be closer than us to the summit. 'Typical' someone says. We spend the afternoon getting all the gear ready for the morning. We will be up at two thirty and leave at three thirty in the morning. Nawang, our cook, surpasses himself and we have Sherpa stew, then potato and rice curry and warm pineapple slices as our sweet served by our boys. The cooks are showing off again, but great getting food as good as this. Of course, we have plenty of tea. Our hot water bottles are filled and we hit the sack about half past seven. Already, the tents are covered in frost. The German team had dropped off our descenders. All of them made the summit and they were in good spirits. It only lifted mine slightly as I was worried about the climb the next day.

Saturday 18th October.

I don't sleep too well, probably nerves about the climb, or too much tea. I can hear the cook up getting the stove going for breakfast and preparing our packed lunches at one thirty. We have our bed tea and there is a lot of frost on the inside of our tent again. It is almost completely white. I have not been cold, using both my silk and fleece liners. Our head torches light up tiny ice particles, like dust, in the air of the tent. I put my boots inside the sleeping bag to heat them a bit. Someone says it's minus eighteen degrees and that is the temperature of most people's freezers! It feels like it too here at two in the morning! Today, Nima and Kami, two of the porters are coming with us - not because we need them, but they want to come with us as it will be a feather in their cap for climbing Imja Tse. I suppose it goes onto their Sherpa CV. Norbu will be climbing the mountain for the eighth time! Both Davy and Derek have bad coughs. The Khumbu cough and it gets worse. John says he is too ill to come with us and suspects he has viral pneumonia! Not good news for him or me.

We have porridge in the dining tent. There is no wind at this hour, but it's very dark. Norbu tells us that if it looks like we will not be on the summit by ten o'clock, we will have to turn back, as the katabatic winds will become too dangerous to be on the summit ridge for us to be safe. As we are getting ready, and it seems to take ages, we see three lights in the gloom, far away but heading our way. They turn out to be a guide with a French couple who have set out hours earlier from base camp. They shout a greeting and are soon lost in the dark as they head towards the steeper rocky area ahead of us. We leave at 4.00am exactly, all of us now with climbing harnesses on and kitted out with slings, ascenders, descenders and karabiners. Our ice axes are on our rucksacks and crampons inside. The boys are carrying more gear and some ropes for crossing the glacier, along with a big thermos flask for hot tea later. After about twenty-five minutes, we passed close to the Americans' camp. No sign of activity. They had asked Pasang if they could also use the fixed ropes but he said only if they paid him, which they didn't. So they can't.

Our head torches show up the rocky steps, which will lead us around the rock face and we follow Norbu, twisting and climbing higher. At some points there seems to be a lot of nothing at one side but whatever void is there, it's still too dark to see. We realise half-way up the rocks that John didn't give Norbu his video camera so there will be no summit film. Norbu leads us on, twisting and climbing over rock. All of us are breathing very hard and we need frequent rests. I am worried about what is ahead as I feel as though this is a real struggle. All of us now have a cough. We pass the French couple and their guide who have stopped to rest and look exhausted. After half an hour they ask to pass us on a narrow section, obviously wanting to beat us to the top I think. I don't, at this point, care as I am exhausted.

Eventually dawn breaks and the torches are put away. There is still no wind and amazing sights up here with glaciers around us. Some snow now on the rocks as we cross a narrow rock section, really like the mountains in Skye. We stop here to get the crampons on and rope ourselves together. This is where I am glad I have my own boots and crampons. The hired crampons are like my old pair and are a fidget to put on with a mile of straps, especially with cold hands. You can't do them with gloves on. Ahead is a massive snow-covered glacier with some unstable cornices above it in the distance. I can see a faint track reaching across it. Norbu leads us, roped together, across narrow snow bridges and across the glacier. We climb up and around this to see ahead of us the start of the summit ridge. In the distance we can see the French party. They seem to be very slow, but we are also going slowly and stop for frequent rests.

As we approach the big snow wall, we can see the French couple are really struggling and one of them is seemingly actually lying down, across the fixed rope. They only seem to be moving a couple of steps upwards then stopping. This is not encouraging. By the time we reach the bottom of the first fixed rope we can see a problem with bergschrund - rotten ice - and also hard to get around. Here we get our safety rope taken off but we are only half-way up. There are four consecutive fixed ropes as it's a long way up. The ropes must be at least one hundred feet in length and appear to be eight millimetres, which is pretty skinny. It looks a bit frayed as well! We clip on using the ascender, which is attached by a sling to the harness. When we reach the end of each rope at an ice screw we have to clip onto the rope above it before unclipping below it and in some cases there is no ice screw, just an old ice axe hammered into the hilt, using a karabiner on a sling. All this on near vertical ice, balanced on crampon points. It certainly concentrates the mind. And this is best done with bare hands! We all rest before the final steep section.

The fixed rope is very narrow, probably eight millimetres and our club would use eleven millimetres, which is slower through the figure of eight but gives more control. It proves to be excruciatingly hard work. Davy leads and Marguerite is in front of me. Arguably the fittest members of our club and we can only manage five steps without having a rest. The sun is now up and I'm regretting wearing so much warm clothing. The ascender is pushed up the rope, the ice axe digging in above my head. For what seems ages. At this section, Davy and Marguerite are up before me and all of us just lie, exhausted in the snow. Davy is coughing hard and can hardly talk. We are on a small snow platform and the French couple with their guide are just starting the next section. I don't think I can cope with much more pain at this point and ask Norbu, how long till we reach the summit. He says half an hour, maybe more and points to a distant white mountain. I despair but the peak I'm looking at turns out to be Lhotse Shar, one of the world's highest mountains and of course much, much further away. I thought it was ours and knew I would never make it, so a big relief! Away down the mountain we can see the Americans crossing the glacier towards the first climb.

We rope up again to cross an exposed but thankfully short section to reach the next fixed rope. Then we all have to unclip and re-attach ourselves, as before, one at a time to climb a not so steep section of about a hundred and fifty feet. From here we can see the summit dome and I know we'll make it. The weather is just perfect. A photograph was taken of Neil and me, tiny figures near the top.

The last fixed rope is up the steep dome and after a few minutes we are on the top. Not a lot of room here and the French party are getting ready to abseil off. Exhausted but elated, we congratulate each other and the rest of the team. Kami and Nima are delighted, but they are always happy anyway, never complaining about anything and always willing to help. Norbu stands and names every peak around us and we can see the mountains forming the border with Tibet. We take photographs, mostly with Lhotse in the background, the fourth highest peak in the world. We are an island surrounded by the Imja and Lhotse glaciers and that is how Shipton named Island Peak - surrounded by a sea of ice. I look at my watch - it's nine fifteen and the wind is getting up a bit. It has been a hard five hours to get here. Was it worth it? Oh yes!

It's time to go down and Norbu is anxious that we don't hang about. My ice axe is now slung in my belt for the abseiling sections, Alpine style. The trickiest of which is the first one. I captured the moment, with Neil, Norbu, Kami, Derek, Nima, Marguerite holding a Saltire and Davy all in the photo. Next it was my turn on the summit, posing with Ama Dablam in the background.

The descent is quite steep, but a small crevasse has started to appear at the bottom of the rope, necessitating a swing out from the summit over a very exposed drop to the dome, but it's over in a few minutes. We get roped up again to cross the exposed snow ridge and soon reach the big snow wall. This is Derek getting roped up to abseil. Not a lot of room.

The abseil down this big section is quite tiring and takes time, having to take off the descenders after having secured a sling to the rope protection, then re-attach the descenders and remove the karabiner and sling. Four times I have to do this - and on a snow wall. When I reach the end of the last rope, I actually have to cool my descender in the snow before I can touch it because it is so hot. The thinner rope was certainly potentially faster and took a bit of controlling.

The Americans were using their own ropes and we can now hear them whooping loudly to each other as they reached the summit. It seems out of place up here in the quietness. 'Typical' someone says. Interestingly we don't rope up to cross the glacier and we walk along back to the flat rocky area. Presumably if no one fell through the snow into a crevasse on the way up, we wouldn't on the way down. As each person comes off the ropes, they walk slowly back on their own. Feel strangely alone here - no one to wait for, no one to wait for me. I feel nature couldn't care less as we are not needed or wanted here.

It's good to get the crampons off and the harness, although we still have to carry them in our rucksacks. I have hurt my back somehow, probably the strain of a big abseil - it must have been about 1,000 feet or 350 metres in total. I feel good though apart from that. The highest I have ever been in my life. Derek has sore feet from the crampons as well as his boots. From my packed lunch I have a hard-boiled egg and half a Bounty bar. I don't feel like eating more than this. My water was almost done, but soon the boys were passing around hot black tea for us to share. Throughout, they have, as always performed brilliantly and Kami is also carrying Davy's rucksack and Nima has Marguerite's to make it easier for them. All the gear is stowed away and we head down the rocky 'path' we came up in the dark. Neil is finding the going hard in his hired plastic boots. It takes us until after one o'clock to get back to high camp. All of us are pretty exhausted. John congratulates us all for making it to the top. I am badly dehydrated and glad to get water and tea down my throat but feel that Tiger beer would be better!

While the boys pack away our tents, we eat the meal the cook has prepared for us outside. We have noodle soup followed by fish and chips he says - of a sort. The chips are OK but the fish is cold, tinned pilchards in tomato sauce. I eat the lot but neither Davy nor Marguerite can take anything. The yak boys asked John for headache pills this morning as not all Nepalese are immune to altitude, but they seem OK now and are getting the yaks loaded to head back to Chukhung. We have a long trek back - first to base camp and then on to Chukhung and at base camp we give Pasang a bottle of Bagpiper whisky for his help and he shakes everyone's hand to congratulate us.

From here though, it will take over three hours to get to our lodge for the night. All of us are suffering from exhaustion now. It's after five o'clock when we arrive back at Chukhung and I have stomach cramps on top of being thoroughly knackered. I've been on the go since three o'clock this morning and had a hard fourteen-hour day. When we arrive at the lodge, it's the last thing I need to hear - John and I have no room. It's like a nightmare, but we get sorted out in an outhouse with a low door, full of paraffin containers and boxes of potatoes. They are tiny single rooms filled with a tiny bunk, but who cares. We are reunited with Tache and Diane.

The dining room is very busy and very smoky too. I can't eat anything as my stomach is still sore so it's some black tea, a quick game of cards and off to bed. We have decided tonight that we can't do another six really hard days to head off for the Cho La pass and Gokyo Ri. Instead we will head down to Dingboche, about a couple of hours away and have a rest day there. Unusually, we don't place a breakfast order and there is no time set to get up. The lash is off and we have done what we came to do and that feels really good. Diane says she has enjoyed the rest and feels good.

Sunday 19th October.

I sleep very well, probably because of exhaustion. Despite not being on Diamox now, I had to get up twice to pee. At seven on the dot, Tache brings a basin of hot washing water to my room. I really need to get some clothes washed as well. Breakfast is toast and red jam, but I only manage half a slice. I still do not feel totally cured and after going back to my room in the dark to the outhouse, I forget about the low door and knock myself onto my back, nearly giving myself concussion. So, a sore head and a sore stomach now. The only injury I've had and it's in a dilapidated potato store!

The walk to Dingboche is easy and mostly downhill. Although the wind is still a bit chilly, the shorts are back on. My back is still sore too and when we stop, I take a couple of painkillers. I bought a bottle of coke this morning and another Bounty bar - life's little luxuries. Lunch is Tibetan bread with chips. I stick to the coke only as my stomach ain't right yet, but I manage some tinned fruit.

I sat outside at the lodge this afternoon in the sun writing my journal. The rooms are actually OK and I'm sharing with John again who is only coughing slightly less. And whatever he's had,

I've not caught it. The toilet is an outhouse, quite a trek from the rooms and the usual hole in the floor type. No electricity or showers here. We watch some people separating barley and chaff by collecting it in a basket and throwing the grain in the air repeatedly, almost biblical in its antiquity. Not a good night and I have to really run to the toilet at half past four. I felt awful and didn't get back to sleep. I get up early and go outside to brush my teeth. Everything is covered in frost. I don't take any breakfast to reduce any risk of upsetting my stomach again. Maybe I'm getting allergic to black tea?

Monday 20th October

We leave at the usual time. The plan is to get down to Phortse, which involves a trek right round a few mountainsides. We will stay high but have some serious ups and downs. At Pangboche, we have lunch at a really weird place. It is someone's house but also some sort of temple, with a monk in the dining room doing consultations and there is a small queue of people waiting to see him. I risk some noodle soup. I would rather be outside in the sun. Derek, sitting next to me, doesn't make me feel better by ordering bloody garlic soup. Pangboche is the highest year-round settlement in the valley. The Gompa, or monastery here once had the skull of a Yeti apparently. It was stolen in 1991. From this small area, about forty local Sherpas have reached the top of Everest.

The soup has done no good and I still have a sore stomach, but have no other symptoms. According to the guidebooks, there is only dormitory accommodation at Phortse, but the lodge is quite alright and again, John and I share a room upstairs this time. No electricity except for two bulbs in the dining room and solar powered as normal. I bag the first shower and the usual hot water into a bucket in the roof technique. The shower walls this time are translucent plastic and I got some washing done as well and hung it outside to dry. Nawang, our cook, spots me and sets up a washing line over the stove in the dining room and brings my washing inside. Later the boys will hang the really wet stuff over a couple of chairs in front of the stove overnight. This is real Chinese laundry stuff.

Back in the room I ask John for the same antibiotic magic pill that I had before and wash it down with afternoon lemon tea and some biscuits. Sit and read my journal this afternoon in the dining room. There are not many others staying here tonight. I have chicken soup and an omelette for dinner and a bottle of coke, with tea and hot chocolate. Davy's cough is now very bad but all of us have a cough now from the cold, dry air. Have to make a loo trip at four in the morning but don't feel too bad. Maybe the pill is working.

Tuesday 21st October.

I manage tea and toast, with yellow jam this morning and feel pretty good. The sun is shining in a clear sky as we head to the Mongla Pass. This involves a steep pull but first we must descend to the river, making the ascent even longer. The views are breathtaking as we reach Mongla, where we stop for tea. Sitting here with outstanding views, wearing only shorts is wonderful. It is really warm now we are lower. We are all benefitting from the lower altitude. We watch a huge, eagle like bird with long, white patches on each wing. No one seems to know what it is. A Lammergeier I think. After Mongla, we head off on the higher of two paths, which will take us to Khumjung, where we will spend the night. We see a pair of Himalayan Tahr, really quite close to us, like a big shaggy goat. Cracking looking creatures and apparently protected and rare. One poses on a rock for us.

The trek takes us down the famous 'monkey steps' which

40

are steps of a sort cut into a cliff edge. Yaks can come up this way but cannot return - they use the lower path. It is very steep followed by a short pull up and into Khumjung, where we end up again in the Everest Bakery for hot apple pie and milky coffee. It is only eleven fifteen. Here is the original Hillary school, founded in 1960 by Sir Edmund. It's very impressive what he has done for the region including building the airport at Lukla. Although I was expecting to be staying in a hovel here, where we had tea before on the way up, we are actually in a really good hostel with en-suite facilities but you could 'pee only' in a small cubicle set into the corner of the room, but one of the outside toilets had a real toilet pan of sorts! There is also electricity in each room. Well, a light bulb anyway. The dining room even has a TV, which the boys sat round, about two feet from the screen - just like I did when I first saw one at my Mum's uncle's house who had the first one in our wee town actually. A few of the kids in the scheme could go round and watch it. These guys are fascinated but it's sad to think it will eventually engender Western ideas, though who would deny them the things we take for granted. I wonder what they make of shampoo ads from India TV.

After a chicken soup lunch, we decide to walk up to the Everest View Hotel. It is owned and probably only patronised by the Japanese. It's a half-hour walk, very pleasant and I feel really good. We have a beer on the veranda outside and you can actually see Everest today. By this time it's usually in the cloud. We have another beer and it's so good even if it is expensive. There is apparently an oxygen supply in each room and a decompression chamber somewhere in the place. It's not been busy since a Japanese visitor collapsed and died on the steps after getting out of a helicopter. It was caused by sudden exposure to the altitude after flying here straight from Kathmandu. It is really good to sit here, the job done, with a beer, in the sunshine looking back at Everest and Lhotse. I feel strangely homesick.

It is a perfect afternoon, and we take a long detour back to the lodge. The boys are ready with the four o'clock tea and biscuits. Tomorrow will be an easy day but John plans a detour. Tomorrow we will be back in Namche. It almost seems like civilization. We headed down by the Syangboche airstrip, built to service the hotel, but now looking as if it could only take helicopters. And an old looking helicopter arrives as if on cue.

There are mountains of plastic bottles here, wrapped in mesh to be flown out, we are told. They are a big problem here. Over dinner, John mentions that we will have forty-eight hours in Kathmandu, but as we are flying out on Sunday, we will only have a day. I think Neil said his Sunday flight was cancelled, but our tickets were clear, we will need to sort this out but nobody can do anything until we get back to Kathmandu on Saturday morning and check the tickets.

Wednesday 22nd October.

The walk to Namche Bazaar in the morning was extended by a couple of hours as we trekked around a mountainside. There are very bright blue Gentians everywhere. Diane takes some to press without any singing involved. We stop for tea at a remote house and are entertained by a couple of women throwing wet yak's dung onto a wall to dry. Entertaining, but at least it wasn't lunchtime. We are in the same hostel in Namche, which is fine. We get our rooms sorted and go down for lunch and I have chicken soup. All of us have different things to do in the town and I head to an Internet café to try to let the family and my company know I'm OK. The account my son Finlay set up for me doesn't work at first, but I eventually send an e-mail home and to work. Finlay will check at home regularly for my emails. I wander round the shops, avoiding the yak trains that come right through the narrow streets and buy a few souvenirs. Most of the stuff I buy from Tenzing, the girl who posted my cards for me. She is still lovely.

We all agreed to meet at the Everest Bakery for coffee later and I have some carrot cake, followed by more coffee and marble cake. I have to get more cash and change £30 into rupees just in case and agree to meet the others at the pub later. At a stall on the street I look at an incense holder but ask the price and put it down. The attractive girl runs after me and asks what I'll pay and I end up buying it. I say I'm going for a beer and she says, "Why don't you take me with you?" And to this day I don't know why I didn't. As could only happen here, there is a big white horse standing motionless outside the pub door like in a western! You couldn't make it up. It's a good feeling though, sitting in this pub, the same one we sat in on the way up a couple of weeks ago having achieved what we set out to do. We have a long game of pool and another couple of beers. The boy serving us looks about twelve and probably is. I couldn't see him at first and had to look right over the bar at this wee guy. Marguerite laughs at my reaction to this four-foot barman! Someone carried this pool table from Lukla! I can really feel the three wee cans of Bud, because of the altitude I suppose. The atmosphere is really good and everyone is pretty relaxed. Happy even!

Neil, Derek and Diane polish off a couple of bottles of red wine at dinner, which is a special treat - yak steak. And it's really good sitting here with good food and good craic. This is the most meat I've eaten in the past few weeks. We only had this as the yak had apparently fallen off a path and died. Yeah right! We have a noisy game of cards until after nine, a really late night for us as we are usually in bed at eight. Tomorrow we leave for Ghat where, once more we will be staying at Norbu's house. I have a great sleep but the weird dreams have returned.

Thursday 23rd October.

Feeling great and we left Namche spot-on at eight o'clock. It would be possible to get to Lukla on a big, seven-hour, up and down, day trek from here. The sky is clear and the sun is already warm. We drop down about 2,000 feet quite steeply and cross the river, but we will be in the shade for much of the way. The path is very busy with lots of loaded yaks in both directions. They are really quite like highland cattle and are very docile, however they have large horns and on a narrow path with steep drops, it's advisable to give them some space. And always stand in towards the mountain, warns John. We cross the high bridge and watch trekkers clear rapidly off the bridge as five fully loaded yaks make their way across. Actually we have seen only a few 'real' yaks, with their long hair and hairy legs. Most 'yaks' are in fact crossbreeds with local or Tibetan bulls.

We stop for tea at Jorsale. We had lunch here on the way up. It's nice sitting out in the sun for half an hour. We will have lunch further down and then make a detour to a Gompa, a monastery high on the hillside, where Norbu's father is the Lama. When he dies, Norbu will assume his position and it's a great honour to be selected. The walk to the Gompa is quite long and really out of the way, and Derek comments that he won't get many visitors! Much of the Gompa is being renovated and we watch stonemasons chipping at stone in a way that will not have changed for centuries. I think it was called the Rimijung Gompa. We get to see the Gompa, which is ancient. Apparently, locked in a secret place inside, is a solid gold figure of Buddha. Some Tibetans tried to steal it some time ago. Inside we see the usual figure of Buddha, not gold and some other figures and scripture books and instruments.

Norbu's father, although an old man with long white hair, looks pretty fit and you can see the family resemblance. All of us are given a silk scarf - a kata - which is put around our necks as an honour to us. A tray of cups arrive and we are given milky, very sweet tea - probably yaks milk. I manage to pour mine away, unnoticed. The walk back down is steep, and we cross the river again and head for Ghat, stopping for lunch outside in the sun and probably taking a couple of hours. At Ghat I have my own room again and electricity but no light bulb. I don't care and I get to the shower first and wash a couple of pairs of trousers for wearing in Kathmandu. Maybe to nightclubs!

I am first into the dining room and sit reading, but not for long. As the others appear, so does the chang. 'Fresh', we are told! Somehow it doesn't taste so bad and as usual the drinks are constantly topped up. The big risk is it uses cold water to ferment, maybe not boiled so a potential health hazard. For dinner tonight we are to have a special feast, with Norbu doing much of the cooking. We can see our cook chopping up and battering yak meat for the boiled momos, similar to small, filled dumplings. Quite similar to warm plasticine I would imagine. We all have chicken soup as it helps speed things up when we don't all order different things and we have tried to do this during the trek. Next up is the dish of the yak momos, with fried chips and a dish of slightly hot, dipping sauce. It's fine though. The centrepiece however is a huge dish of raw carrot and radish with lettuce and tomatoes from Norbu's garden. It is all delicious and we leave nothing. After that it's Norbu's home-made apple pie, with fruit, nuts and cinnamon and we are all very full after this. What a brilliant meal.

I gave Norbu my lion rampant flag, which I carried up to Island Peak summit, but forgot to leave it there, or even take a photograph with me holding it. Only Marguerite remembered the

Saltire flag at the top, she even brought shortbread when I remember! The meal is followed by a shot of whisky from the plastic half bottle I bought in Abu Dhabi and I've carried it all the time, unopened. Naturally, we finish it and have more chang. We head to bed at just after nine and I sleep very, very well.

Friday 24th October.

No pressure for an early rise this morning, but I nip down to see if my trousers are dry. The boys had hung them above the stove last night, as they slept in the dining room. They are perfect. It's a mild morning and great having no breathing problems and all of our coughs are getting better. Getting everything re-packed almost every day is a pain but only one more day of it to go. For breakfast I have porridge and black tea. I hear that Nima has left at five this morning to go back to Namche.

The yak boys have left the climbing gear there instead of bringing it here last night. He will have to carry it straight to Lukla as we will be leaving for there just after a very early lunch. Unbelievable! It is very different weather today. I'm used to clear skies from early morning to mid-afternoon but it's cloudy and mist clings to the hillsides like smoke. In the far distance I can sometimes see a plane leave, or come into Lukla through clouds. Hopefully the flights won't be affected. There is a lot of hanging about this morning, which would have been fine in the sun. Derek has gone for a walk and the rest of us read or get our diaries up to date.

Lunch is at eleven thirty. It is homemade spring rolls with cabbage and a potato cake with a fried egg on top. It is very different, but good and very filling. There are also some carrots and radishes and more tea to wash it all down. Best not to think of human fertiliser that helped the carrots grow. Bad news as, the closer we get to Lukla, the more it's starting to rain. It's also now very cloudy. If Kathmandu or Lukla have mist or low clouds, they often won't fly at all. We stop in a bakery in Lukla to let the others catch up. It's apple cake and milky coffee again and it's great and at only eighty rupees really cheap. I buy a few things in a bookshop and then head up to our lodge - the 'Shangri La' -, which it certainly isn't. There are no lights but a candle in the room. The toilet is at least a sort of pan and a bucket of water for flushing. The dining room has a view of the airport, but no form of heating at all. And it's bloody cold and raining more.

Some of the party head to a pub. John and I sit and read. It's a dump. There are no locks on the room doors so I've cable tied everything with my steel combination lock. Some doors have no handles. Some rooms have no doors! After dinner, we give the lads their tip, about twenty-odd quid each and we buy them a few beers. Kami is back with the climbing gear from Namche and looks tired but says he isn't. Some whisky is bought and Norbu orders weird looking containers with a straw - it's fermented millet seed and gets topped up with hot water to bring out the alcohol - a few times in fact. It tastes awful. It's called 'tongba' I think. In fact it is like drinking vomit. I give Nima my watch to keep and Davy and Marguerite give theirs to the other two guys and this leads the rest to hand over stuff as well, including clothes. It's a nice end to the trek and a good way of showing our appreciation for guys who have never let us down and just keep going and do it cheerfully. I think they are quite appreciative of our gifts. It is still raining.

Saturday 25th October.

The rain wakes me up at three in the morning. This is not good. It sounds torrential on the corrugated tin roof. Despite this, at seven thirty, from the room, I see the first Twin Otter come in and this will be Yeti One. Over the next hour another six or seven come in, unload, reload and head off. Our check-in time is nine o'clock. When we fly is anyone's guess though and the visibility is getting worse. The rain is constant and there is fresh snow quite far down the hillsides above us. It's probably white back in Namche. Nothing seems to be happening and it's after nine and we should be checking in by now. Norbu says he is waiting for the next three aircraft to come in, and then the next will be ours, one of another three. There is a feeling of depression in the team after the success we have had but no point getting upset.

We head down to the airport at half past nine and it is total chaos, and cold. Some money changes hands between Norbu and the female lodge owner who seems to control check-ins and our bags are taken past about twenty people ahead of us in our queue - there are other queues for other operators and the hall is full. We have to then open the bags up again for a cursory security check and move through security, which again is cursory. We wait in the 'lounge' which is really cold and two planes come in, a Yeti Airlines Twin Otter and a Ghorka Airlines Dornier. Apparently, there are two Yeti flights to come in and we are on the second one. We are all aware that they usually don't fly at all after mid-afternoon and the clock is ticking. People have been stranded here for days I remember.

After two hours of hanging about cold and bored, we head out of the airport and back up to the lodge for hot soup. We have left the lounge area and no one challenges us as we walk out past security. We pass our kit bags lying in a corner, again unattended. The weather is worse with really poor visibility and we can't see across the valley. I feel really pissed off about this. We could have been here yesterday. The rest of the team feels the same I know. We head back after one thirty and the mist is now very low. There are only a couple of people in the building and no one knows what is happening and there is no information anywhere, and no staff about to ask. The rain is constant. Suddenly one of the army guards runs across the tarmac, a siren sounds to clear the runway and through the open doors and windows we can hear an aeroplane. The Twin Otter makes two attempts to come in and lands on the third, taxis up and a very unhappy looking pilot jumps out. This flight is a new 'Yeti One'.

As Yeti One takes off with a full complement, we despair of seeing Yeti Two later this afternoon. This is not good as cancelled passengers then go to the end of the queue - not at all a priority - the next day. And, we think, what if the weather gets worse - we need to fly to London tomorrow night. We are losing hope after over an hour when the siren sounds again, but it's at least half an hour before we hear the drone of Yeti Two coming in and it's the same pilot who has come back for us. This will be the last flight to Kathmandu today. It's now three thirty and we have hung about for six hours. The pilot has only stopped one engine at the loading side and as soon as the bags are on we are turning and hammering down the short runway and into the mist, which fortunately clears after we clear a couple of ridges. I am sitting watching the co-pilot. It feels like being on the last US helicopter army flight out of Saigon. I think the three of us have taken this harder because of the time-scale for our flights back.

At Kathmandu, the afternoon is pleasantly warm, which is nice after the cold and wet of Lukla. Amazingly, the boys with the minibus have been keeping tabs on events and are there to meet us and we are soon back in the comfort of the Harati Hotel. I get a room to myself again. We are meeting for tea at reception to get the flights home sorted after leaving the bags unpacked in our rooms. Things slide a bit when we hear that our flights from Kathmandu are confirmed for Monday, not Sunday night and we have connections booked from London to Edinburgh, on non-transferable tickets. This would be a problem even at home but a bigger one on the other side of the world. The hotel doesn't seem switched on about email and Internet stuff. I call home and send a fax with the new flight details and my wife Margaret replies later that night to say all is sorted, but we have to pay for new tickets at London. John agrees to refund these flights. After the stress of this I have a bath, get into clean clothes and feel pretty relaxed - at least we will have a full day in Kathmandu tomorrow and that will be a good and relaxing end to the trip. It's great to have my own room again and plenty of space after the lodges. I remind myself to get the slide film from Davy although too late now!

We eat this night in the Third Eye to celebrate. It's an Indian style restaurant, and the food is great. I can't finish the starter and have chicken korma with rice and naan bread washed down with a litre of Tiger Beer. The meal comes to just over a fiver at 600 rupees. No Macdonald's or Starbucks here, not yet anyway which is good. We then go to the Himalatte Café for a coffee and Neil and I have a large whisky each for a nightcap. Slept well and my first time in a real bed for nearly three weeks! This is the longest I've been without female company in my life! Fall asleep thinking about the good-looking girl in Namche. Ah well!

Sunday 26th October.

John has organised a sightseeing trip for us early on Sunday morning, and we leave in a minibus with Yogi, our guide who is a driver, not a bear. At the Monkey Temple at Swayambhunath, to the west of the city, I made a deal with a woman selling bangles after asking the price of individual items and bought all she had for 500 rupees. I could have married her for less probably! We are both pleased and this will make part of Margaret's Christmas presents for years to come! Amazingly there is a Hindu temple here to the Goddess of smallpox! Or that could be a wrong translation by me. Some of the street sights are amazing, highlighted by this being the start of Diwali, the Hindu Festival of Light and firecrackers are going off at nights...or is it gunfire? We are taken to some markets and the fish market is amazing, considering Nepal is nowhere near the sea. These must be freshwater fish, or more likely, farmed. The guys are de-scaling the fish. As we have left early, we have missed some of the crowds and we're back at the hotel before eleven.

Davy and I sit at a table out on the lawn and order two San Miguels - litres of course. We also order chips as we feel we have lost sufficient weight to justify this! It is bliss sitting in the warm sun. We have another two and lovely relaxing here in the sun going over the trip and what were both our highlights. In the afternoon we wander down to Durbar Square, You need a permit to enter this historic area but it's only 200 rupees for the day. Look at lots of shops but don't buy anything. Neil has bought a hat which seems to single him out as an easy touch and he is constantly hassled to buy things like flutes. He always talks to them though and that's fatal. I buy some incense, which is really cheap. The name on the packet says 'cocaine'. That might be a challenge at Heathrow.

Back at the Harati, we all have another beer. Tonight we

are going to the Sherpa Society for supper, but first we go by taxi - always precarious - to the big temple at Boudhanath, or Bodhnath. It is a really big stupa and about a hundred and thirty feet high, one of the largest in the world. There are hundreds of people here and lots of monks in orange robes. There seems to be some sort of ceremony and we go to a second floor café to have a drink and watch. We should have been here at sunset apparently. Sit here thinking that maybe this society, with all its poverty is maybe more viable for the future than our energy greedy, all-consuming operation. Are we happier?

At the door of the Sherpa Society we take our shoes off as usual and sit in the pleasant room and have some punch, which tastes really strong. The supper is a dish we have had many times on the trail and what our porters and Norbu had to eat continually - dal bhat, but with spicy chicken as well. I think I have come to hate dal bhat! Again a lovely night talking to these friendly people. The plan is to take two cabs back and go to the famous 'Rum Doodle' bar for a drink as recommended by our baggage guy in Edinburgh airport. Our cab gets pulled by the police, for having no licence and our next taxi then hits an army road-block and is diverted and ends up just going back to the hotel, having lost the others and lost the will to look if not live.

Monday 27th October.

Wake up with Kathmandu waking up at five o'clock. What a racket as the city wakes up. For a change we go to the Himalatte Café for our breakfast, which is OK and it's fine to watch the world go by, but the hotel breakfast was probably nicer. This morning is the last opportunity for shopping, and it is good fun haggling, but the reality is, most stuff is really, really cheap and as today is the Hindu Diwali celebrations, trade is slack. I really feel at home here, wandering about, having the odd stop for a drink.

Davy, Marguerite and I meet up with Neil for a Tiger beer and wait for a shop-owner to complete our celebratory T-shirts of Island Peak. We get talking to a Chinese girl in the bar who has heard us talking (and swearing!) and we talk about Britain and China. Typically, her English is excellent. It's still sunny and warm as we collect our T-shirts and head back to the hotel and start to get packed up for the journey home. All of our bags feel very heavy. After that we all meet in the gardens to order lunch and beers and the white suited waiters are back and forward like something out of the last days of the Raj, bringing drinks and dishes of food. I have Peshwari Murg, much nicer than it sounds. With the beer it's less than five pounds.

We are collected by our taxi at three o'clock. Only four of us are returning as Diane is staying in Kathmandu for a few more days, Derek is off to Tibet and John meets his next clients to climb Lobuche East. We say our goodbyes and we're off through the chaos to the airport and get checked in and have a last beer in Nepal. I feel we were a really close team and regret that we are all going our own ways. The flight home is via Abu Dhabi, where we have to wait two hours. I buy Margaret two lovely gold chains, which you pay for by weight, one for when I get back, the heavier one for Christmas. Then off to Bahrain, although we don't get off here. It makes it a long flight and we get into Heathrow at six in the morning.

Tuesday 28th October.

Our connection to Edinburgh isn't until early afternoon, so there's even more hanging about, but as I am actually working now, the mobile gets switched on and it's back to the world of work. Everyone's brilliant at Hyundai and there is no problem with being a day late. Everyone wants to know all about the trip. Margaret is at Edinburgh to collect us and we drop Davy and Marguerite off. Get home at last and a big cuddle from my four boys who are quite taken by my beard - they want me to keep it and Alastair actually brings his friends in from school to let them see me. Decide to leave it on till the weekend as a link with the rest of the month. Turns out I've lost nearly a stone in weight, in spite of the Kathmandu beers. The experience, which was to be a 'once in a lifetime' will have to be repeated but I regret not having a dad to tell all about it. The experience of course will always be more than just the photographs and the souvenirs. It's been a journey in more ways than one.

Book Two

Annapurna And Chulu Far East 2005

Friday 30th September.

After our Island Peak expedition, when we collected over £2500 for Cancer Research and held a slideshow in a local church hall which was well attended and raised £1000 for Nepalese charities, everyone was asking what we would do next. With two other climbing club members, Ivan and Tom, I had been climbing in the French Alps and climbed Mont Blanc so the precedent was set for others to come with us back to Nepal. Well, this time again there was going to be few members from the club interested in going to Nepal after hearing about our trip two years ago and Mont Blanc but the reality was that there would be four of us and the same team as last time plus Donald, a recent member of the club. What Donald didn't have in terms of equipment either we or the club could lend him. It was likely he said that he wouldn't climb the mountain with us but go for the adventure. But he still did the practise ropes in winter with us on Tinto and bought an ascender just in case. I had been talking to my new friend Sunir from Far-Out Nepal since meeting him briefly last time in Kathmandu and lots of emails back and forward over the year. Basically we wanted to do some of the hardest parts of the Annapurna circuit and climb another big mountain. We would plan to travel to the start by Land Cruisers to Besisahar, trek the Annapurna Circuit to Jomsom and fly back to Kathmandu from Jomsom via Pokhara.

We agreed after a lot of discussion about which mountain to climb with Pisang Peak looking the most obvious choice as it was closer to our section of the Annapurna Circuit, but ultimately we decided on climbing Chulu Far East and Sunir would sort out the permit. Again a 20,000 foot mountain, very rarely climbed it seemed, as I couldn't get much information on it. Again, trying to get our money's worth! This would be our own expedition and I was expedition leader, at least for the paperwork. There was still an issue with the Maoist guerrillas and more chance of meeting them where we were going! Again, our club member, the ex-Gurkha Captain advised us against going. The Chulus form part of the Manang Himal, which is included in the larger Damodar Himal. The largest peak is Chulu West at just over 21,000 feet. Chulu Far

East is almost exactly 20,000 feet but easier to get to given our timescales of three weeks.

The BA flight from Edinburgh down to Heathrow was uneventful apart from there being no catering because of a strike - just a sandwich. As always when you are not in a hurry, the flight landed early. Like last time, we decided just to walk to Terminal 3 as it isn't far. With a couple of wayward trolleys, we headed off. Davy and Donald guided them as best they could. Marguerite and I warned pedestrians ahead. Davy changed some Scottish notes for Bank of England ones, and I bought some dollars. Just for bribing the Maoists not to shoot us. Although we were about three hours too early, we got booking in at the Gulf Air desks and then upstairs to one of the food places. We got four seats OK and then I went for a big pizza slice. I bought a bottle of red wine for Donald and I to share and Davy bought a bottle of white. We justified this by saying we could take them onto the plane if there was some left. There wasn't. By this time the flight has been called and soon we're boarding the plane. We have the middle row of four, away up the back, and after drinks and dinner we all get some sleep.

Saturday 1st October.

At Abu Dhabi we didn't have a long wait for the flight to Kathmandu, unlike last time. I used the dollars to buy some drinks and biscuits and it seems a lot busier than last time, but soon we're heading again for the gate and through security. This time we are split up, with Donald and I on the right as we enter and Davy and Marguerite on the left. That should mean if the weather is clear, Donald and I will get a view of the Himalayas. The reality, of course, was that it was pretty cloudy and although we did see some big peaks, the landing seemed to be through big storm clouds and it was a bit bumpy on approach like last time.

As we already had our visas, we got through passport control and immigration quickly but then waited a full hour for our bags, unsure which belt they were on. The usual chaos I suppose but anyway, now on two trolleys and out to face the mayhem of Kathmandu. Looking at the myriad faces we search for a sign saying 'Wilson' or 'Far-Out Nepal', but nothing. I hesitate about going out into the throng of eager, too eager porters and hangers-on but as we move out the main doors, a voice shouts, "Over here Mr Jim"!

It's Sunir! And, of course, he recognised us from our copies of the passport photos we sent him for the climbing permit. Nima is here too, our guide for the trip. With lots of helping hands we are soon across the car park and into the mini-bus, and we are handing out British money to the porters who accept the pound coins OK. It's now getting dark, so we don't get to see much. Donald is amazed by the Kathmandu streets and the driving as it's his first time here. Soon we are at the hotel Vaishali and it looks pretty smart and has a really nice bar and lobby area. We get checked in and take the bags to the room and will meet some of our team in ten minutes downstairs. The room that Donald and I are sharing is adequate and has air conditioning and en-suite facilities. In a few days this will just be a pleasant memory. The other bags arrive, and the porter is showing us how the TV works but it doesn't matter as we won't be watching it. Downstairs we meet Sunir again and Nima arrives too, with his assistant, Dorge, one of our climbing Sherpas. Som our senior climbing Sherpa, is here as well. We go over the climbing gear and we get a couple of bags for the gear. Sunir says there is a change of plan for tomorrow. No Land Cruisers for us, instead, a coach! So, we can all travel together, he says.

To save the porters and cook having to travel separately and have all the hassle of being stopped at police checkpoints every few miles, we will all travel together. We will leave at 6:00am from the hotel, collect porters along the way and all the gear and food from Nima's storeroom. We all shake hands and they leave and we're just happy to be here and it's all been fairly smooth. "So far" I think. We decide to go to the famous Rum Doodle restaurant for a meal and as it's nearly eight o'clock, I ask the clerk to change some money. Only with a lot of persuasion and pleading will he change £20 Scottish notes and I get £200's of rupees. Davy changes some money - his English notes - no bother but the clerk has only just over £100's of rupees left. We will need more cash.

We also need to get our passports and British cash into a safety deposit box, along with mobile phones, which are useless here and while the others are doing this, I order four large Heinekens from the bar. We don't even finish the drinks and carry the bottles across the street to one of many moneychangers. This guy says a definite no to the Scottish notes but makes a couple of calls to check. This is not looking good. While this is going on, as I take a last swig from the bottle, I can see the other hotel clerk at another moneychanger across the road and as if it was a movie, I can see him hold up one of my £20 Scottish notes and the moneychanger definitely shaking his head to say no. Not good I think. Our moneychanger is now saying no Nepalese bank will accept them. I say that they did two years ago - I had no problem. "That was then, this is now," he says and he suggests we try an ATM. So we wait in a queue but eventually I try my card and it fails, Davy manages to get another £200. I try another card but no joy there and we try a few other moneylenders but find only one that will give me money against my card. But only £100 maximum, and with an extra 5% charge. When we get back to the Rum Doodle, just round the corner from the hotel and try to think of a plan. Basically we have enough money between us for the trek we agree. I order a round of Everest beers and think about things and that we will have the garbage disposal money refunded when we get back and that is $350. Surely a main bank will accept a credit card OK? Maybe even in Jomsom or Pokhara? This is when Donald admits he hasn't brought a credit card with him. Only cash. Scottish cash! I pay for the meal with my card to save our rupees. We have enough rupees between us but only just and we're away for over two weeks. We go to the hotel bar for a nightcap. It's not a quiet drink as the clerk at reception is demanding his rupees back and has my Scottish notes in his hand. He is apologetic, but adamant so I have to say I have spent all of it hiring porters and paying for transport. I casually tell him to put it on my room account but he can't or won't. I say it's 'only' £200. A few minutes later the other younger clerk asks if I'm a rich man and I regret not being more subtle as that is a lot of money for them and a big lack of cultural awareness for me.

Lots of discussion and phone-calls and we have another beer while we wait on his boss making a decision and he arrives after a few minutes and agrees it can go on my card but with a 15% charge! I have no option but to accept and I get my £20 notes back. I have £400 to leave in the hotel safe, all useless here now. While this is going on, an Indian party arrives, all of them in either bandages or on crutches. It appears there has been a bus accident bringing them to Kathmandu. And four people are dead.

They were on the road that we will be taking tomorrow. We finish our beers and head off to bed. What a night! During the night there is a power cut and the emergency generator starts, wakes me up and I can't get back to sleep.

Sunday 2nd October

We are up at 5:00am and I get the final packing done for my kit bag and climbing gear. We have all the stuff downstairs before Nima arrives. We also organise bags with a change of clothes to be left at the hotel for our return and get a packed 'breakfast'. As we hang about at the hotel door waiting on the bus. Marguerite spots a big shrub as she asks if I have seen the wee different coloured fruits on it? Yes, like an opal fruit tree, but no they are little lights - so a good laugh at her expense and for days to come!

Well, the bus is certainly big, and colourful, and a very, very old Tata. We sit at the front and head off to collect the camping gear and the porters. Even this early the city is really busy and because it is the start of the Diwali festival Nima says. People are heading back to their villages for the celebrations. At Nima's place, his young daughters come up to thank us for the presents we brought over with us, from friends in Scotland and the gear is loaded and we are introduced to the porters individually with lots of smiles from them.

Getting out of Kathmandu is a nightmare but eventually we are heading out of the city with our driver overtaking everything he can and some he can't. The horn is used a lot. We are heading west on the Tribhuvan Rajmarg. The bus heads down some tortuous bends and you can see several places where a landslide has occurred. Lots of traffic coming the other way, ancient Tata trucks, all heavily decorated and coming from India says Nima. Just like the crashed bus last night I think and a lot of breakdowns too. A bus passes us with live goats on the roof! We stop twice while the driver checks the wheels or tyres. At one point a tyre gets some air. Not inspiring confidence but after about two hours, we slow down and pull into a sort of truck stop, with two fuel pumps, a café and a shop of sorts. Our packed breakfasts are unpacked which is OK. It has two boiled eggs, some pastries and a carton of orange juice. From where we sit, we can see the spare tyre coming off the bus and some roadside operation is going on with a guy trying to fix it. The equipment looks ancient and another guy has a Stanley knife and is cutting bits of an old inner tube to pack somehow into our tyre. It's good to watch, and it seems to work.

As I turn around a lorry driver is at his truck at the pumps, filling up with diesel and smoking away happily. Just a different world and we wander about and take some photos. The toilets look pretty awful and I don't use them. The river we follow now is the Trisuli, good for rafting and I bet it's safer than this road. We get back on the bus and another four hours of high drama to come on the roads. After half an hour we pass a bus on the outskirts of a village lying crushed, on its roof, still on the road and this is the bus that the injured Indians had been on. It makes no impression on our driver who thunders on. We are on the Prithvi Rajmarg now, built in the 70's with Chinese finance.

Eventually we turn off the main road onto an almost single track road, but we still thunder on, the horn going at every blind bend to warn the unwary. At one point a young ox is running ahead of us with a bloody nose from some injury, maybe it fought to get loose. Eventually we stop for a lengthy police check and we all get out. It's really quite tropical down at this level and rice is growing in the fields. Quite soon after this we enter Besisahar and this is the administrative centre of the Lamjung district and we're at just 2,700 feet. It has a bank, school and post office. It also has a police checkpoint we have to visit. This is the end of our bus ride and we will have a light lunch here which Nima has organised and he also mentions that we might be able to take the 'service bus' another few kilometres to save some walking. I mention this to the others and I'm for it as I don't like walking on tarmac I remember saying. So we order lunch but it takes ages. I have an Everest beer while we wait and lunch is vegetable soup and then fried rice - with vegetables. Nima comes in to sit with us and says we have spaces on the bus and that's good. It will take us on to Bhulbhule, which means 'place of the spring' which sounds encouraging and we start trekking from there. As we walk up the street, luggage is being loaded onto the roof of an ancient bus and even older than ours and there are lots of people milling around. It doesn't look as if there's room to me. As I walk to the bus door a voice says, "Jim, give me your rucksack"!

It's Dorge and I pass my pack through the window to him. We just seem to get on and no more and the bus is packed and I can hear a hen squawking somewhere. Next to Dorge, a porter gives me his seat and some of our team are actually travelling on the roof. We were never ever on tarmac and it was a road for a rugged 4x4, not a bus. As I stick my head out of the window there are people holding on at the front and back and, more tightly, on the roof. The road is incredibly rough and I'm glad that at my side I can't see the sheer drop to the river as we plough on through streams with all sorts of bangs and creaks. Twice I thought we were over and later Nima tells me he thought this too and he was on the roof! So after almost an hour we come quite literally to the end of the road, and where our porters get all our gear down from the roof and sort out their loads. While we all take photographs of the bus we notice someone has laughingly painted 'speed control' on the front bumper. If the first bus journey was exciting, this was terrifying, but some experience.

We have tried to keep our kit bags under 15kg, so a porter

will not have to carry in excess of 30kg, but we can see one of our porters with three bags on his back. There are some heavy looking loads and one guy has a folding table and four chairs as well as other stuff on his back. To start the trek we have to cross our first rope bridge and we wait until some donkeys come over with big packs on their back.

After walking up stone steps we pass through a village and meet up with children coming from school. Three girls walk with us asking where we're from. They haven't heard of Scotland. They are laughing a lot and we ask them lots of questions too. One girl spots Marguerite's furry toy dog tied onto her rucksack and asks its name. It doesn't have a name, says Marguerite, but asks the girl her name. "Ritoo" says the wee girl and that, says Marguerite, is what the wee dog will be called from now on. The girls are delighted. It is very hot and humid and we walk past lots of rice fields, which have rows of soybeans running through them. The beans are grown on the ridges holding in the watery soil, the rice is grown in between. There are also some banana and orange trees growing here and they are very subtropical.

We reach our lodge for the night in Ngadi, which Nima says is pronounced Nyadi. We are only at Munro height - 3,051 feet. Almost 1,500 feet lower than Kathmandu, so it's going to be a slog to get to 20,000 feet in just over a week! The lodge is right on the only street in the village and we sit on the small terrace and have some tea. After an hour I head for the shower out the back and pay 50 rupees for hot water. The shower, inevitably, is cold. Anyway, there is erratic electricity, which is a bit of a luxury, and it's nice to sit outside, writing up our journals but in the distance we can see lightning and hear far away thunder. We have our meal outside with a wee bulb for illumination. Davy and I order two large bottles of Tuborg lager to share, and at one point the lights go out and we get a lantern and some candles. Nima and Som join us after dinner to talk about tomorrow and the possibility of using our 'spare' day at base-camp to help us acclimatise.

Inevitably, we have another couple of beers and I bring down the patented Talisker/Southern Comfort mixture, I call it 'Nepalese Nectar'. The woman of the lodge I think is going to object to us drinking our own, but no, she brings out some shot glasses and Dorge and Som join us in this nightcap. It's only 9:00pm but it's been a long and eventful day and as will be the norm, we order our breakfast choice before we go to bed. We will have breakfast at 6:00am; mine will be apple porridge and black tea. About an hour after we are in bed, there is a heavy downpour and amazingly, even with the rain banging on the tin roof, I sleep fitfully.

Monday 3rd October

I am up at 5:30am and the rain has stopped and the back

courtyard even looks dry. We all have our breakfast on the terrace next to the road and by the time we leave at 6:30am it's already warm. This lodge is where something bit me and unusually for me I had a few red lumps. I hope it's not malaria! The trek today is going to be around six hours and Nima says we should go slower than yesterday to "keep our fluids". In a way of course he's right and I know I haven't been drinking enough water. Before we leave I've filled my bottle from the street tap and added iodine. After five minutes and some vitamin C to kill the taste, at least a bit, but my tablets take ages to dissolve in the very cold water.

We set off at an easy pace, lots of up and down and following the river but inevitably we stop soon for tea before plodding on to the next village, Ghermu, where we have lunch and for me this is spicy vegetable soup and rosti. The soup is fine but the rosti I was thinking of was what I had in a mountain hut in Switzerland in the summer. Now that was good - this, on the other hand, is like under-cooked wallpaper paste. We sit in the sun for almost two hours and watch an amazing display by huge dark blue butterflies, sometimes three of them dancing in the air next to us and I get a few photos of them. After lunch and high above the river now we walk past wild cannabis plants and some growing taller than us. It's everywhere but of course illegal here as well. At one point we spot reddish brown monkeys on the other side of the river.

At Jagat (4,311 feet) we stop for the day and we're staying in the Mont Blanc Lodge, which sounds very grand but is pretty basic though OK. To get to the rooms we go up a rickety wooden stair on the outside of the building with a badly painted white arrow to guide us. Apparently, the village has a school, three campsites and once was a customs post for the Tibetan salt trade. The room Donald and I are in is quite good though, apart from the outside staircase! As I go down for a shower, Nima pulls me aside and says the Maoists are in the area and may come tonight or tomorrow. He looks awfully serious and says it may cost us 1300 rupees each. This it seems is the going rate of 100 rupees for every day we are in 'their' territory. I let the others know but I don't think anyone is too worried and not much we can do about it anyway.

Dinner tonight, outside in the backyard, is noodle soup,

indeterminate flavour, followed by well, just chips and lots of black tea as well. After dinner we get the cards out and order some Tuborg and we play till 9:00pm and finish the Nepalese Nectar - the Talisker/Southern Comfort mix. No Maoists. No monkeys and no gunfire and breakfast ordered. I have a great sleep, thanks to decadent western alcohol.

Tuesday 4th October

It's been raining during the night but it's dry now as I meet Nima after having been for a wash and he says the Maoists will be here soon. We were down having breakfast in the yard when they arrived very quietly through the outside door. A tall serious-looking guy with a pistol comes in first and a second in command who keeps looking about. The guy with the gun looks at us and asks Nima a question and I wonder if it is who to shoot first and I'm startled a bit when Nima points at me. But he has asked who the expedition leader is and that is me! It's all quite formal as we sit at a table and Nima pays the money and we actually get a receipt. I give the leader a wee metal hammer and sickle badge from my rucksack I bought in Prague last year and he puts it on and shakes my hand. No discount for this Scottish comrade though. So, the Maoists leave, and I get on with my porridge. A weird experience but Nima says they are harder if you lie about how many days you are in their territory and we are likely to meet more of them further on who will check the receipt!

It has started to rain again a bit but by the time breakfast is finished it stopped and we sit with yet another cup of tea. Nima says it will be another six-hour day. We are passed frequently by mule-trains and then flocks of goats and sheep, heading to the markets in Kathmandu for the festive celebration meals as it will be Diwali soon, the Hindu festival of light. The rain stays off but there are a lot of ups and downs this morning. The scenery is still subtropical and mist is clinging like smoke to the highly vegetated hillsides. We climb quite steeply from a rope bridge up to a wee lodge at Kangrung for black tea and an hour's rest. From here we climb quite a bit before inevitably heading down again and we leave the Lamjung area and enter the Manang area and, as we pass through a concrete gateway and come round a bend, I am stopped in my tracks. Suddenly the scenery in front of me is totally different from the deep vegetated gorges and we are now in an open valley with the river, now wide, running through it.

At Tal, the next village, we stop for lunch at 5,700 feet. Lunch today for me is noodle soup and an omelette and is possibly the best meal I've had so far. And, of course, there is plenty of tea to wash it down. The area around us is quite open compared with the deep gorges and valleys we've travelled through. As we sit here it begins to drizzle again but after an hour it goes off and we have clear skies. We're back in a wide gorge with the Marsyangdi river beneath us. We walk for a couple of hours then cross the river by a long rope bridge and stop for tea at the "Dorchester Hotel" - it says it on the lodge sign and we take a few photographs and of course the sign as well. Nothing like the one in London however!

From here, it's a short walk to Dharapani at 6,450 feet, where we stop for the night. Our lodge here is just outside the village but at least it's quieter and the accommodation is again OK. We haven't many other trekkers in the lodge, no doubt because of the Maoists. After a cool shower, made possible only by using my head-torch - no lights are working; we have a beer at a table in the front courtyard and the place has lots of flowers and huge cannabis plants on the path outside. I take a botanical leaf specimen and keep it at the back of my guidebook and a specimen for the others too. Almost wish I smoked. Dinner is in a small dining room, which is quite well lit and we have another beer to go with it and after dinner we play cards until about 9:00pm. Then headed off to bed and slept well again to the sound of the river.

Wednesday 5th October

Slept till about 5:00am and still dark at this time. When it got light I wandered down to a street tap about 500 yards away to wash and brush my teeth. I didn't notice the lodge tap till I got back and Nima was laughing as he had seen me wandering away and had a look to see where I was going. Breakfast is two cups of really nice black tea, with cinnamon and the porridge is the best yet and is served with chopped apple on top, which is a wee luxury! I feel pretty fit today. From here we will climb to Chame at 8,760 feet and this is potentially a sore head day as we gain a lot of altitude. Again, on the way we pass sheep being herded from the high border with Tibet to the Kathmandu markets. It seems a crazy distance to take livestock but the old Scottish drovers did it with cattle!

Not far outside the village, Som meets a porter whom he knows and is heading our direction and they are from the same village, but the porter crosses the Marsyangdi and heads in the direction of Tibet. This was, according to Som, an important trading route before the Chinese invasion and this is the direction the sheep are coming from and it must take a couple of weeks to get them to Kathmandu and their ultimate fate. In the far distance we get a fantastic view of Manaslu, a very big looking mountain.

We are now passing lots of mule trains, going down empty, maybe as far as Besisahar to pick up loads. Inevitably we stop mid-morning for tea in the village of Bagarchap at about 7,000 feet. The trail has been really busy today and some parts are congested where there have been overnight landslides. People are working here and there to clear the path and where we stop for tea is on a raised terrace and we sit outside and watch the world go by. There is a big French trekking group we keep catching up with, but hopefully not in a lodge - as that would really complicate the feeding regime if everyone orders different things, which then have to be cooked individually usually by one cook. I took a picture at the "Tibetan Guest House" of Davy, me, Marguerite and Donald, all looking relaxed.

I am watching three Nepalese children playing and Davy gets a couple of good photographs with his long lens. I would have to get closer with my camera. So, as we leave, I steal Marguerite's pen. I'm fed up with her constant journal writing anyway - she's always a way ahead of the rest of us by a day or so. I say I have an idea, then walk up to the kids and hand them the pen and take a couple of shots of these lovely wee girls. She eventually saw the funny side and the photos are really good. As we leave here, we are walking only with Som. Nima and the rest of our crew are still at the teahouse. Som questions a porter who is passing about the route and hears about another, bigger landslide, which means we will have to divert to a higher route. But what about the rest, how can we tell them? Som draws an arrow in the mud with a stick to indicate which way we have taken, so the others can catch us up. I'm impressed at these Nepalese trekking skills. Tonto would be impressed too but, needless to say, we don't see the others till we stop for the day, much later. They didn't see the arrow and took another route. Following Som we head uphill onto a very wide but still very rough track. This is to be part of a new road, which will go from the road end at Besisahar right to Chame. It will totally change this largely unspoilt area but we can't complain if poor people have their lives made easier. A lot of the trees have debris marks from flying stones as they blast the new road through.

Lunch is outside in the sunshine and I decide to go for the same menu choice as yesterday. The difference is though, that yesterday's omelette was made with two eggs. So is today's, but three are sharing it! The place is really busy and it takes a while to get served. Some of our guys arrive and our cook is helping out in the kitchen and some others are helping with serving as well. By now the wind is getting cooler and it's fleeces on. We are fed and ready to go, but Som and some others are also helping in the kitchen and they haven't been fed yet, so more hanging about. It's getting really cold and I leave the other three, sleeping on a seat, to wait on Som and I as we head downhill and out of the wind, to a rope bridge. In front of us, is the weird and massive pure rock

Pisang Wall, which must be miles long. Apparently, it's an upturned seabed.

When we all get started, Nima says the walk this afternoon will be three hours and although we stop again for tea, we will arrive into Chame at just after 3:00pm. Overlooking us is Annapurna 2 but in the cloud. We can, however, still see Manaslu. There is an army checkpoint and it takes half an hour to get past it. We all have to show our passports or copy passports and sign a book. There are soldiers in green camouflage uniform and police in blue camouflage uniform and all armed with really old looking semi-automatic rifles. I notice one soldier's gun has only three bullets in the clip, which must take at least ten. As we walk into the village past a long Mani wall with prayer wheels, I notice a young soldier is walking with us, talking to Som and the soldier has a red flower pinned to the arm of his uniform. I ask Som to ask him if this is a standard army issue, as a joke. In response and to the delight of the group, the soldier takes the red flower off his arm and hands it to me. So the joke is on me now. Anyway we get talking and it turns out he is twenty-two and has been in the army three years. He asks about the Maoists and in good English. I tell him our story and he seems to think we paid the going rate. No Maoists in this area he says. I handed the flower to Marguerite.

The lodge is quite new with a good dining area and has chalet accommodation. However, we couldn't get in here, so we are in poorer sleeping accommodation in a wooden building next door. Upstairs and with no lights anywhere and the outside wooden steps are quite steep. Just one toilet here along a dark corridor and a hole in the floor type as usual. After we leave the bags in the room we all go for a walk. Som said Chame was a big place but it's just a big village. Some really primitive looking wooden shacks, a few lodges and some shops, including a sewing workshop where boys are using the type of sewing machine my mum had forty years ago. There is a safe drinking water station here so you can refill your water bottles rather than buy plastic ones. I go back with Donald and have a beer in the lounge with him and then go for a shower. And it's quite warm so I must be the first! The dining room is small and the place is quite busy, so I get down first to keep us seats. It's just after 5:00pm. And it gives me the chance to write up some notes and as usual order a Tuborg and a litre this time.

The rest come down about 6:00pm and we order more beers and dinner. Tonight I have noodle soup and pizza and all pretty good. As usual, after dinner we have a game of cards and another round of beers and this is when we christened Donald with his new Nepalese name, 'Minu', as he was always asking if it was his turn to play at cards, "me noo"? Nima and Som have a good laugh at this. Later on I ordered two glasses of chang for Donald and I and these were in half-pint glasses and cost about 18p each I think. Amazingly it didn't taste as bad as I remembered from last time in Nepal. It was only the next day that Som gave me a rebuke and said it was dodgy stuff, made from cold, un-purified water. No bad effects though. I passed out as soon as I got into my sleeping bag and slept without waking up until 2:30am, when a barking dog woke everyone up. I got up for a pee and really needed the head-torch to get me to the loo and back, but couldn't get back to sleep.

Thursday 6th October

I got up at 6:00am and felt really lousy, a combination of dehydration, lack of sleep and now, of all things, a sore throat. At breakfast I forced a litre of water down my throat, had two cups of tea and corn flakes of a sort with apple and hot (yak's?) milk. I can taste nothing and my nose is running as well. We set off under pure blue skies with Lamjung Himal, at 21,500 feet, shining white high above us. Again today we follow the river and sometimes on the foundation of the proposed new road to Manang. In some places though, the path is only a few feet wide and the cliff face above the river has been carved out to allow passage. We go down to the river then climb steeply through warm pine woods before levelling out as we come to our lunch stop for the day.

The lodge we stop at is quite big and the whole team is having lunch here. The sun is warm and the atmosphere very relaxed. Today I will have noodle soup and an omelette again and it's quite good. No rush to press on so I have the chance to look at the map and write up some of my journal. The scenery is quite alpine now. This is the first time I put sunscreen on and I can feel myself burning. When we set off we are heading down again, which is a disappointment as we have just came up. The next valley we enter is much wider than before and just a bit bleaker looking.

We are heading to the village of Pisang at 10,449 feet and the walk is under two hours so it's not a big day. The wind is stronger though and we are glad to be in some shelter at the lodge which seems really busy when we arrive, but we are sitting in the sun at a big table having tea as the porters get our bags into our rooms and again, it's very relaxed. The room this time is the usual size but for the whole place there is only one shower and one toilet, the hole in the floor type. I have a shower eventually but don't feel well and take a couple of painkillers, and my first Diamox, just in case it's altitude related, although we're only at

69

10,000 feet. I have to go and lie down late afternoon and fall asleep straight away. Donald wakes me at 5:00pm to get dinner ordered, but I don't feel hungry at all. All I can manage at dinner is a bowl of soup that I couldn't finish and I'm off to bed at 7:00pm feeling feverish.

Friday 7th October

As Nima has said we are in no rush today, we haven't ordered breakfast last night and we have a long lie. Just as well as I have slept for ten hours and even then don't want to get up. And I've slept fully clothed because I was cold too and to help sweat whatever it is, out. Eventually I get up, and head for the only shower, which is empty. I get stripped off and turn on the shower, which is freezing, so no wonder it's empty, but needs must. Bracing is one description. Nima said last night that we will have an audience with the chief Lama for the area. Nima has organised it and the Lama is at the lodge this morning. After this we will go for a walk to a monastery high on the hill outside the village. Breakfast is muesli with apple but though it's good, I can't finish it but have two big cups of black tea. Our audience with the travelling Lama will be half an hour after breakfast. Nima says we should make a donation of about 200 rupees and I notice that he is really quite serious about the whole event. This will be our Puja a blessing ceremony for good luck on the mountain.

When the time comes to go in, we have to take off our shoes and we go in and copy Nima, sitting cross-legged on the floor. The Lama sits behind a big desk and is wearing a dirty looking down jacket, not robes and his baseball cap is hanging behind him. Warmer than the robes for a travelling Lama but not what I expected. With a pen with a peacock feather on it, he sprinkles holy water about and up to heaven. He first blesses, and then hands Nima the prayer flags that we will fly at base camp and then we get rice grains thrown over us, the prayer flags, and again to heaven. Nima looks very solemn.

The Lama reads from holy scriptures, and we are each given a kata, a silk scarf, which we accept with hands together and get an individual blessing and a bow and give the Lama the 200 rupees. We all got a photograph after the event. I felt better for it.

70

The climb to the Nipara monastery takes us over a wood and stone bridge over the Marsyangdi and up a quite steep hill where there are views up and down the valley and across from us we can see the snow slopes of Annapurna 2. It's still misty though and there are some spots of rain and certainly not the consistency of good weather we had two years ago in the Everest region. Som is telling us that the Nipara monastery was a wreck but with Japanese sponsorship, it's been almost re-built. I have no idea why they would want to sponsor a monastery away out here, but we meet the guardian and he uses a big key to open the doors and let us in. The decoration, as always, is very elaborate and looking at the roof, I nearly fall over Som, who had decided to prostrate himself on the floor to pray. Not a place to shout out an expletive. I wish I could say a prayer that would get me some Coldrex. The others seem really interested but I'm not so I just put my donation in the box and go outside.

There are people in the fields threshing what I think is buckwheat and almost every field has people working and children playing. We walk slowly down and we all take some photos and I shoot some film as I've not been doing enough filming, trying to conserve the batteries for the mountain. We head back across the river and we are now heading towards Humde at 11,115 feet, where there is a STOL airstrip (short take off and landing). It's possible to fly here from Kathmandu, but acclimatisation would be a major hazard and possibly life-threatening. As we pull up to the top of a hill, through scrub to meet our porters and Nima, inevitably we go downhill from here and in the distance we can make out the airstrip. This will be our last stop in a lodge as we head off the trail and towards Chulu and off the Annapurna circuit trail. As we walk into the basic town we pass the usual shrine with prayer wheels - the longest set I've seen yet with 250 wheels - sore on the hands as we pass, of course, on the left hand side as always.

Before we stop we pass a sign advertising a safe drinking water station. You can fill your water bottle at these stations and it's to prevent the use of bought plastic water bottles. Next to the sign someone has helpfully nailed up a buffalo head. Our lodge tonight looks OK and seems pretty quiet and in the courtyard is a big blue plastic sheet with buckwheat spread on it and sparrows stealing what they can. It must be to dry it, but it is soon taken away. Nailed on the balcony leading to the bedrooms is another bulls head but this time with coloured lights in its eye sockets. The Eagles song 'Welcome to the Hotel California' comes to mind but it's actually the 'Hotel Gandaki'. That word may of course be Nepalese for California. As usual we all have lemon tea as we wait on our porters with our bags. We are in a dining room upstairs, overlooking the road into town we have just walked up. It's quite cold and windy here and the only other person here, a Danish woman, asks me if we are heading to Manang. I say no, we are off to climb a mountain from here then rejoining the trail. It turns out she is waiting on a helicopter to take her to Jomsom. Her husband and two kids all got over the Thorung La, but she developed acute mountain sickness and on medical advice came back here, some of it on horseback. She has no other options. She was upset that no one could tell her if the helicopter was coming tomorrow or not. From Jomson, she would again walk back to join her family, maybe at Muktinath.

I'm reminded that we also have to get over the Thorung La and to put it in perspective, it's 1,900 feet higher than Mont Blanc, the highest mountain in Western Europe. It's also, for us, the only way to get back to Kathmandu without taking another ten days, maybe more, to get back the way we came, plus, we would have extra costs. Lunch today is chicken soup then mashed potato with cheese, which is so dry, it won't mix with the potato but I manage to force it down. The weather still isn't great and there is no sign of improvement so to pass the time we are going for a walk with Som for a couple of hours. My nose won't stop running, oh for Coldrex! We get some good, but fleeting, views of Annapurna 4 and we can see some of the Chulu peaks as well and they look very far away and very big! In the late afternoon the lodge is still empty. The bedroom is really big compared to what we have had and the dining room is quite nice, if cold. Before dinner, Nima and the porters check the portable decompression chamber, which they are carrying, just in case of severe altitude problems. They check it works by putting one of our personal porters, Pasang, into it. I suppose it could save a life. The chamber is then pressured to mimic high altitude and then brought to normal. Pasang is brought out to applause with nothing worse than sore ears. Makes you think though.

I was first in the dining room, which was unlit and freezing. I switched on the lights (as such) to work and a boy from the lodge came up and lit a Chinese kerosene stove, which initially produced eye-watering fumes then, disconcertingly, he put the stove under the table I was sitting at and eventually, the worst of the fumes cleared. But now I am waiting for the table to catch fire. The others and the Danish woman came in and the boy appeared again to take the heater out from under the table as he had a big kettle to put on it. Dinner was duly ordered and I had more chicken soup, followed by fried noodles, which I couldn't finish. Only one beer tonight, and two cups of tea but before going to bed I took another Diamox and drank at least a litre of water. Then a wee Strepsil for my now sore throat and I have to say that I have felt better and a bit worried about climbing the mountain in a few days' time.

Saturday 8th October.

In the morning, the weather looked worse with lots of low mist, and still feeling cold. I feel a lot better though after a good sleep and some weird dreams. My throat is still sore but I have a good supply of throat lozenges and if it doesn't get worse than this I can handle that OK. Breakfast is lemon tea and cornflakes, which looks and tasted like Weetabix that had been left in milk for an hour but it tasted fine. Today the plan is to trek to Yak Kharka, which means just a sort of open area or corral for Yaks about 13,000', and near an area where there are huge waterfalls. No more teahouses for a good few days as we will be in tents from here on. The going is fairly slow and in under two hours we come to a big farm for early morning tea.

As we are standing about waiting, a barn door is opened and about thirty black and white goats run out. As I start to film this, a small door next to me is opened and more goats pour out, then another door and even more goats and they're running everywhere. I don't know how that coincided with our arrival but it is chaotic but quite funny. For our tea we climb up two primitive wooden ladders to come out on the flat roof of the farmhouse. No sun and the wind is really cool up here and we huddle up with our cups in our hands and we are here for almost an hour. We watch our porters leave about half an hour before us with all our kit and when we climb back down and get our rucksacks to continue the trek and only Som is with us at this point. From here we cross a river and follow it as we climb higher and after only an hour walking we hear a shout through the trees from the riverside. It's Nima and the porters who have stopped to prepare lunch. It's only 11:00am. The scene is amazing and there are pots, pans and stoves being unpacked and a huge pot is being heated over an open fire. Other pots are on kerosene stoves. And some of the porters are washing pots, some are fetching wood, some water, some unpacking foodstuffs and one is mixing flour and water. We have never seen them working together and we are really impressed.

A table with four chairs is set up for us and we get black tea while the sun is just coming out and we can feel the heat as we sit with our tea and watch the lunch preparations. All these guys are here just to put four people on top of a mountain. The meal was certainly different, with fresh chapatis, some tuna and thick cut chips with tomato sauce. It was so good I had a second helping and of course, more tea. The remains of the hot water we get for our water bottles but I still pop an iodine pill into mine, just in case. I keep thinking that the pace will have to be harder than this from here as we will need to be up to at least 14,000 feet or preferably higher to make the next day, on steeper ground, bearable and safe. However, we don't climb that much higher and it's only after 2:00pm when we stop for the day. In the distance are the twin waterfalls, falling hundreds of feet and like a scene from Lord of the Rings. While the porters are getting the tents up we decide to go a bit higher to help with the acclimatisation process. With us we have a kitchen tent, three, two-man North Face tents, a dining tent and a toilet tent. As well as tables and chairs. The porters already have a fire going in a stone howff.

Although it's only 12,750 feet here, I don't think we're high enough so while Donald stays at the camp, the rest of us walk up to a ridge which takes us to 13,200 feet, maybe a bit more, before we decide to go back down and the sun is still out so it's quite pleasant. This will be our first night camping. The downside of an easy day today of course is that tomorrow looks like being really hard and we can see where we will need to climb. The other factor is the increase in altitude. A safe maximum at this height is 1,200 feet per day however we need to get to base camp which is at 14,800 feet or thereabouts. The day after that is a rest and acclimatisation day, and I think we'll need it. It gets pretty cold as soon as the sun disappears behind the mountains. Dinner tonight, cooked fresh, is vegetable soup and dal bhat, not my favourite meal, although the staple diet of the porters which they eat with their right hand. I can't even manage half of it. We have fruit salad next and a few cups of tea. Tonight is the first time I use my silk liner in my sleeping bag and keep a pair of socks on too. We're in bed by 7:30pm, which will be a pattern and soon after this it starts to rain but it doesn't stop me sleeping.

Sunday 9th October.

In the morning, being first up, I walk sixty yards down to the river to wash and fill my water bottle. The water is ice cold and it takes my breath away. Coming back up I move quickly up the hill until the altitude slows me. The camp is busy with breakfast preparations, although we have already had 'bed-tea'. And now we have a bowl of hot water each, to wash. I don't mention that I walked down to the river to wash in glacial water. The table and chairs are set out and breakfast is great. We have tea and hot chocolate, muesli, and cornflakes with hot milk. To follow there are fresh chapati with peanut butter, jam and honey. After breakfast we have a pretty stiff climb for over two hours but at a slow and steady pace. It must be really hard going for the porters but as usual they are all smiles and laughter, even from the guy carrying the table and chairs! We pass them and they pass us - all morning! Again that will be a pattern.

I am always looking for signs of the altitude affecting me as we get higher but so far, so good. Donald is suffering a bit though and Davy is feeling it a bit as well. They both have a sore throat like me too. We reach the site for our base camp after a hard four-hour slog. It's a bleak looking place. The sun has never managed to get through so far. The other life here is four yaks which is odd away up here. While the porters get our tents up, we get some shelter behind some rocks, as the wind is really cold. Although it's cloudy we can see some of the Annapurna range behind us and in front of us, none of the Chulu peaks are visible. This, as they say, is harsh reality.

The porters bring us over foam sleeping mats to shelter ourselves better and we sit on some, lean on others. Tea is soon made and it heats us up a bit as we watch, the small dining tent is soon up and we get better shelter in there. Although we are expecting nothing more than more tea - especially after a big breakfast but lunch is being prepared. This was more indeterminate soup, then hot potatoes with coleslaw, sardines and the hardest cheese imaginable, followed by Tibetan bread, then more tea. We do our best but Donald and Davy are struggling with sore heads so I give them Diamox. Marguerite takes one as well although Nima says he has plenty and will give us some more later. Davy has to go and lie down but the rest of us decide to go for a walk and get a bit of acclimatisation and we walk towards a ridge, which will bring us back round to the camp. It can only be a couple of miles but we will get a bit higher too.

After about an hour of walking and the pull up onto the ridge, Marguerite is sick suddenly and loses her lunch. I feel for her because ahead of us is Chulu Far East and our best view of it. This is what we set out to do and we're so close now. Not a good time to be ill. The walk was pretty easy, but, on the way down, Marguerite slipped badly before I could catch her. It could have been worse than trousers ripped at the knee and a bruised thigh but I just think that this is so different from our last trip in more ways than one. Chulu looks menacing but close.

After a while we meet for dinner in the dining tent. It's really cold but at least sheltered from the now freezing wind. Donald and Marguerite still have sore heads and Davy doesn't look too good. I ask Nima for small portions for dinner as none of us are hungry and we agree on just one small portion of Sherpa stew. I know Nima is wondering if that will be enough fuel to get us onto the mountain. The Sherpa stew is better than it may sound and certainly better than it looks with what looks like stewed cauliflower and carrots in greasy dishwater but it tastes fine. Marguerite has to go and be sick again just after this and I give her another Diamox. After dinner, Davy and Donald go and lie down just after the meal. It's 5:30pm and despite a couple of cups of hot tea it feels bloody cold! Marguerite and I are left with two candles burning in the dining tent brought by the porters. It should look romantic, but doesn't, and it's almost surreal to be sitting here at this altitude with snow flurries outside. We talk about the trek and about life in general over cups of black tea, but we're both tired and we're in bed by 6:30pm. It took ages for me to get to sleep. It can only be the altitude - or lack of Tuborg!

Monday 10th October.

This morning we got bed tea from Pasang, smiling as usual. As I sit up, my head touches the skin of the yellow tent and there's a whoosh noise. It was snow sliding off the tent and when I looked out, everything is white and it's a bit of a shock. I get up to take a

77

photo of the campsite looking white and bleak and it's really, really cold so I'm not out for long.

Apart from the weather though, I feel pretty good. Donald has been sick this morning and complains of feeling dizzy and that's not good and I'll have to keep an eye on him. Chulu Far East is stunningly clear and we can almost pick our route up. I took some more photos and some film too.

This was fortuitous as everything disappeared half an hour later. Dorge and Som are getting ropes together and will take a couple of porters to carry the gear as far as the start of the glacier. The plan is for Som and Dorge to climb as high as they can and get as many ropes fixed as possible, so tomorrow, we don't have to hang about. Today for us, of course, is mainly hanging about. Although Davy looks better, Donald and him go back to their sleeping bags after breakfast. Marguerite and I are left in the wee dining tent writing up our journals, changing batteries in cameras and head-torches and generally preparing for tomorrow. At one point, Pasang and Robi come in with late morning tea and sit and watch us writing. All smiles and they are a pair of great guys. The tea is welcome and as they came in, we can see it's started to snow again. The porters and Mingma the cook are preparing lunch and generally cleaning up and they never stop laughing and sometimes sing too. Fortunately Marguerite doesn't know the words. My feet feel like ice and even with a down jacket on and a hat and in a tent it feels freezing. I've been trying, and failing, to drink four litres of water a day, but this morning, as well as tea, a diuretic, I've had hot chocolate and now we're sitting with lemon tea. Robi comes into the dining tent with four toilet rolls for us and we have a laugh about this. What is it he knows that we don't? The weather has cleared again and the sun is half out. I have a plan to shoot some film of me talking to the camera with Chulu Far East in the background.

After lunch, Nima has a plan for us to walk almost as far as the glacier, which will take us a couple of hours and this will take us to about 17,000 feet. I'm glad of having something to do and it will also help acclimatisation as it must be about 1,200 feet higher than base camp. However, the weather is not improving and the wind is getting up. No sun now and I think about the two climbing Sherpas on Chulu with the ropes.

Lunch is mushroom and vegetable soup to start and this is followed by Spam, yes, Spam, with roast potatoes and pasta with sardine sauce. You couldn't make this up. The whole lot washed down with a couple of cups of tea. But with lunch over, Donald goes back to the tent and won't be coming with us. We're all taking Diamox now. It's really cold as we head up towards the big col between Chulu East and Far East and it's hard going even though we're going slowly and I'm breathing as hard as I did running in preparation for this trip. Davy is struggling at the back and we have to wait for him a few times. We aren't even on the mountain yet.

As we head up, we are met by Som and Dorge, coming back down. They have only been able to fix one rope because of the conditions. The mist was too heavy for them to see much and it was too risky to go higher because of the danger of crevasses hidden under the recent snowfalls. After a short discussion with them, Nima says we should set up an advance camp further up, closer to the glacier. It will save us a couple of hours coming up and of course shorten our time on the mountain. The three of us agree.

We soon reach a plateau and Nima and Som go off to look

for a water source. We will set up camp in this area tomorrow. It looks like the surface of the Moon, it's just endless moraine, a stone desert. We might have to melt snow for water if they don't find water. However Nima soon comes back and says they have found "a blue lake", away over a couple of ridges, so we have a water supply, even if the water really is blue but better than yellow! Soon we head back down, a bit happier that we will have a shorter day than we planned to do the climb. It means however that we are using our 'spare' day, but I suppose that's what it's for. Still very cold and there has been no sun at all this afternoon, although the overnight snow at the camp has now melted.

Not much to do the rest of the afternoon but mooch about the dining tent. Davy has gone for a lie down and Donald still hasn't surfaced. Again, Marguerite and I catch up with our journals. Outside is freezing and it has become misty as well, and there are some snow flurries too. I wonder if we will see an improvement. We have some more tea of course to keep our liquid intake up. Later the wind gets up and   batters the tent. How much can you take of this I wonder? The plan for tomorrow, we discuss with Nima in the dining tent. We will have a late breakfast and then pack up three tents and the dining tent and go to make the advanced camp. As it will be a very early rise for the climb, we will be having a very early dinner. We think the plan sounds fine, as long as the weather improves.

Donald and Davy join us, feeling a bit better. We have some really good soup, indeterminate again though. I have a second bowl too and this is followed by fried rice and boiled momos, filled with tuna and a sauce I can only describe as red. My last association with boiled momos, was a memory of eating plasticine, but these were good although I still prefer the fried ones. To add a flourish to the end of the meal, Mingma has produced warm grapefruit slices. All we need is a glass of port! So, we sit about a while discussing tomorrow and Nima brings in four hot water bottles in some fetching colours. It looks ridiculous, but we all have them inside our jackets, relishing a source of heat. Donald has said he will go to high camp but will not attempt the climb, which I think we all expected. It's not long before we're all in our sleeping bags and my down jacket makes a fine pillow. It's great to snuggle in and not to have freezing feet. However, up for a pee about midnight and my head knocks against the frost on the inside of the tent, the particles like snow in my torch-beam. It feels awfully cold. In the morning our water bottles will have turned to ice. Minus fourteen someone says.

Tuesday 11th October.

This morning I am determined not to move until one of our guys brings the bed tea and just lying here looking at the inside of the tent, white all over. The top of my sleeping bag is damp with condensation or at least I hope its condensation and not Donald getting out for a pee a bit late. Lying here I'm thinking I don't want to do much more of this. It's too hard, too cold although I slept well. However, as if to make up for the recent miserable weather, as I hoped, there isn't a cloud in the sky this morning when I look out. Although it looks fine, there has been more snow and the sun isn't over the ridge in front of us and it's back into the tent until the tea arrives and a bowl of warm water to wash. It's still only 6:30am and a long day to come. Breakfast is out in the sunshine and the table and chairs have been taken out of the dining tent and sit forlornly in the snow. This is style! Here we are having breakfast at this height, this early, and outside. We had heard Som and Dorge getting ropes sorted out for another attempt to put them up on the mountain and they leave soon afterwards, a bit happier with the weather today.

Breakfast at 8:15am is brilliant! I had tea and then cornflakes with really hot milk followed by two mini chapatis with a slice of scrambled egg in between which is luxury. I keep one chapati for a peanut butter roll-up. Another mug of tea and I'm ready for the day ahead, although, if the peanut butter runs out, I'm going home. The plan is that we stay here till lunchtime then move up to advanced base camp. So to pass the time I go for a walk back the way we came to this camp where I can get a few photographs of the Annapurna range, clear of the ridge surrounding us. Everything is spectacular and I don't feel cold at all now, and no headaches, which is good news. In fact, everyone is well today, which is a first. I put a new battery and tape into the camera and sort out some other bits and pieces. As we sit in the sun for hours at the breakfast table, Nima comes over, points to Chulu and says, "look, Sherpa". And sure enough, away on the mountain we can see two tiny figures on the start of the snow crest. They are on Chulu Far East at last and we can see them a bit clearer with the binoculars and everyone has to have a look through them. It now feels awful real and, well, tomorrow is our final shot at it; we have no spare days left.

After lunch we get packed up to move camp, and we are taking the three North Face tents and the wee dining tent will become the cooking (and sleeping) tent. As we head up it gets colder and windier and the visibility is deteriorating as well. Everyone is going at an easy pace but Donald is taking it very slowly. He is the only one who has not been up here before and this will be the highest he's been in his life.

As soon as the tents are up we get inside as it's too cold to hang about in the wind. This is about survival now for the next twenty-four hours. However as we hear Som and Dorge are almost back we go out to get their news. They have managed to put up three fixed ropes. The first two will get us onto the glacier and another, higher up, on the first steep section. Som and I have discussed the possibility of avoiding the final steep part by moving around to a more exposed but less steep section. It's the last steep section that he is worried about, so worth a try tomorrow we agree. Dinner is early and served in our tents. Soup, which is fine and at the same time a big plate of spaghetti with a hint of tomato sauce, but It's cold in minutes and I have to force myself to eat most of it as I have no appetite. Next we have tea and a very welcome hot water bottle. At 6:15pm we get bedded down as we will be up at 3:00am to leave at 4:00am. I get my stuff ready and try to do it quietly as Donald is sound asleep in his sleeping bag. I'm not surprised he won't be coming tomorrow. Still it's a bit lonely up here on your own, knowing what a big day is coming and no one to talk to about it.

Wednesday 12th October.

I don't sleep much due to a combination of adrenaline and altitude. It's really cold and annoyingly I can hear snow flurries hitting the tent. I might have just been getting over to sleep when I heard the clang of stainless steel mugs and a shout of "bed tea". It's only 2:55am and again the inside of the tent is white with frost so I lie back with the tea and mentally check I have everything I need. Donald, lucky bastard, is sound. Breakfast arrives at 3:30am and it's cornflakes and warm milk, chapatis with scrambled egg and more tea. I can only manage the cornflakes. No appetite at all this morning. Robi comes to the tent door to offer me hot water but I say I'm OK.

Then it's socks and boots on. My boots spent the night in my sleeping bag to keep them warm. Rucksack packed and water bottle in and my cameras. Same boots as last time, Scarpa M4's then down jacket on and fully clothed for a look outside. I can see nothing as it's as black as anything and there are no stars visible. It's not snowing though it's at least minus fourteen degrees inside the tent and we're going 2,000 feet higher. At just after 4:00am, Nima, Dorge and Som arrive at our tents. This is when I wish I was Donald still in his sleeping bag and warm. Gelu, one of the young porters, is coming as far as the foot of the glacier with us carrying ropes and gear and here we will get into our climbing gear and put on our crampons. Having experienced the hassle of putting on a harness in the dark and outside, I have put mine already on. Attached to it are my ascender, descender and a couple of slings and karabiners. My gaiters are already on as well. Everyone has a head-torch on.

Before we leave, Nima gets us all in a circle in pitch blackness and we hold hands as he recites some Buddhist mantra with his eyes closed. This is our own Puja ceremony for luck on the mountain - a sort of back-up from the one the Lama gave us I suppose. Suddenly he raises all of our hands to the sky and scatters rice in the air with a shout. We're then off into the pitch-black Annapurna night. How Som found his way in this darkness is a mystery, even with a head-torch. We are walking over frosted and icy shale and it's hard to keep your feet. The boulder field seems to take ages but we are walking slowly as well but eventually the ground starts to rise and we are all slipping about. It's hard going and I can feel my heart pounding. Slowly I can start to make out shapes in the darkness but all a bit ominous.

At one point I feel as if my legs are restricted and my movement limited and for a minute I suspect something serious but it turns out my harness has slipped off my jacket. This is a real hassle, as I have to take off my down jacket and with bare hands, re-adjust the harness to fit under my jacket. So now I'm colder with numb hands and I'm not happy about that. Eventually we reach a rocky platform at the edge of the glacier, where it meets the rocky slope we have come up. Here we get our climbing gear on. This takes the other two ages, but all I have to do is put crampons on, but the others have boots to take off and plastic boots to put on then gaiters and harnesses. My hands are freezing with just putting on my crampons and they are semi-step-ins so quick to get on. Marguerite looks to be struggling getting her plastic boots on. Dorge is helping her but after putting her crampons on, she realises she hasn't put her gaiters on first. No matter she says but Som says they are a must, with deep snow up ahead in places. So she has to take the crampons back off. There is two feet of fresh snow in places he says. I'm cold hanging about and as I look across to where the first fixed rope is, Gelu is waving for me to come over to it where he is waiting. I have to pass the others carefully and of course it's still quite dark. I lose sight of Gelu but with some trepidation I clip my ascender onto the rope and look up into blackness. My ice axe is now in my right hand and I push the ascender up the rope and swing the axe into the ice and kick in the front points of the crampons. This is it. My heart is racing.

As I look over, the rest are still involved with their gear. I climb another five or six steps then have to rest and I wonder at this point if Som will be annoyed at me going on, but he could see what I was up to and even now the others are still on the rocky ledge. It's a hard climb up to the top but not too long. As I come over the crest at the top of the glacier, I am shocked to see Gelu there, smiling down at me. I look back down and no one has moved to the rope yet. Between gasps I ask Gelu if he has an ice axe as I can see none. No, he says. I tell him he can't go any further without one but he's cool about that. How did you get up I ask and he says he ran up holding onto the rope. He had no crampons either and he's laughing at me shaking my head at him. What if he'd slipped? I say I will walk ahead and he will wait on the others coming up. There is a fixed rope here too but it's not steep and as the ridge rises I get my video camera out to film the rest coming over the crest. It's getting light now but feels colder and I suppose because of the cold, the video camera won't work. A Himalayan glacier at 5:30am is too much for the battery. That's the reason I bought the bloody thing but my other camera should work.

I manage a couple of shots with my digital camera, which works fine. The rest catch me up and after a break we head up the snow slope. The views over to the Annapurna range are spectacular and everything is in full morning light. It's very cold with a stiff breeze. I feel better now than I did walking up the boulder field from the camp. I seem to have settled into it now. Gelu, as expected, has gone back down and there are just the five of us on the mountain. This will be the first ascent this season apparently. We can now see ahead the major obstacle of the domes - two steep snow slopes, which look quite lengthy, but I am confident we can do it. In fact, I actually feel pretty good and the summit is about two hours away from here at a slow pace. However, although the sun is up it feels colder and colder. I wonder what the wind chill factor would be here. So Som leads the next pitch, quite steep and about 200 feet. We stop every few steps for a rest and to get our breathing under control. I look across the white slope against the blue sky and I would say it's nearly sixty degrees, not forty-five as I read somewhere.

Half way up, and the first rope is tied to the next. This is a bit disconcerting, as you have to unclip off one rope and onto the other on this slope, with only an ice axe to break your slip on the slope. I'm thinking we did this more efficiently on Island Peak. The wind is now stronger than ever, but I'm not cold except for my hands and feet. I only wore my inner gloves coming up the last pitch; maybe thirty-five minutes and I can't feel my fingers - or toes. My over-gloves were too big to use with the ascender. This wasn't clever though. When we stop for a rest, Dorge grabs my hands and starts manipulating them so hard it hurt, and they were less sore just being freezing. Then he gets me to batter my hands against each other and eventually, I start to get some feeling back. The big gloves go back on and he nods approvingly. When i climbed Mont Blanc earlier in the year these gloves were too warm, even at the summit! We walk slowly up another snow slope and Som is saying he might try the route he and I discussed at base camp, when we looked at it through binoculars and it looked feasible. Maybe a bit more exposure, but again, quicker too and with the wind rising that would be important as well. The three of us are left to wait on the easier slope while Som and Dorge climb off up to our right and out of sight. We eventually stand huddled up against the wind here at well over 19,500', our axes rammed into ice, our only protection.

It feels as if the wind would rip your skin off. And I can see

Marguerite is suffering. Not long after we talk about all the recent snow and the risk of avalanche, I shout "look, Annapurna 2", and we see the end of what must have been a huge avalanche sweeping down the slopes facing us. Impossible, at this distance away to gauge how big but big it was. Som and Dorge are making their way back and the news isn't good. There is a huge crevasse almost at the summit and on the alternative route, which we wouldn't be able to pass so this means we can't have fixed ropes but they decide to try and get us higher. So they start pulling ropes out their bags and ice anchors. We have no option but to watch and wait and it's now 9:15am. We try to cheer ourselves up by saying we are only 200 feet or less to the top and with luck, could be there by 10:30am. But we are now held up on a slope before the steep dome section to the summit and it's bitter cold.

I remember that the other night I dreamt of an avalanche and it was on this last bit and the snow broke into wee slabs when my ice axe went in. Hmm. Then I think of what Som said about there being two feet of fresh snow. If this was Scotland, we would have been more aware of the risk I think. If this was Scotland we wouldn't be on a mountain with a big avalanche risk and the fresh snow makes it more likely.

Som started off up the slope with the rope but almost immediately is struggling getting his axe into the soft snow to get a grip. It's now 9:45am and I now have to turn my face out of the wind. Marguerite has started to shiver quite uncontrollably. This is not ideal and not the place for hanging about, but we are. It goes through my mind that if my hands are too cold to grip the rope going down, I'm in trouble and have still to go up. Som shouts to clip in and follow him. By 10:00am we know we have a problem. Som is not so far above us but for the last five minutes has made no progress although he is swinging his axe a lot. Dorge looks uncomfortable about the situation. I haven't felt my toes for over an hour and my hands are getting numb. Marguerite is all huddled up and at almost 10:30am, when we should have been on the top, Som is coming down, bringing the rope with him. We are I think less than a hundred feet from the summit.

He says the top of the dome is crevassed and unstable and could avalanche. Maybe one or two could get across he says but is shaking his head to reinforce the risk and he doesn't want us to take that risk. We tell him about the avalanche we have seen and he nods. It's not usually an easy option to turn back, especially being so close to the summit but this time an easy decision to abandon the attempt and go back down, although if we had insisted, I think he would have taken us, but that risks his life as well and not fair. Anyway another half-hour and we would all be hypothermic. Our disappointment is quickly forgotten as we are shocked a bit when Som says we will walk carefully down a slope I thought we would abseil. It's quicker he says - yes, but I think steeper than we would all consider as OK at home. The actual abseils, of course take ages as the first person puts so much strain on the rope, so that no one can clip their descender on until they are unclipped at the bottom. Davy goes first, then Marguerite, than me. The last Sherpa then unties and take out the ice screw protection and comes down on a double rope. Not slick, or quick.

We manage to get some photographs now that we're a bit lower and out of the fierce wind, but nothing like the quantity we all took last time. The hanging about in the cold at that altitude had certainly sapped our strength and it was the right decision not to force ourselves on at risk. When I bring out my water bottle for a drink it is frozen solid. Then I remember Robi offering hot water - it was for my water bottle. I thought it was for washing. What an idiot. By the time we are down to the final wee abseil down off the glacier, I start to feel OK again. I go down last again and we're back on the shale ledge where we now take our climbing gear off. We are a bit subdued and Som comes over to apologise but we tell him it was the right decision. We're here and alive and that's a better outcome. I know we were certainly fit enough to have got to the top. As we get the gear off we can see Nima and two porters with baskets coming up to take the climbing gear and ropes from us. I am just staring at Nima in the distance trying to make out what he was carrying. Eventually we identify it as a one-gallon aluminium kettle and our stainless steel mugs. Full of hot lemon tea and on its way! And it's really welcome. They had watched us coming down from the camp. Nima has walked almost a mile with a full kettle!

Except that there now is no camp as we walk back. Everything is packed ready to go back down, however, a tarpaulin is spread out for us to sit on and we all get a bowl of soup, which none of us can finish. Sitting here looking at our mountain, I realise all I've eaten since 3:30am has been some cornflakes and a Bounty bar. And because my water bottle froze, I haven't drunk enough either. I drink all of the water bottle now. Again, I can remember early this morning, Robi offering me hot water for my bottle, but I said no, I'm fine and that was stupid, and I bet he thought that too. We're all pretty tired and my back is sore from the abseil, as it was last time. Or was it from using the ascender? Despite this, discussing the rest of the plans for the day with Nima, we agree to head not just down to base camp but down to where we camped before coming up to base camp. Or further if we are up to it. For us three who climbed the mountain and our Sherpa guides, this means a descent today of over 9,000 feet. At least it's mostly downhill!

The sun is still out and our mountain looks tantalising. The porters are getting their loads sorted and as we head over a ridge we can see, far below, our other porters collapsing the big green cooking tent. They will be ready to leave by the time we are down to them. The porters are in high spirits and having a right laugh as we all leave from base camp to head down towards the twin waterfalls and down to the river. The sun is strong and we are in good spirits. We could do no more than we have done. On the way down, Nima asks if we are fit enough to continue to the farm where we had tea on the roof on the way up and we all agree to go for it. It will add another hour and a half but it's a better camping spot, but a long plod and at the end I'm almost beyond it. By the time we arrive the guys have the cooking tent up and the rest of the tents are up within half an hour. Inevitably, tea is on the go but none of us feel at all hungry. It's 5:00pm and we could easily just go and sleep. We've just walked down the equivalent of three Munros and only Donald slept last night, and three of us have climbed a mountain. No wonder we're all feeling past our best.

Donald and I get our gear into our tent. Last night we'll sleep in one and I could just lie down here on my sleeping bag and pass out but Gelu pokes his head in to say tea and biscuits in the dining tent. Big deal I think, so what. I'm too tired to be kind. I look up at a white mountain in the distance and it is Chulu Far East and is where we have just walked down from and we were close to the summit. Marguerite has passed out but the three of us wander down and over tea we decide we need to speak to Nima about the tip for the porters. We will all split up tomorrow with most of them walking back to Besisahar and then bus to Kathmandu. Our two personal porters, Robi and Pasang, Nima and Mingma the cook will come with us on our trek on the Annapurna circuit to Jomsom. I mention to Nima that it's Donald's birthday today.

From Jomsom we will fly to Pokhara and the porters will take our kit bags back to Kathmandu from Pokhara but will walk there to get the bus to Kathmandu. Nima and Mingma will fly with us to Pokhara and then get the bus back to Kathmandu. Back in the tent we talk to Nima and things get sorted. Because we are short of cash, he will pay the porters tips for us, and Dorge and Som. We will square him up back in Kathmandu. He is telling us about a reunion party and his daughter's 10th birthday party, maybe not in that order of importance but we are invited. It will be the night when we fly in from Pokhara and we accept of course. Although none of us are hungry, dinner arrives with soup to start and Marguerite arrives too and the soup is actually really good. Next course is a kind of pizza and I can only manage about half of it. We can hardly keep our eyes open during the meal.

Davy says goodnight and heads back to his tent and we sit with one candle burning and we are all about to go when Nima sticks his head in, notices Davy isn't there and goes back to get him. I did have a feeling something was going on but this is now confirmed. With Davy returned and with a flurry and maybe ten faces now at the door of the tent, Nima brings in a big cake with white icing on top and a single candle. I get Donald to ceremoniously blow it out and Dorge cuts through the faces to produce a half bottle of 'Bagpiper' whisky and some cups. The atmosphere is lifted and it's great and so is the cake and of course, so is the whisky. A fitting end to a hard day and brilliant what these guys have done. How do you bake a cake with icing on a kerosene stove?

Thursday 13*th* October.

This was the first night I wasn't up at all and slept from 8:00pm right through till 6:00am next morning which was wonderful. In the morning we had a laugh with Donald telling us about his Spiderman dream climbing up on Glasgow tenements. He reckoned there was something in the cake, and maybe there was, but it might have been the whisky, or both! There is again this morning a heavy frost on the outsides of all the tents. We have bed tea at 7:00am and a leisurely breakfast at 8:00am. The plan is that we will be leaving at 9:00am but today will be easy. I give Dorge and Som a watch each and Davy gives Dorge a book about Scotland and Som, a tartan scarf and we take a few group photos as well, some with Chulu Far East in the background.

By 7:30am, the sun is up over the mountains and melting the frost. Breakfast is outside to facilitate the dining tent being packed up and at the table we have chapati and scrambled egg and a slice of, well, Spam. I keep a chapati for my favourite, and final, peanut butter roll-up. Lots of tea as usual and it really feels like an expedition this morning as I have to sit at the table and sign various forms for Nima. The climbing permit is a big document and we have to estimate our garbage disposal and methods so I can reclaim our $350 back in Kathmandu from the Nepalese Mountain Association. We will also get certified to say we climbed Chulu Far East, only we didn't quite so not sure how that will work out back in Kathmandu even if our climbing Sherpa, Som says it counts as a summit. Everything is pretty laid back this morning, and I ask

Nima where they got the whisky from last night and he says, we sent a porter to the village. I nod, but only later realise the village was about four miles away at least.

We leave at 9:40am and it's a beautiful day, blue sky, no clouds and the sun is strong. Away behind us are the Chulu peaks and I take a last photo and turn away. It's hard not to have a wee sense of disappointment that we didn't get to the top. We all take the last photos of our porters, before they get loaded up. And quite emotional but we will meet most of them again in Kathmandu at Nima's daughter's birthday party. All these people put three of us on a mountain. At the first split in the path, long after we have passed the farm where we had tea on the way up, we all shake hands with the guys who are off back to Kathmandu. They have been a great team and more than often lifted our spirits with their cheerfulness and laughter in spite of their hardship. We also hear later that a team of four French climbers on a mountain close to us are all missing. So are all of their climbing Sherpas who were with them. I think it was Kangtega. We will later learn they all died in an avalanche on the day of our climb and when we saw the huge avalanche on Annapurna and we remarked that we were taking a risk. With hindsight it looks like the idea to abandon the last hundred feet on Chulu was the right one. Experience though, as Hamish Brown once said, is just the sum of near misses.

We walk on, a smaller party now, with the wind at our backs and head towards the village of Braga where we will stay overnight in a lodge. No tent. And not missed by me one bit. As we approach Braga along the dusty track, I'm walking with Donald and there are a few people on horseback and one old man rides quickly up to us, pulls his horse up and shouts to Donald, "European"? And when Donald confirms this he shouts, "what age"? Donald replies that he is sixty. "Seventy seven", shouts the horseman riding quickly away, laughing. I think he meant us to be impressed. The lodge is great, well, it would be I suppose after the tent existence, but the room has a sort of en-suite - a side-room with a hole in the floor toilet. But there is electricity, though very intermittent, and apparently, hot showers. Off the dining room is a big veranda with a hard plastic sheet at one side to shelter us from the constant wind.

The boys get our bags into the room and we go out onto the veranda for tea, imposing ourselves a bit on other trekkers to get seats together. We take turns going downstairs for a shower. I let Donald go before me, and this is a mistake. When he comes up, he says the electricity has just gone off and for me this means a bloody cold shower - and now by candlelight and head-torch. Not really good. Lunch is on the veranda in the sun, which is lovely, and we're all clean as well. First course is something called 'ministronia' soup, which is OK and quite like an Italian soup with a similar name! My next course is an omelette, for safety, with lots of tea and to avoid monotony, a bottle of coke. This is quite indulgent and the first soft drink on the trek.

We spend the whole afternoon up here in the sun until it disappears over the Annapurna. We have heard that as part of the celebrations, two bison have been slaughtered in the next village and that today and this week there will be lots more 'sacrifices'. We hope we are not part of them. Nima suggests that we go up to the local monastery for a walk before dinner. There is a ceremony going on of sorts and it lasts all week - twenty-four hours a day. A kind of Autumn harvest celebration perhaps and it sounds interesting so we get wrapped up and head off. The monastery, or gompa, is over 500 years old but everything here looks that way.

The village is really ancient looking, built into the rock face and hanging there sort of. We take our shoes off and enter the darkness of the monastery, lit by candlelight. I end up sitting cross-legged in the semi-darkness, watching and listening. The singing is like a Scottish Western Isles Gaelic hymn. I try to film but the light is too poor. The service is a bit confusing and at some point tea is given out, but not to us. Then apples are handed out and we get some small green ones. There is a bit of chanting and everyone looks relaxed. It is mostly Tibetan looking women in the congregation.

At a break, I think we are leaving but Nima says we are to make an offering to the head Lama. We do this by buying a kata, or silk scarf, and put some notes in it and hand it to him. The deal is this - he opens the scarf, takes the cash, gives us each a coloured, knotted thread which goes over our heads. We need to keep it on for six months apparently, and you must wear it always. Mine is orange and it's called a 'soongdi', and is placed over your bowed head, he then places the kata over your head, while blessing you. I thought I felt better for it this time too, and I kept it on for six months! As we leave, Nima has organised with the curator to take us upstairs to see, in a locked room, a huge figure of the Buddha. It has been here for over 500 years and not everyone gets to see it and definitely an interesting wee trip this evening.

I take some photographs going back as the sun disappears over the mountains and the wind, relentless as ever, is colder now. It never seems to die down at all here. As we make our way back past yaks to the hostel some look worried. I am first into the dining room, which is freezing and the owner comes in, Karma I think he's called and he is quite amiable and can see the problem. I ask about the room at the front, which has a stove and he says he will light it and we can eat in there. As the rest appear, we watch the owner bring some burning wood through to get the fire started. The stove is an elongated steel box with a makeshift chimney, not at all like the Chinese cast-iron wood burning stoves so prevalent in the Khumbu. This is a homemade job, but quite clever as we soon realise - it can take long pieces of wood! Donald comes in and feeds the fire from the collection of wood beside it, all of our seats are around it and the place soon heats up. Marguerite comes back and says that when she asked the owner for menus, he said that yak steaks were available tonight as a special. No surprises that we all go for it. Too much vegetarianism lately!

So here we are, cosy around the fire with glasses of Tuborg, eating real meat and with both heat and light and after the freezing tents this feels like luxury. After we have finished and have ordered more Tuborg, Nima arrives with Mingma and the porters, Robi and Pasang and they join us and we order more beers. Suddenly the lights all go out and we are sitting in candlelight for ages. The electricity goes off at 9:00pm. The craic is great though and we sit talking till after 10:00pm. This is the latest night so far on the trip. I feel brilliant and sleep well and my first night not in a tent for five nights.

Friday 14th October.

I still wake up at 6:00am but feel really refreshed and go down to get a shower - this time hot and with light. Upstairs to get all packed up for 7:00am and then go in for breakfast. Two slices of toast with peanut butter. I could be addicted to this stuff. I have three big cups of black tea to wash it all down. This morning Nima is taking us on a wee acclimatisation walk up high on the mountainside to the rear of the hostel and a bit out of the village, well above the tree-line, to a monastery of sorts where a monk lives in total isolation and we will meet him. As we climbed steeply through warm, scented pinewoods, I realised that it is the place I had spoken about on the way into the village yesterday - we could see some of the path and thought it might be a route onto the Annapurna. As we round a corner, we can see prayer flags everywhere and a brilliantly white shrine ahead of us. All around is what I expect of Nepal with the pristine mountains and a deep blue, cloudless sky. But the walk has been a lot harder and longer than we expected and takes almost two hours to get here.

The shrine itself contains a huge Buddha figure which was apparently helicoptered up here in one piece. Nima tells us the story of Milarepa, a yogi, Tibetan poet, and eccentric who lived here in the 11th century in a cave near here and how he met Kero, an archer, hunting in these mountains and how he became Milarepa's disciple and a holy man. Then we meet the monk, a tall lean sensible looking guy and he's been here on his own for nine years and has still another nine years tenure, but wants to stay here all his life. We visit the small monastery, give a donation and then the monk makes us tea and we offer him biscuits and a sense of peace as we sit here in the sunshine, Nima and the monk have a long discussion. The viewpoint is amazing. We can see Mansulu, Pisang and the top of Chulu Far East, where with better luck, our own prayer flags would be flying. Going down is really quick and we take just over an hour. Now we are back in a pasture setting with horses and yak dotted about. Back at the lodge, our rucksacks are locked in a room. Nima decides we will have lunch here before moving on.

We manage to cajole others into us having seats together on the balcony and the sun is warm and it's nice to sit and soak it up and order lunch. I have chicken soup and an omelette with 'finger chips'. Marguerite orders a slab of apple pie for us all to share and it looks pretty heavy-duty stuff, with nuts and grapes as well. Plenty of tea first though. The rest of us manage to eat everything and then demolish the apple pie, which is excellent. Nima comes through and says it's time to head off and as we get our stuff together, the owner comes through to present all of us with a kata, which is a really nice touch. Nima reckons we will only have a walk of just over two hours to the next lodge. The boys have taken our bags away this morning, and they will be waiting for us at our next lodge in Gunsang. The trail today, although short, has been very dusty and windy. At least the wind has been behind us.

So, we have left Braga at 11,483 feet and head up through Manang, the district capital and as we leave, we pass a field where a yak has just been slaughtered. The grass is stained red and not much remains of the animal. Once through Manang, we stop to photograph a wee lake, with its turquoise-grey glacial water. Gangapurna towers over it too. A few minutes later we hear, and then see, a huge avalanche on the mountain. Makes us think of Chulu and how risky that was for us all. It's a fair hike up to Gunsang at 12,000 feet and the sun is only just holding up above the mountains when we arrive and this though is the second time today we have been at this height! As expected, the boys, all smiles, are waiting on us at the lodge and our bags are in our respective rooms. And a good looking lodge.

Tomorrow we head, with some trepidation, to the Thorung La pass, highest in the world apparently at an altitude of almost 6,500 feet higher than we were in Manang and the plan is to get to Thorung Phedi at 13,800 feet and if we are all right with altitude, to press on to a high camp before tackling the pass. It's already getting cold here and by 5:00pm, the sun has gone down behind Gangapurna. Marguerite has had to go to bed as soon as we arrive and all of us have had something or other ailing us and I'm still sniffing with the remnants of the cold. The rest of us go down to the dining room and our crew are all sitting around a stove with the woman who seems to run the lodge. Also in the room around a big table are two Israeli guys, and then just us. We order some tea and get talking and it turns out one of the Israeli guys has been to Glasgow!

Half an hour later another guy arrives carrying a huge pack. It turns out he's Russian and has just come over the Thorung La with that pack. He has no porter and has walked from Muktinath, which for us is another day and a half away, and with our porters! To heat the room, a sort of metal firebox with embers from the stove is put under the table. It doesn't seem safe but it soon heats us up. We order the food, which for me is, chicken soup and tuna pizza and I order a couple of bottles of Tuborg and we share them with Nima and Donald who have less drinking capacity than the rest of us it would seem. Despite it being pitch dark, half an hour later, another traveller arrives and asks, with desperation in his voice, if there is a room and the woman says yes and he looks pretty relieved. Shortly after he comes in and sits beside me and we get talking. It turns out he's Danish and works in Kathmandu for the Danish government for a sort of NGO (Non-Governmental Organisation). He's been here for five years helping to set up pro-democracy institutions. It's interesting to hear his opinion on the current political climate and between the heat, the food and a few more Tuborgs, we have some good craic and set the world right. His talk of spies being everywhere and to be careful what you say makes me feel as if I'm in a John Buchan book, which is no bad thing. He also is fluent in Nepali and Nima has some conversations too. It's a late night and it's after 9:00pm when I get into my sleeping bag. I had to get up twice for a pee - combination of Tuborg and Diamox. On the landing I miss a step and come so close to falling over the balcony into the courtyard. That was though maybe just Tuborg.

Saturday 15th October.

The boys make us a cup of tea in our rooms this morning and it's porridge for breakfast and another three cups of tea. A fairly big walk today, probably about six hours and we must get at least as far as Thorung Phedi to have any chance of getting over the pass tomorrow. Outside the lodge I photograph and film, lammergeiers sweeping above us on the track. For lunch we stop at Churi Latter, at 13,780 feet, which is just a collection of wooden shacks and we just have soup here and watch, across the dirt track, women chopping up chunks of bloody yak meat. I ask if I can photograph them and the two, younger women are OK about it, but the older woman says no so I don't.

We have a laugh with them though and they all lighten up. There is a baby there as well and when the women are finished chopping yak meat, one of them puts the baby on their back in blankets and they all have bags of bloody meat and walk away. Nobody has washed their hands. Hmm, is it just us in the West who are a bit hyper about cleanliness? Donald with some clowning around, has some great photos, and entertained us all. Before we leave I look at some stuff a guy is selling next to the village and I buy a turquoise stone, real I hope for 250r. He wanted 1000r for it. And he also had coins from everywhere in the world and lots of other stuff but we can get them in Kathmandu, or even Pokhara. As usual, there are lots of ups and downs. I can't say my mood is great on this walk and get a bit fed up when everyone charges ahead, as if there was a rush and maybe just nervous about tomorrow. Anyway, we soon reach Thorung Phedi, at 14,598 feet, which is really just two big lodges in reality. But they are both full to bursting. No room here so just as well we are all feeling OK enough to head to the higher lodge or tea house. The climb is only 1,000 feet higher, but hard going at this altitude. We will have a break here and have some soup first and meet the Danish guy who is a bit pissed off as he only has a bed space in a dormitory with 5 others. At least he has a space. We don't as yet.

Initially we sat outside but as the sun disappeared, it was too cold and we went inside. Donald has ordered chips but the soup took ages and you just knew the chips would be another half an hour - and they were. We arrived in shorts but now I have a fleece, gloves and trousers on. Then we are out and climbing higher on the trail. When we reach high camp there are, again, two lodges. We are told they are full. Mingma had been sent ahead to sort it out but it seems, has failed. An interesting proposition as it's now dark, freezing and dangerous to go down to Phedi. However, it turns out Mingma has asked at the wrong lodge - the best-looking one it has to be said, with a big fire and laughter and music! Inevitably we are in the other one down the hill a bit and looks like a bit of a dump. After we get our bags into the other lodge and soon realise why there is room here. The room is freezing and there are big gaps between the window frames and the stonework. So not very hospitable and of course, no electricity, so no lights. The toilets are somewhere out the back - and very basic. No music or fire here!

The dining room is actually in another building across the track and the heating is an electric two bar fire under the table we are eating at. It's quite warm though, if not too safe. None of us are 100% but we all order food, even though hygiene looks really suspect and a cold inhospitable place but for dinner I order chicken soup and almost against my better judgement, egg fried rice. I surprise myself by eating most of the rice. It feels later but we have finished dinner by 6:30pm and head across the track to our rooms. It's a freezing cold night but inside my bag I get warm quite soon and only have to get up once for a pee and I don't even think about going round to the toilet.

Sunday 16th October.

I am woken at 5:00am by our boys and breakfast is half an hour later. Across in the dining room, which was obviously the sleeping room for the guys across there and a grandfather figure is still sleeping on a bench and later we notice another old guy sound asleep under a table. I've ordered porridge but can't finish it, however I feel really good this morning. Nima says for me to lead us off at exactly 6:05am at a slow, steady pace as I think someone has to set an appropriate pace. Even so, it's a hard pull and I notice that even this early, Marguerite is struggling. She's hardly eaten for days and that is not a good combination for today. Nima stays with her at the back, and that makes me feel marginally better but today will be a big test for her. Almost exactly two hours later we are at 16,500 feet. It's just cold and windy, not particularly scenic, just a slog and to be truthful, it's a bit of a disappointment.

There is nothing here at the top of the pass, just a shack, but it sells tea! The most expensive tea in Nepal it turns out. To the south I can see Khatung Kang at almost 22,000' and can just see Dhaulagiri in the south west.

About half a mile before the top I am watching a guy in front of us. He was actually staggering about in circles and looked as if he might collapse. Quite selfishly I was annoyed that this guy isn't up to it and he might collapse and need our help. However, he makes it to the top of the pass and here he looks relieved sitting down on his pack. Marguerite looks a bit better but she has put mind over matter to get up here so we take photos with her Saltire - the one I took to the top of Mont Blanc earlier this year and the one which we took the top of Island Peak two years ago.

Nima has got us all a cup of tea and we finish this quickly and don't hang about. I lead us down and from here we will descend some 5,000 feet and although it's a sunny morning, it's still really cold as we descend. I feel as if I'm walking too fast but I just want to get lower where we will all feel better hopefully. We stop after an hour for a drink and a snack. It's just after 10:00am. It's quite steep in places and at one point we have to stop to let a big mule train up past us.

We stop for a drink at Chabarbu at 14,070 feet - a really basic shack again, but it's nice to sit in the sun. I feel though that we all need a longer rest. From here it's less than an hour to Muktinath at just over 12,000 feet. Nima tells us that it is to Hindus, what Mecca is to Muslims, and if you are a Hindu you should see this before you die. The Tibetan name for it is Chu-Mig-Gyr-Tsa-Gye, meaning place of 108 springs. Nima is taking us on a tour but I have to say it's not impressive. Carfin grotto is probably better, but India is only around 200 kilometres away, and the place is busy with pilgrims or Sadhus who have travelled from there and we will pass lots of them. The others are too tired to walk round the site and I go with Nima, and as could only happen here, there is a Buddhist monastery as well, and it's called the Jwala Mai temple. I don't take any film or photographs - is it just tourism fatigue? But I did see the 108 water spouts, all with different wee metal animal heads and in the Tibetan style gompa, a natural gas flame which burns through a spring. Now that is impressive. The miracle of water burning!

It was just after 1:00pm when we all met up and headed down to the town. Our hostel is the charmingly named 'Bob Marley Hotel'. However, the rooms look pretty good and, we notice, western style flush toilets - a first on the trek, but we find later that both of these toilets are blocked, and the shower room - cold shower - is flooded. Ah well, nothing changes. On our return, I am first up to the sunny veranda and order a litre of Tuborg. This is brilliant sitting here watching the world in the warm sunshine. I can see Nilgiri, Annapurna 1 and Dhaulagiri and what a view and no wind here on this side of the pass - at least so far. Away behind me at the foot of the pass we have come over is Khatung Kang, huge and white with snow at the very top.

The rest join me and we are all catching up on our journals and we order lunch. We all have potato soup and I order something unheard of in the last two weeks - a ham sandwich. Only to be told there is a problem - no bread. So it's a chapati ham sandwich. Marguerite orders more Tuborgs, despite being sick twice today and not the recommended way to re-hydrate. The village itself is the usual shanty town look, but some more modern looking buildings and has a police check point Nima will need to visit. There are lots of people on horseback here though and good to watch it all from this veranda and you can hire a horse to take you over the pass. I must have sat here for at least two hours, some on my own as the rest go for a lie down. I watch horses, mule trains, cows, dogs and lots of other trekkers and it gives me time to think - and have another couple of beers. And I think this is what I need. I watched some trekkers walking in with fleeces, hats, gloves and even gaiters and I'm sitting here in my shorts. Tuborg warms the parts other beers don't reach? It was really warm and I could have stayed here all day, watching the world go by. The team appears and we decide to go for a walk down into the village and there are stalls everywhere selling mostly the usual stuff. I bought a bracelet from a cracking looking Nepali girl and didn't haggle too hard. And just on the other side of the village I buy a ring - and did haggle hard - so much so the stall-holder's wife starts to give him a big row for selling the ring too cheap, and then she asks me for more money and I politely decline. A deal is a deal I try to say. Real silver she insists. I doubt this and the tell-tale greenish stain on my finger next morning proves that silver it is not.

We head slowly back to the Bob Marley Hotel. In the room - with electricity - I've managed to get my video camera charged and unusual to have a plug point. The supply is, of course, erratic. Both Davy and Marguerite have gone to lie down. Donald has toothache - an abscess he thinks and he wants to rest as well. So I'm off to the veranda again to write this. The sun is still shining and to cool things down, I order a Tuborg. After a while I go for a shower because it's now empty. Turning the water on and it started warm but soon ran cool then cold. However, none of the water was running away but I am committed now and it's freezing. I had to paddle out the cold water and get back to the room and into my sleeping bag to try and warm up so not a good experience. Just after six we meet to eat and go upstairs to the dining room. There are no seats together at a table and it's really busy and we end up in seats, four in a row and order the food. And it's cold so we all have carrot soup which isn't good. I have an omelette which comes cold and we all feel a bit miserable so it's an early night and in bed for 7:30pm. This for me is maybe the poorest meal yet so not a great night. Anyway, I didn't feel cold as I fell asleep and would feel fine in the morning. I got up for a pee at one point and looked out the open window onto a biblical landscape. If you had a pee here 2000 years ago, it wouldn't look so different I'm thinking.

Monday 17th October.

The plan is to get away early without even breakfast and stop somewhere early on. Nima says we will have breakfast on a rooftop in the village of Jharkot so I shoot some film outside the hostel in the morning and some Tibetan chants playing from the hostel are a perfect soundtrack as I film horses with their steamy breath in the cold morning air getting ready for their duties today. Also on the soundtrack is Donald behind me loudly commenting on a horse's fart, which wasted the ambience of the film. So, out of the village down to the Dzong valley and it's a cool morning and people are just starting to get about, getting their stalls set up. After about half an hour we come to Jharkot, which looks like a collection of hovels and a sort of mud and stone ruined fort. A real medieval type village and we go into, well, a house and Nima is talking to the owner and soon we are going up rickety stairs onto a sort of mud roof. A plastic table and chairs are brought up and the sun is now just over the mountains, heating up the morning air and as we look about we can see the people in the village getting ready for the day ahead. It looks like a very primitive place.

The breakfast is surprisingly good with tea and boiled eggs and a chapati and of course peanut butter that looks ancient and suspect. We all take photos and I take some film. Marguerite takes a few shots of me with my camera and it's really warm and again, we watch the world go by. On another rooftop we watch a beautiful girl tend to her baby in total contrast in this remote and bleak place. After more tea we leave in the sunshine and walk out of the village into a more desert-type environment as we head today for Jomsom and the end of our trek. We all took lots of photos on the way and I filmed some children who were taken by Marguerite's wee dog mascot on her rucksack and it almost vanished in their excitement. There are quite a few people here on horseback. I almost wish we were too. The trek is now over dusty trails and there is only the odd oasis of green where the mountain melt-water has been harnessed. Away to our right is a route into India but it looks very steep. We take a detour to the historic village of Kagbeni and we will have a lunch stop here before we cross the dustbowl of the wide riverbed leading to Jomsom.

Nima has already warned us about the high winds and dust. Planes don't fly here in the afternoon because of it. Kagbeni is an oasis on the gateway to the forbidden kingdom of Mustang. I have to say that looking towards it I wonder why you would want to go. It's so bleak and desert-like, but unspoilt and also pretty expensive as there is a daily tax on trekking. There are routes here to Tibet and India. As we head downhill towards the village we can see all the cultivated areas above the village growing basic produce and an oasis in this yellow and grey landscape. The wind is getting up and we can see big dust-storms. As we enter the village we pass the river Jhong Khola which runs through it. The hostel is the usual basic place and for lunch I have chicken soup and French toast. The soup is all right but obviously has been 'extended' and is a bit watery. After lunch Nima says we are going to a 600-year-old monastery, the Thupten Samphel. But Marguerite has no lunch and isn't up to it nor the others. That was a pity because not only is it interesting but I get to see ancient scrolls in a locked casket, which look like vellum and are beautifully written. I remember an Incredible String Band song, which feels appropriate:

In the golden book of the golden game
The golden angel wrote your name
When the deal goes down you'll put on your crown
Over in the old golden land

The views from the red ochre monastery rooftop are amazing and there are two big mastiffs up on the rooftop but not near us. The walk round this village is amazing too and not much has changed here in centuries and soon we are close to another ancient ruined fort and through narrow back streets full of animals and children. No fear, no risk, only a wonder that these people can exist and not only that but look happy. How long before they think they need all the stuff we take for granted. Is their existence more sustainable for our planet? Of course it is but will I give up my 4x4. Well, no, not yet.

Another thing we notice is that the wind is even stronger and back at the hostel, Marguerite says she feels a bit better. For days now she has hardly finished a meal. This is the final stretch and the trekking and climbing will be over this afternoon. Davy has brought masks to keep out the dust on this next part and Nima and the team all have bandanas on now and we set a fast pace to get this bit over with as soon as possible. I have my tartan scarf around my face. We head out into a strong wind into the Kali Gandaki valley and soon we are on a dusty trail. The other three plough on and I am at the back with Nima and Mingma and I stop to take a few photos but the wind and dust make it unpleasant. Soon the other three are out of sight. Now I don't mind being on my own but just feel a bit left out on this last stretch. This area is famous for ammonite fossils and was once a sea.

Eventually it is me now away in front and it's just a case of making this a march. When I finally stop at the end of the narrow valley to wait, I am spitting dust out of my mouth. Nima has also caught up with us and the pair of us have another forced march into the outskirts of Jomsom, a long drawn-out town. At one point he shouts and points ahead to a dust storm rushing towards us and we have to turn around against it as it sandblasts our backs.

We pass lots of lodges and a school before crossing the river and up into the main part of the town and I have some craic with some soldiers about comparing the IRA and the Maoists as Nima shows them our papers.

As we reach our hostel for the night, this is effectively the end of the trek and we all head inside and a miffed Marguerite asks if we are going to take photographs as it's the end of the trek. And, of course she's right. I think we are all just glad to have got here and we all take a photograph and we get one of the boys to take all of us. None of us looks very happy. The strain of the afternoon march is there to see.

The lodge is quite big and Donald and I share a room again but with an en-suite Nepalese hole-in-the-floor toilet and a shower. The shower is electric but at this moment the electricity seems to be cutting out every ten minutes. I manage a fairly warm shower using my head-torch to see, which is different. As we head along to the dining area for an end of trek beer and Nima and the team join us, the atmosphere is very relaxed and Nima says there is a special dish on the menu tonight - fried chicken! I can't explain how wonderful that sounds after our largely meat free diet and we all order it.

So, after a beer, I head down into the town and end up buying a couple of bracelets and some apple and apricot brandy in glass bottles. Jomsom is famous for it and it's distilled here at the Nilgiri distillery. Nima says the apricot is best and the cost is about £1.20 each. One bottle is clear and so is the liquid inside. However, there is no sign of any banks open to try and get some more cash. It's quite nice just walking about on my own, but is getting cool as I walk back to the hostel. It turns out the fried chicken is in fact chicken pakora but at this stage, who cares. It tasted wonderful and we had a few more Tuborgs to wash it down and some craic with the boys. Only Nima and Mingma will fly out to Pokhara with us in the morning. The boys will walk to Pokhara and catch the bus back to Kathmandu. It's almost 10:00pm when we go to bed so a really late night. I slept well and was if anything too warm and I had a crazy dream - residual Diamox? Anyway, it was about a strange alien craft landing in Scotland to take us over. I was hiding behind a stone dyke just outside East Kilbride and then one of their spaceships landed silently next to me and I'm caught I think. But it turns out they are actually friendly Tibetans and I join them to take over the world.

Tuesday 18th October.

The reality is being woken up by Donald coughing out yesterday's dust. It's 6:00am and daylight so time to get up and get packed. The two bottles of dodgy brandy makes my pack heavy. From the bedroom window I watch Shangri La airlines Twin Otter land at 7:00am. The first flight of the day and from a rooftop veranda next to the dining area, we all watch the Cosmique (our airline today) land at 7:50am with a Dornier, a bit bigger than the Twin Otter. All the fights are morning only as the dust storms are too bad to land in the afternoon as we now know. Breakfast is two cups of tea and toast with peanut butter and just before this I get ready to film the departure of the Dornier and get a classic shot of the plane coming down the runway and I should then be panning round to catch it lifting up through the narrow valley, but Donald has placed himself in the frame by walking in front of me. I need a Donald filter.

Next, we now have to take all the bags down the street to the wee airport offices and for some reason, Mingma insists on taking mine, leaving me just with my rucksack but the rest are left for them to carry themselves. Before we get in, there is a security check and all the bags including our rucksacks are physically checked and even almost emptied in some cases. I've wrapped the bottles in a pair of climbing socks but this seems OK and they don't even look inside. Donald just manages to get his Leatherman tool kit out of his rucksack and into the hold luggage just in time. Then we have to hang about for about half an hour and the place is pretty bleak inside but soon the Dornier arrives and we get packed and loaded. The flight isn't too busy and I have a seat to myself. Disconcertingly, as we head down the runway, I'm thinking that this isn't fast enough to take off but then realise we are turning and we will fly out in the opposite direction to the other flights. I remember now that the Danish guy told us that the pilot has to make the decision to clear the first mountain range from one direction, or to play safe if the plane is heavy and head over the dried lakebed we walked over and then turn around once height is gained. I got some good films of the area we walked over yesterday.

The flight is spectacular right through the mountains and we can see some of the really big peaks, which are always above us. I film what I can and we are then soon over the sprawled out suburbs of Pokhara, a really flat area surrounded by massive Himalayan mountains. The airport building is a bit bigger than Jomsom and we are soon collecting our bags. Nima has organised a minibus from the hotel Barahi - one of the best in the town he says - to pick us up. We are there in about twenty-five minutes and as we head along the 'main street', it doesn't look promising, less so as we turn up a dirt track, past a cow wandering down past us. However, as we turn into the hotel gates it all changes and there is even a wee swimming pool! The rooms are all air-conditioned and it is a haven from the chaos of the streets. Nice big gardens too. Nima and Mingma say goodbye as they are now also heading by bus back to Kathmandu. We are on our own here in Pokhara and Nima gives me our flight tickets for tomorrow. The hotel minibus will get us to the airport.

Donald and I get some washing done in our shared room and I have a hot shower and get changed and meet Davy and

107

Marguerite for a walk down the street. Although not planned, we all buy stuff from the stalls and shops. Everyone wants you to look at their stuff and I get my son Finlay a cracking ammonite fossil for a few pounds. The plan is to head back to the hotel and sit by the pool for a beer. In the distance in front of us is Machhapuchhare - the fish-tail peak, and 23,000 feet and a holy mountain that no one has actually stood on the summit of Nima says. The sky is pure blue and we watch some large eagle-like birds. Marguerite still isn't 100% and she heads to her room for a sleep. The rest of us order lunch at our poolside table and another round of beers. The lunch is excellent and it's great just sitting relaxing in the sun. The hotel seems pretty quiet.

Later on, we have a swim while Donald sits soaking up the rays. There are only another few people in the pool and we sit until the sun disappears and head to our rooms. The plan is to go out for dinner somewhere. Time for me to do some catching up and I send a fax back home to Margaret from reception. The plan is to head down the main street and I have a couple of small Cohiba cigarillos. It feels quite safe here even if it's a bit dark in places and we walk the length of the street, which, even in this direction, must be half a mile. We find a big bank and the plan is to come here tomorrow morning and get some cash. By chance we choose a restaurant across the road and upstairs. As we get the menu, we order and get a round of beers too. Just as the food arrives there is a power cut, but the staff are nonplussed and have candles on our table pronto. There are now no street lights either and we can see at least one cow has wandered into the middle of the road. With no lights surprisingly there are no collisions. We plan how we would rob the bank if all else fails.

The meal was really good and I ordered a coffee with rum to go with my last Cohiba cigarette and the bill for all of it for the four of us comes to about £14. Downstairs, I buy about fifty red and gold, plastic bangles for about 50p from a passing vendor and I still wonder why I did that. Back at the hotel, Donald and I are the only ones up for another beer and we sit at the bar at the pool and it's still warm and it's nice sitting out at this time in the evening and I could easily have had another couple. Just after 10:00pm, Donald heads for the room and I go into reception to see if there is a reply to my fax, but nothing.

Wednesday 19th October.

Before we go into the restaurant for breakfast, I check again for any faxes but still nothing, so I send another. There is a good choice for breakfast and this is a real luxury compared with camping and lodges and we get talking to the manager who is really friendly. I check again for a fax after breakfast, but nothing and I head back to the room with Donald to get packed, as we will fly out late afternoon. The plan is to have a last walk down the street to buy some more stuff. Firstly, we hire a rowing boat to take us out on the Phewa Tal, a lake, to the island where the sacred Varaha temple is. Nice spot and despite Donald nearly colliding with another boat and sinking us, a really good wee trip. We are just tourists now. The first port of call is the bank and I get sorted out, but I have my passport with me. Davy hasn't but they accept a photocopy and suddenly our money worries are over. The guards only seem to have kukris as weapons.

In one shop, Marguerite buys a shirt and soon we are all being measured for this and that and I buy two shirts - one is almost made for me. Some items need more adjustments and the others will have to come back at 1:00pm to collect the finished clothes. The minibus is booked for just after this to take us to the airport. I buy quite a bit of jewellery and other bits and pieces and a wee Lowe Alpine rucksack for about £6. A fake no doubt but it does the job. Everyone has made a few purchases and the pressure is off about money and we still have $350 to get back in Kathmandu, so we are OK. I go to the hotel reception but there is still no fax so I decide to phone from the room phone and get through to Margaret. She has sent a fax but there was no number on the hotel headed paper so she phoned and they gave her a number, so a big mystery where it went. I ask right away how my mother is doing in the hospital and as Margaret tries to get the words out I know then that she is dead. And died two days after I left the UK, just when we started trekking so there was no way to contact me. I can't get much more out of her as she can't speak for crying. I say I'm OK and will phone later and from Kathmandu.

Donald, who was in the room with me, asks what happened and I tell him but meant to say not to tell the others. This is my grief not theirs. I wander out of the room and up to the bar and order a beer and go into reception and ask them to look for the fax, which duly appears. I don't even read it. Donald comes up with the others and they ask if I'm coming with them, but I say I'll just sit here. It feels really lonely, here on the other side of the world knowing my mother has died while I'm out here, and nothing I can do about it. I order another beer. When the rest return, Marguerite gives me a big hug and you know, that made me feel a bit better, and of course there is now plenty to do and we get the bags up to the reception and the taxi arrives and soon we are on our way through backstreets to the airport. Everything goes OK but again all our bags are physically checked and we are waiting in a pretty clinical big departure lounge for our flight. The schedule is to take off at 3:10pm but someone comes in and shouts something in Nepalese and people head for the door. We are hoping it's the right plane - a twenty-eight seat Saab. Just as well it is as we taxi out at 2:55pm.

I had joked about in-flight service but there is such a thing and the stewardess gives each of us a packet of nuts and a plastic cup of Fanta from a two-litre bottle. The flight is only forty-five minutes into Kathmandu but it's quite misty all the way. At the airport, Sunir is there to get us and our bags are pretty quick this time and we have a minibus and a driver to get us through the crazy traffic to our hotel. It feels great being back here, but a bit sad that it's all ending and it's a bit drizzly too. I try to get some film of the traffic chaos out of a side window and we all have a laugh about how frenetic the traffic is. As we slow at lights, I see some kids run across the road in front of us then a bang and Marguerite is screaming and unbelievably, in front of our eyes a car has hit a wee girl and ran right over her, and drove on. We all shout stop! We all get out and help to carry the girl to our minibus and her two pals come with us. Not another car has stopped. I think the wee girl is dying and her legs go rigid but maybe shock. Marguerite is shouting behind me and we are all talking and Sunir lifts her up and brings her into the minibus with the other two kids. The girl is on Marguerite's lap and she looks about eight or nine and she's screaming. We are on our way to a hospital.

The wee girl has blood all over her face and I'm leaning over using paper hankies and my water bottle to clean her up. Her mouth is all blood but her teeth look OK. Davy holds her still as I clean the blood and talk to her to try and calm her, but I'm not much good. The other two kids just stare at us in shock.

Eventually she looks a bit better but I'm sure her legs must have been broken. Blood is still coming out her mouth as we arrive at the hospital and we are all covered in this wee girl's blood. Sunir carries her in and we are all relieved that she is at least in good hands. He comes back and says she's been admitted to the hospital. We are all a bit subdued and we each have our own thoughts as we head for the hotel, no more filming and the traffic just isn't funny now. I think back and realise that no one seemed to take much notice of the accident except us.

At the hotel we get checked in and I'm relieved to see that I didn't get the two reception guys sacked with the currency issue. Nima is here as well and we are to meet him later to go to his daughter's birthday party. So we go to our rooms, get a shower and change and soon we are downstairs again and ready to go. A taxi takes us through dark unlit streets and I wouldn't like to have to have to find my way back to the hotel. Nima we all expect to be relatively well off and I think we are taken aback at the condition of the housing. Basically he has a flat in an apartment block, but it is very basic and cramped.

Anyway, we are well received and almost the whole team is there. All of the porters are here, Som and Dorge, except Robi or Pasang who will catch up with us tomorrow. Nima has filled a big fridge with Tuborgs and other beers and there is a real party spirit. Donald is introduced to Nima's three aunts, which is a potential risk and at some point one asks Donald if he is related to the King. I bet he said yes. There is a constant supply of snacks and cooked food for us. We have brought wee cuddly toys for Nima's girl and there is a huge birthday cake for Sumi, the wee girl. She's ten years old today. Soon we are dancing to an unreliable CD player out on a terrace, sheltered from the evening drizzle by a big blue tarpaulin. I have a few dances with Nima's sister who is quite attractive. It is a great atmosphere and we really feel part of it. I'm glad we were asked and glad we came. At some point tongba is produced. I've tried it before and it is a jar of fermented millet onto which hot water is poured and you drink the alcoholic result. Similar maybe to drinking vomit I thought last time. Anyway, Donald is photographed having a sip. We are all quite tired when we leave as it's been quite a hectic day and we are partied out.

111

Thursday 20th October.

Next morning I went to reception to get the number of the hospital where we took the wee girl. This takes ages, but eventually back in my room I get through. It's a nightmare as no one knows about the wee girl and of course I have no name, just an admission time. I eventually speak to someone in a neurology department, but they can't help. We have a really super breakfast in the hotel and there is quite a mixture of nationalities in here and quite a few cups of tea and we all are ready for a morning's shopping. I buy presents for my boys and it's great just wandering about and we end up at Cherapati roundabout to show Donald the chaos but it is a brilliant place. I get offered cannabis on the way back. After lunchtime I have to go with Som to the Nepalese Mountaineering Association to get our certificates and hand in the climbing and garbage disposal paperwork. And get my $350 garbage disposal deposit back. So we met with him, Nima and Sunir at the hotel reception. I also have to get money to pay Nima. So with all our passports, Som and I jump into a taxi and say to the others that we will be back shortly.

Well, this is Nepal and the whole process took about two and a half-hours. The certificates are hand written in script with our names. I'm given two cups of tea waiting here. But then a problem, our certificates says Chulu East but we climbed Chulu Far East. Som says we can't change it as Chulu Far East is a sacred summit and there would be a problem getting permission so it says East, not Far East. I can see he is embarrassed and worried but I'm not sure I'm convinced. I don't want him to lose face and it might be credible that the summit is sacred - there are such mountains here. Was this the reason we didn't get to the top? I'm really confused but don't feel I can argue in case it gets Sunir and Nima into difficulty. It was only later that Sunir gave me the original climbing permit to take home and it said on it Chulu East. So the permit and the certificate for a successful ascent both say Chulu East and I now know why. Chulu Far East was not on the original permitted list of mountains back in 1981 but Chulu East was, so we all have a certificate to say we climbed a mountain we were never on. The certificate also says the climb was successful, when we didn't actually get to the top, but someone has painstakingly written with a calligraphy pen, our names on the certificates as we waited and they are stamped with our spare passport photographs. I decide life is too short and accept them. I didn't get the $350 back either as the paperwork wasn't completed by Sunir, but Nima gives me the money later. We are back into the taxi and through the now monsoon rain back to the hotel to find everyone has gone out. We eventually meet up and the four of us have lunch in the hotel bar and it's really good.

We all try and go out later to shop but the rain is unbelievable. I'm offered cannabis on the street again, but we are soon at the hotel to sit with a couple of drinks. Later, in the room, I try the hospital again and it's one department then another until I get someone who can't speak English and I hang up. So, showered and ready to head back out to the Third Eye restaurant, where we had eaten a couple of years ago and thought it brilliant. The same guy offers me cannabis again. What is it about me? Well, the meal was OK this time and we are all relaxed and the rain is off so we go into an Irish bar in search of Himalayan Guinness, and find it at £5 for a wee can, but, hell, it's the last night. And it tastes good too. We have some Bailey's and a Jack Daniels for me. Back at the hotel we go to the bar and I get a glass of wine that is off and give up trying to explain this to the barman and go to bed.

Friday 21st October.

So, this morning, I tried the hospital again. I say I'm a British doctor, for credibility, and I admitted a young girl who was a road accident victim at 4:30pm two days ago and wished an update on her condition. They can't find anything but then the voice says, "You may have admitted her but maybe we didn't accept her."

I feel devastated and wish yesterday morning I had just got a taxi down to the hospital, if only to punch that voice in the face. So I have to give up and just hope she is OK. Time to get packed up and worried about the weight of my big bag, I taste the apple brandy, which is a heavy bottle and it goes down the toilet and the marginally better apricot stuff into an empty plastic water bottle. It might dissolve it I think. So we have another super breakfast and we have all morning and a good bit of the afternoon free. Donald and I head down to Cherapatri where I want to film but we buy stuff on the way. Coming back I go into a shop to buy a Kukri knife for Richard, my oldest boy and discover the guy makes Skean Dhus for export to Scotland. We get talking and he has only one but says it will be too expensive to buy, but after some haggling I get a cracking example with a yak horn handle and sheath with solid silver mountings for $50. We would become friends in later years. All of us meet up in a bookstore and all buy stacks of stuff. More stuff to pack away and the weight does worry me a bit, but we get our bags into storage and go off in a taxi to take Donald to the monkey temple. We enjoyed it last time and it's a big tourist thing. Our driver was asked to wait for us - maybe an hour - we say. Although last time there were people trying to sell stuff, this time they were really persistent and I bought more than I should, and more expensive too. It's hard going getting up the million steps to the top past them and then we have picked up an unofficial guide who is harmless but still a bit of a pest.

The total bill for the taxi comes to about 90p. We give a tip of course. Back to the hotel and we have lunch, which is really brilliant on the rooftop of the famous Rum Doodle, and in the sunshine. What a change from yesterday and back at the hotel I'm buying more stuff from the hotel shops which is a pantomime when Robi and Pasang appear with a kata for all of us and I give Robi the watch off my wrist as a gift. The others have gifts as well, and then Nima is there and our minibus to take us to the airport and we say our goodbyes. And of course the airport is chaotic and it takes about an hour and a half just to get into the departure lounge after paying departure tax, queuing, filling out the departure form, queuing and through two sets of security and more queuing. I even queued at the bar. The flight is OK to Abu Dhabi but we have a good few hours to hang about. I have a few plastic miniatures of Jack Daniels, which are useful after dinner is served on the London flight to induce sleep and I wake up with an hour to go to Heathrow and breakfast just being served. I am thinking now about my Mother's funeral and that it will be two days after my return. And Margaret has had her body kept for me returning and that is on the limit for doing that.

Saturday 22nd October.

By the time we are through immigration control and passport stuff at London, our bags are already on the carousel and we are now walking to terminal one and haven't a lot of time before our flight to Edinburgh. But the catering strike means we have a voucher to get a sandwich and a drink and the queue is crazy and our flight is about to be called when I'm asked to pay another 60p towards the voucher, I lose the rag at the stupidity of all this after having travelled halfway round the world without hassle. At Edinburgh airport, Donald is still wearing beads and me too. We are just a pair of old hippies but good to be home too. So, another great trip to the Himalayas and again, no thoughts about going back.

Book Three

Mera Peak Expedition 2007

Saturday 13th October 2007.

Early 2006 I climbed Jebel Toubkal, the highest mountain in North Africa, in winter conditions with another two guys from the club, Tom and Ivan and in August 2007 completed a full traverse of the Julian Alps in Slovenia, including Triglav, its highest mountain with the same two guys. But I kept thinking about the Himalayas. When there was a discussion about going back to Nepal, I decided to go with a known expedition company and it was Himalayan Kingdoms. I would still book my own flights of course. The other two Marguerite and Davy were again the only ones eventually up for it. At one point, it looked as if Davy wouldn't make it, having developed a neurological disease that delayed his decision but he insisted he was fit enough. It did mean he missed out on getting the same flights as he had to get the medical OK. He would fly via London and Delhi to Kathmandu. We were going to climb Mera Peak, the highest of the permitted 'trekking peaks' but with no technical climbing, just ropes and harnesses. This would be another three-week expedition.

Edinburgh airport was busy as we arrived with Rickie and Margaret, our respective spouses. But we were stopped at check-in by a girl from British Midland who asked if we had an onward connection in London. I said we did but lied that it was earlier in case the flight was going to be cancelled, but all she wanted was for us to agree to take a later flight. Not a problem as we had plenty of time at Heathrow, and we would get £100 in cash each which was fine considering both of our tickets only cost about £45 each so that was a good start. Although everywhere was as busy as you expect on a Saturday at lunchtime, we got seats in the bar with Margaret and Rickie and the first pint of Guinness downed in the knowledge we were now in no rush and that we were a few quid better off. So, we are now booked on the three o'clock. I couldn't book this flight at the time because it was full fare only. Later on my oldest son Richard joined us too as he worked in Edinburgh so it was a good family farewell. We still have to go to the gate for the one fifteen, the girl said, then they would probably just call our names and that would be us being told we were on the later flight. However, we were boarded and in our seats when other people came up and said we were in their seats. Apologies from the staff and we were unloaded and had to go back downstairs to check in. As we left the plane, the stewardess said to just go downstairs to the check-in desk as they know all about the change. They didn't of course and then the hassle started.

As it turned out we weren't even sitting together, which I lost the rag about. And we had to queue again and then we had to go somewhere else to get the cash. All of this took so long we only managed to get a glass of white wine and then we were again on a plane. This time it's an Embraer, so no room for our packs in the tiny overhead lockers, but the stewardess sorted out seats together for us, so I'm a bit calmer. A good smooth flight down and I'd been on lots of these planes and I've always liked them. We're a bit late in leaving but no worries for us. At Heathrow, we are on our own and a big adventure ahead of us when we leave London and a million things to go wrong of course. We walk through to the luggage carousels in terminal one and soon all of our bags are through and we have our trolley fully loaded. And off now to terminal three - the way to it we can both remember but a bit of a walk and it must have taken us at least fifteen minutes. The check-in area was really busy and it was hard to spot Qatar airways check-in desks but soon we are at the start of the queue, except for four or five in front of us. However, it was the wrong queue and lucky we asked as it soon became an even bigger queue, but they opened the other desks early and soon we were checking in. Very efficient and quick. It should have been electronic tickets but there was a problem - always stressful - and we were given replacement paper tickets and of course seats together and window seats too. Not that we'll see much tonight as we leave at 9:00pm.

I've booked the Servisair lounge from 5:30pm for three hours and we lost about an hour queuing at security. However, soon we are at the lounge but it's really busy and we have to stand for a while. Eventually we got a seat, which was fine but soon moved to a corner seat when some people left and the lounge got quieter. Marguerite had made sandwiches, which we shared, and a quick couple of beers and crisps and so glad we had this haven, as it just seemed mayhem outside, with people sitting in corridors. We took turns to choose the drinks, so we had Bacardi and coke and then added Kaluha, which was lovely. Oh,

117

and some white wine as well so fair to say we got our money's worth. At just after eight we boarded the flight to Doha, suitably relaxed and although we are far back, we are in two seats to ourselves, which is great. Not long after take-off, dinner is served and we have another couple of glasses of wine with our chicken and rice. We must have slept well as we both missed breakfast but a great way to travel. Everyone else just seems to be waking up too but a good flight and no noisy kids.

Sunday 14th October.

Sunday 14th October.

With just fifteen minutes to run, there is just desert below us. The landing was exceptionally smooth and we arrived in Doha, bang on time and despite the quantity of alcohol, we both felt OK, but we drank plenty of water and juice as well. This is a new country for me. As we went down the aircraft steps and onto the coach, the heat was impressive and it was only 6:30am. It was great having no bags to collect as they go straight through to Kathmandu. As we queued at transfer, I realised we should be going through immigration as we are going outside the airport. The desks are empty as most people are transferring to other flights. But I had planned to be different. So we stood in front of this girl in a black burkha and we thought she was talking to herself but must have been on a microphone headset. We asked for two tourist visas - the first hurdle I think, but it's straightforward and I just handed over my credit card, put in the pin and duly got my passport stamped. This is when Marguerite realised she couldn't remember her pin and one of those awkward moments as you must prove you have funds to even be here a few hours.

So I said, just put in 1234, which failed of course and then I gave Marguerite my card - you are supposed to have sufficient funds to enter the country personally - which seemed to work fine. When we got back home she found that the money had been taken from her card anyway and not mine. We walked out through an empty bit of the terminal, no customs or any other check and to my great surprise, there was a guy holding a big sign reading 'Mr Wilson'. He pointed to the exit and met us there with the hotel minibus. Just as they said they would. So, after landing in Doha, fifteen minutes later we are in a minibus heading down the gorgeous Gulf Corniche in the early morning sunshine and calm seas. I still can't believe it's that easy but of course our luggage is booked straight to Kathmandu so we only have our rucksacks. In the distance, across the water are the skyscrapers of Doha City.

I've booked an early lunch at the Rydges Plaza on the outskirts of Doha and we can use all the facilities. Our plan is to stroll back along the Corniche, apparently a beautiful walk and that will take us back to the airport. A pal of Marguerite's said she should do it. The hotel is surrounded by desert and it only takes twenty minutes in the bus and of course, the hotel is well air-conditioned and has twenty floors and the pool is on the roof. We check in and have the use of the changing rooms, but, again, in some Islamic tradition, the male and female changing rooms are on different floors so we leave our bags at reception and go for a wander. Even at this hour the heat on the roof by the pool is fierce, so after a shower we sit in the foyer checking cameras and tickets and our itinerary and funny to think I will be sleeping in Kathmandu tonight.

Lunch is light with salads and soft drinks but really good and very relaxed and we decide to check the temperature so we go back to the roof. It's too hot even for me so no way could we walk for miles with heavy rucksacks back to the airport. The girl at reception organises us a taxi and thinks we were mad to think of walking. The taxi takes us back along the Corniche and the sea is deep blue with the odd dhow sailing along. And the taxi only costs 25 Rials. Outside the airport we take a few photos before the heat gets to us, however, it's been a wee adventure rather than sitting at the airport all day. We fly at three and go through security and there are no shoes or belts off stuff as there was at Heathrow. Then we head to a café where Marguerite has tea and I have an Americano, in the absence of Guinness or any other alcoholic drink. A serious expansion is being made to this airport, like in Dubai. In the usual fashion we plan to be first on the plane, as we know now the Nepalese who are heading home from working here will take on board as much as they can carry and the lockers fill fast. Most of the rest are trekkers like us with big rucksacks.

However, we are to be taken to the plane by coach, so Marguerite takes one door, me the other so whatever door opens first, one of us will be among the first on. We're in 15a and b with an English woman beside me, but we are surrounded by Nepalese guys going home after their stint working in Qatar and we're on the right side to see the stretch of the Himalayas later but of course it will likely be too dark. We leave on time and it's a smooth take off and soon we are over the desert and the stewardess is offering a pre-dinner drink, which is white wine and then more with a lamb and rice dinner. It looks like we might get in at 10:15pm Nepal time, which would be good. The flight lands on time again, which means we can get to the hotel for a catch-up beer as Davy should be there already and get a good night's sleep but we both forget that even with a visa an immigration form has to be completed and then our bags will take half an hour, which is very fast, going from previous experience.

As Marguerite goes to find a trolley I notice another guy with a Himalayan Kingdoms bag, still waiting at the carousel. Outside, there's the usual sea of faces and chaos but we can see two guys with Himalayan Kingdom posters and after fighting off would be 'porters', we get our bags loaded onto the minibus, which is not quite as plush as the Doha hotel bus! Apparently the guy I'd seen at the carousel, Steve, has lost a bag and he's on our expedition and our driver and assistant go to help but there's paperwork too so it means we've lost almost an hour sitting on the bus waiting. It turns out that Steve has lost his bag with his crampons and boots and they are probably still in Doha. He will have to come back tomorrow, as ours was the last flight to land tonight. The journey to the hotel takes only twenty minutes and as we enter through these big gates, it looks really good. Inside we get our rooms sorted and try, as arranged, to get money changed at reception. Dave, our leader, has to get involved as there isn't enough cash and we can only get £200 changed and we need at least £300. I had faxed this request to Himalayan Kingdoms, our expedition company and they said this would be OK. The exchange rate is 125 rupees to £1.

It's now midnight and Dave assures us more cash will be available in the morning and it seems Steve will have to catch us up somehow but we are flying again tomorrow. Anyway, as I get my key, Dave says there is a 4:30am alarm call and we fly to Lukla at 6:15am, which isn't great and I've still my bags to repack and leave a bag here. I haven't really slept much since Friday night. However, on the plus side, the room is good and huge and on the first floor with two bottles of water but only one with an unbroken seal, so it gets two iodine tablets for a drink in the morning. I finish the other one and do a quick repack and get into bed. Of course, I can't sleep.

Monday 15th October.

I must have eventually fallen asleep as the alarm call came as a shock and then another quick sort out with my kit and then a quick brush of the teeth with the bottled water and downstairs with the bags. I put some cash, my mobile phone and passport into a hotel security box and left a spare kitbag with clean clothes for travelling home. At the airport there are the usual 'porters' ready to take our bags and it's still a bit dark but I grab my own stuff and push through the throng. Some of our party think these guys are part of the HK arrangements and end up being asked in one case for $5. Good try I think.

Inside, nothing has changed except security isn't as tight as two years ago and no need to worry about the 15kg limit as all our bags are dumped onto the one big scale for weighing. And next to a sort of conveyor belt are boxes of smashed eggs, ignored by everyone. We kind of get to know each other, especially when we are asked to carry white cardboard boxes, which contain our breakfasts! The security searches aren't as thorough as last time and my security guy just asks if I have matches or lighters. I say no and he doesn't even look in the breakfast box. It's only later I realise I have twelve lighters as gifts for the porters! There are nine of us on the trip, plus David Pickford, the expedition leader from Himalayan Kingdoms. We are just in the 'lounge' when there is an announcement in Nepalese - well, just a guy shouting and then he points at us and shouts 'Lukla, Lukla!' Then we are into an ancient bus and along to the Yeti airlines Twin Otter, only it isn't there. We can hear it before we see it with that heavy droning noise as the engines are trimmed for landing and it taxis right down to us and disgorges the first flight from Lukla and then we are boarded within minutes. I'm not bothered about getting any shots with the camera as I've done the trip before. The stewardess comes round with a tray. The last time I thought it was sweets, but it's cotton wool for your ears.

We were on board five minutes when the engines were again fired up and we're thundering down the runway and up through the early morning Kathmandu smog and cloud. Our pilot is a very pretty female and watching her at the controls passes the time but soon we're doing the scary landing at Lukla, surrounded by snowy peaks and below us is the milky white waters of the Dudh Kosi. When we land there are guys - this time they are HK porters - taking our bags and loading them onto trolleys and in front of us, another load of trekkers waiting to board and in less than ten minutes our Twin Otter is turning ready to taxi and take-off back to Kathmandu and a faster turnaround than Easyjet! We meet our Sirdar, Lhakpa Gyalu Sherpa, who is getting porters sorted out and we are following them past the freezing teahouse we stayed in last time waiting to get out. No big military presence here now and unbelievably, there is a red hammer and sickle flag flying from the airport security fence. Changed days indeed from the last time I was here. Soon we reach a flat grassy area behind the main street and all of our bags are put down here on a big tarpaulin and there are loads of gas canisters and big paraffin containers and what looks like bedding. The porters will get their individual loads sorted here and Lhakpa, our Sirdar is in charge of loading. We have three Sherpa guides as well, Nawang the younger, Nawang the elder and Phuri and our cook is called Palden Chosang and we also have an assistant cook, Milan, oh and eighteen porters. One porter will wait here for Steve arriving tomorrow. Two of our porters are female, increasingly common. Naturally, we are having tea and I must have had five cups of black tea, hanging about and some breakfast too. It seems some package is missing as well from the flight.

However, it gave us all the chance to introduce ourselves but to complicate matters Dave was expecting a package, which didn't arrive on our flight. We have to wait for that too, so we sit about chatting, have a look in the nearby shops and generally hang about. I met one of our party members here, Hazel, from Wales, who has just been to Everest base camp, so is well acclimatised already. We don't actually get away until 10:30am and it makes me think how much longer I could have slept back in Kathmandu, anyway, the weather is OK, warm but a bit cloudy and I've been here in worse conditions and good too, to be heading in the opposite direction from most people who come here with most heading to Everest base camp as I did four years ago. Inevitably we stop after less than two hours for lunch at the 'Everest' restaurant in Surke which is just over 7,000 feet and here we have chips, beans and a cold boiled egg and, of course, a few more cups of black tea. After lunch we again traverse around mountain ridges with lots of ups and downs, but the walking is easy at the elder Nawang's pace, our Sherpa leader for today and at some point I must have walked and talked to everyone.

As we've had a later start than planned, the light is slightly fading as we arrive in the village of Poyan at 9,300 feet and a team from Jagged Globe, another expedition company, have eight tents in the only camping area, so we sit outside at a teahouse getting cold as our guys try to sort something out. The decision is that we will stay in this teahouse tonight, with a few having to sleep in a teahouse across the road and that suits me fine, the less time under canvas the better and especially in the cold and rain. We will still all eat together as our cooks will be cooking in the teahouse just for us. The porters sort out rooms and I get a room to myself and two sleeping bags and I say to the porter I only need one but he says everyone will have two of their own and gives me a label for their storage bag. It's just plywood walls with gaps in the room here. We all go down for our first trek dinner together and we are given lemon 'tea' which we have, then order beers, which are litre bottles of San Miguel, which can't be bad and brewed in Kathmandu it turns out. Dinner is mushroom soup and I have a second bowl and then, the dreaded dal bhat, my least favourite food in Nepal, however, it's not bad at all and even has some sort of meat in it and fresh carrots.

All day on the trek here we passed porters taking huge bits of bloody ox carcass in canvas bags to, I presume, Lukla, to sell and in one village bits of the beasts were laid out to either dry or to sell and we had joked about getting oxtail soup but it wasn't to be.

Another round of beers and some journal writing and then Dave is telling us about the plan for tomorrow and a few laughs later at Marguerite's expense as we recall when we watched this huge bird circle above us as the Jagged Globe lot passed us. It's a 'Lammergammer' says Marguerite and a girl from JG looks at me and asks if that's right. No, I say, it's a Lammergeier. The girl from JG says she didn't think it sounded right. Ah, well, it did to Marguerite and it got recorded on Colin's film too! Earlier in the day she'd been talking to me about the yaks with ping-pongs in their ears and it took a short while to realise she meant pom-poms. Funnily enough no yaks so far on the trail.

No one is having a late night as we all have too much sleep to catch up on, so it's upstairs and into this wee room with one wooden bed and just wooden partition walls. It's only 8:30pm when I climb into my bag and fall asleep quickly and then wake up at 12:30am thinking I'd slept all night. I go outside for a quick pee using my head-torch to get me down the precarious wooden stairs and past the sleeping porters. Then unlocking the big wooden door and out into the black night and a sky which is just full of crystal stars and walking back up the stairs smiling to myself.

Tuesday 16th October.

I wake up this time at 5:30am to the sound of the cooks making breakfast, and the horrible smell of paraffin, which is not a great combination. When I go down onto the street to a water stand to brush my teeth I'm met with an amazing sight. All around me are white peaked mountains and one of them appears over the roof of the lodge where some of our party slept last night. When I go back upstairs I get packed, the big kitbag and then the sleeping bags and both are left outside my room door for the porters to collect as they will leave well before we do. Bed tea arrives with two smiling porters and some hot water to wash as well. I stick a label on my sleeping bag just in case there isn't a system. At breakfast I have a look at my altimeter and we are at just over 9,300 feet here. Breakfast is porridge followed by some pretty tough toast and some really good omelette and of course plenty of tea. I feel good this morning after a decent sleep in a real bed. We plan to leave at 8:30am and today will be longish with a lot of ups and downs but not much gain in height. As we walk, the weather just gets better after a cool start and we head down initially to a river and then it's a steep pull up but as we are contouring, the views are continually changing. Eventually I have to take my shirt off and walk in a vest. Lots of mountains around us, all with white tops and they all seem a long way off.

At around midday we stop for lunch at a stone and wood building perched at the top of a deep valley and as we drink lemon tea, Dave points out in the far distance, the building we will be staying in tonight, another tea house and it looks a long way, especially as we have to go down to the river first. There is a wee, cute, gold and brown dog here, which gets photographed by almost everyone while our guys get some cooking done and we all sit outside at benches. It's OK but not that warm now that we've stopped so I get my jacket on and we have a sort of potato cake with, well, Spam, and chapatis and fresh cabbage, a strange combination but it all goes down well. More black tea to wash it down and the dog barks at the approach of what we expect to be the Jagged Globe people, but its locals.

Dave says it's just contouring to get to our stop for the night and his words come back to haunt him as his contouring is our up and down - vertical contouring someone says and a bit of underestimation I think. The landscape is changing too and becoming almost tropical and very moist in the wooded areas with ferns and moss growing on the trees like fine green hair. It's an easy plod down to the river, but much harder pulling all the way back up. After about an hour and a half we stop for a rest at a couple of shacks and the JG lot are there too and we have a chat and a great viewpoint here and we all take more photos.

There are a few kids about, always interested in what we're doing and Hazel, the Welsh woman in our team talks to them very softly and Sheila gives them some pens from her collection and her husband Colin helps out and both from Glasgow. Hazel gets some paper and draws for the children and Dave has given Hazel his big book, which he had been reading, for her to lean on and it's a lovely scene and more photos are taken.

However, after about half an hour and we're ready to go, Dave takes back his book. And the kid who had been drawing starts to scream to Dave's obvious embarrassment and we say we

125

will report the incident to his company when we return but he takes it well. Soon we took a steep and narrow path away from the main route we've been on which is the route to Jiri and onwards from there to Kathmandu and, before the airstrip was opened at Lukla, this was the only way to and from Kathmandu and a few days hike. That trek route was rife with Maoists holding up trekkers four years ago and now they form part of the government.

Like yesterday, it starts to cool in the afternoon and mist is clinging to the hillsides like grey smoke and in the far distance we can hear thunder. No more contouring, this is now just up and steeply in places on vegetated rocks and quite slippery. We are maybe fifteen minutes away from our camp spot at Pangkongma and the thunder is now close, lightning too, sometimes spectacular forks. Big raindrops start splashing around us and its waterproofs quickly on as the thunder is rolling around the valley and Dave says we should try and stay in bricks and mortar again tonight and it's a good idea we all say. Another night not in a tent is fine with me.

The rain is suddenly torrential and we move as quickly as we can towards the dim lights of the village, just a few buildings really and soon we are all huddled into the dining area of a tea house and tea is ordered. Dave goes off to sort accommodation. It's freezing inside the tea house as no fire kindled yet. There are only three doubles, a tiny twin and a room with six beds and the

Sirdar will sort out who's in where. Outside the rain is still really heavy and we're thinking of the porters who are far behind us, and of course, how wet our kit bags will be. But about twenty minutes later as they arrive we can see they have covered themselves and their loads with polythene sheeting. It turns out I'm in the wee twin room with Chris, a paramedic from Kent and the room is tiny, in fact the smallest here. Chris is the tallest guy here at six and a half feet and you can hardly walk between the bunks. Outside there is only one hole in the ground toilet for all of us, in a wee wooden shack. Hmm. I go down to the dining room to write my journal while Chris sorts his kit as there is no room for two of us walking about. After nearly an hour, the rain stops and not long after that the mist starts to lift and we can see across the valley but it still feels cold. We go outside for a look and the peaks we saw on the way up are now really white with fresh snow and it looks great but could have implications for us. Dave reckons that a foot of snow is likely to have fallen on Mera and that is not good for us as it will increase avalanche risk.

We're not sure about the beer situation and there is a small store next to the teahouse here so I get Dave and ourselves a litre of San Miguel while the stove is being lit. This is always a performance and not often initially successful and usually more light than heat. I don't actually feel like drinking beer but after a few sips it starts to go down well and we have another during dinner when I have vegetable soup to start, with prawn crackers and the main course is spring rolls and curried potatoes. Just as we are finishing, a porter is at the door and with him, Steve, who has walked through all the heavy rain coming straight here from Lukla and quite a trek for him and his porter considering we all have already had an overnight to get here. By now the sky has cleared and is full of millions of stars. Marginally warmer inside, we write up our journals and the conversations are good and we have a laugh when Dave says there will be more contouring tomorrow, so a last round of beers are ordered. I share mine with Dave, and we talk about his first ascent of a mountain in Kyrgyzstan in the Pamir Alay range and it is really interesting. But at 8:30pm we are heading to our rooms and a quick nip out for a pee but there is a queue of three so I nip across to a field and of course no shower or washing facilities. So quickly into the single sleeping bag as I was too warm last night and fall asleep right away.

Wednesday 17th October.

Inevitably after the beers, I wake in the early hours bursting and have to creep downstairs and outside into the darkness. Make a mental note to leave out my pee bottle. I wake again at 5:30am having slept well despite the interruptions and Chris says he didn't sleep well. We get bed tea at 6:15am, which I drink in my sleeping bag as Chris is repacking his kitbag and we have no room for two people moving about. He takes ages and by the time he's gone to brush his teeth, I've quickly re-packed my bags and the sleeping bags are packed too. Marguerite pops her head round the door to say good morning and to say she already is having tea in the dining room and I'm ready in a few minutes and go down to brush my teeth and join her. I brought all my bags down as the porters are getting today's packs ready outside and it's a dry day with some blue patches in the sky. I feel good this morning, happy even, however it's not warm and I have my fleece on inside the dining-room. There is no fire lit in the daytime and we have breakfast of porridge and toast with fried egg, and black tea of course.

I haven't used my walking poles yet but today we set off at a faster pace and uphill, so I'm using them this time. We pass some porters from Exodus Travel who have clients staying in another teahouse just outside our village so no camping for them either last night. As we walk, we look back a bit later and can see this group heading up towards a monastery far above us to our left. I'm wondering if they will head a different way or whether we will see them again tonight. I'm pushing hard at the front of the group but sweating hard too but as it's only a three-hour walk I drop back as I don't want to sweat and then cool down too much. I end up walking with Val, the gynaecologist for an hour and interesting listening to all the treks and stuff she's done all over the world. This is where we get our first view of Mera and the snowline I guess is about 15,000 feet, which isn't good but it looks like Dave was right about the fresh snowfall and it could mean camping on the stuff earlier than we planned.

After two hours we stop for tea at a quite well-built teahouse overlooking a huge green valley which we will traverse away to the left from here but won't get much higher. The black teas arrive, all of them sugared but I can still drink it that way. We are well off the usual trekking route here which is great. What used to be the normal route was over the Zatra La, the pass we will return over. The difficulty is that it is very high and risks Acute Mountain Sickness which can be fatal if you can't get lower but once you are over the pass there is nowhere out except by climbing over a high pass! People have died here from using that route in.

Always planning ahead and as we will be in a fairly remote campsite, Marguerite suggests we buy a litre of beer each for later and it's only 200 rupees a bottle which is really cheap. To save weight she starts to pour the beer from the bottle into her collapsible plastic container, which promptly fills with froth and over the next fifteen minutes, only gets half of it in and a truly failed experiment by a drinking expert! Behind the house I film a man and boy working an ox and wooden plough in a field and women walk behind them lifting what looks like weeds. This is a sight which must not have changed for centuries.

From here it's off traversing again and despite the walking poles I can feel a wee niggle in my right knee but this is the first problem I've had so I'm hoping it doesn't get worse as this is an easy day today. As always on big treks you just become so aware of your body. There are lots of ups and downs as there always seems to be on Dave's traversing but I keep at the front with him. At the top of a particularly steep section, two porters have come from the forward camp with a big kettle of warm lemon tea, which is very welcome. The camp is half an hour away from here and these guys are good. The campsite looks good with a couple of big, flat grassy areas and the cooking squad, led by Palden, have laid out a big blue tarpaulin with plates and cutlery. We have arrived before the porters so there are no tents up yet. It's quite a tropical looking setting with only a couple of wooden shacks up the hill, a couple of farmers tending to some cows, and a bloody barking dog. We are back down to 9,500 feet here though from well over 10,000' earlier. And the first view of Mera's three tops and all pure white.

Lunch is served on the tarp and it's good with big potato chips with skin on that taste like Ayrshire potatoes and slices of very pink salami, and tea, plenty of it. Meanwhile our beers are cooling in a stream close-by as we watch Milan, the assistant cook, being very particular about placing the cutlery and the condiments of red and green chilli sauce. It's lovely sitting here in the middle of the afternoon in the sunshine and some sit on the ground, me on a wooden fence. There was talk of a walk after lunch but I want to sort out some clothes to wash, and to wash myself too. Marguerite and Dave go down a path towards where the valley steepens to see if Mera is visible as it was earlier. So I wander to the stream and go uphill for about a quarter of a mile for seclusion and I get socks and pants washed then strip off and wash myself. The water is freezing cold and probably melt-water from the recent snow. As I stand up naked and now freezing, wringing out my socks I see Hazel just downstream and she must have seen me so now freezing and embarrassed!

Needless to say that when I get back to hang up my washing, the sun has gone so I try to get as much water out as possible and hang my clothes on a wall to dry. The porters are putting the tents up and this is our first night camping. The tents are North Face, yellow domes and look good but there are also a couple of taller green tents although mine is a dome. It's great having plenty of room as this is at least a two-man tent. As always from here on, two holes are dug for the toilet tents to cover and a washing bowl, hand-wash and a towel are put out beside them. A sleeping mat and double sleeping bag are put in the tents and then our kit bags arrive and they also go in. When all this is done I get myself organised but will only use a liner and one bag at this altitude. Afternoon tea is served and is announced by the cook banging a stick on a pot and we all sit on the camp chairs and after a couple of black teas I open my wee bottle of cognac and we have a cognac black tea next and very nice too. It gets too cold to even sit and write up journals so we all head back to our individual tents. Before I go back I nip down to get the beer back from the stream ready for dinner later. It's as cold as I am.

This is our first time in the dining tent and it's amazing what our cooking staff can come up with and all cooked with wee paraffin stoves or gas canisters. We have chicken soup with ginger to start with, followed by chicken, roast potatoes, green beans and a white sauce. This is topped by the sweet, which is banana pie with a criss-cross pastry top and with custard! So we sit replete with our beers till about 7:45pm. The porters will sleep in this tent tonight and we don't want to deprive them of their accommodation so we start to leave when the cook brings in a big kettle of boiling water and we have to fetch our drinking bottles to be filled. This is our hot water bottle and in the days to come will become really important to us. In my sleeping bag by eight and falling asleep feeling great and then even better as I realise the niggle in my knee has gone and I wonder if it was the custard or the cognac.

Thursday 18th October.

Despite waking up about midnight and hearing the dog barking, I slept really well and woke up again at 5:30am. No point hanging about so after bed tea in the tent and some warm water to wash, I got packed up and this will be the format almost every day now. I am ready by 6:20am and not a cloud in the sky although the sun won't hit us for another ten minutes but I feel fit this morning and no knee niggle either. Last night I used my silk liner in my sleeping bag and I will from now on. The sun is just hitting us now as the dining tent is now packed up and we sit outside for breakfast, but we still have tables and chairs. Breakfast is porridge with nuts and raisins, then some cheesy toast and a wee rectangle of omelette and again, lots of black tea. We leave camp at 7:45am and its vest and shorts this morning and Dave says today will be around seven hours with lots of ups and downs and the first bit is hard going uphill onto a ridge then down, then of course contouring, then down again. It was like this for a good three hours when we came upon a river running over big boulders. The cooking team have gone on ahead and set up lunch here and plenty of rocks and logs to sit on and a couple of fires are going too for the porters' food. It's really warm and everyone uses the cool river water to wash and cool off. I stick my whole head under to cool down and sit on a rock where I check the altimeter but disappointingly it's still just the same height we were at this morning.

Lunch is puffed potato bread with spicy sliced sausage and fried potato slices and some cheese is handed round too but it is rock-hard. We have lemon tea first then onto the black stuff and we're here for a good hour. The next part of course is just up and the path here is really overgrown and certainly not used much. At one point there are some big stone steps in place but still a lot of sliding in mud and every tree has the hairy moss growing on it. It's quite eerie in the thicker parts of the forest, which is mainly rhododendron, juniper and bamboo. It is a lot cooler in here too. Talking to Dave at some of the stops to let everyone catch up, he says we will get to 10,300 feet today but it doesn't feel like we've got that high and furthermore he's saying tomorrow will take us to 13,100 feet which seems like a big ascent. I think the reality is that we are at 9,700 feet with no prospect of going much higher as we will camp near the river, which we can just barely hear now. And, of course it is somewhere below us.

Getting to the river is a bit of a shock as the river is almost a waterfall and fast flowing and white with glacial silt and the only way to cross it is by a big log. And that is a big bare log with no bark left on it, so not much grip and it's wet from spray. On the other side, the bank has been washed away, leaving a scramble up the bank to regain the path. I can understand why it's not a route used often. I watch Colin crossing with Dave helping him and this would not be a good place to slip. Marguerite was first over, then Steve, and then it's me. The poles are pretty useless here and it takes ages to get everyone across and just as long for everyone to scramble up the rocks at the other side. I noticed that

Sheila has struggled today and Colin and her were at the back almost the whole day. She says she thinks she might have the flu.

From here it's just a short pull up to our campsite for the night and it's amazing with a huge fifty-foot black rock face surrounded by bamboo and lush vegetation and the big rock has a couple of caves. The cooks already have fires going in them and I can hear the hiss of the pressure cookers. It's a bizarre, almost stone-age sight but the dining tent is already up and here and there planted in the undergrowth are places for individual tents some of which are already up. You can hear the roar of the river below us. The cooks have lemon tea and biscuits for us as we wait on our tents being finished. Some porters are behind us but I wonder how they get over the log bridge carrying their huge loads. My tent arrives and is pitched far below the dining tent and I'm surrounded almost, by big bamboo canes and quite a unique location and totally different from last night so it feels like being in the lost world. I expect to see Tarzan any minute. So I get my stuff sorted out in the tent and maybe two bags tonight, as it feels colder and certainly more humid. The sleeping bag cover and the tent is still damp from last night and not much chance of stuff drying here.

I feel as if I'm alone here in the jungle in the tent but after getting sorted I go up to the dining tent for a seat with my journal. So I have a wee squirt of hand-gel as always before anything else. I have felt really good today and before I write, I take some film, as photographs can't capture the magic of this place. Hazel joins me for a chat for about fifteen minutes and I really like her and her no-nonsense approach and we talk about our trek to Everest base camp. Then the improvised dinner gong goes. We keep the same seats for us as last night with us at the far end and everyone has brought their empty water bottles to be filled with hot water later and again, this will now be a ritual every night. The big paraffin storm lamp is hissing but hanging up in the middle of the dining tent, it gives a great light and it has a really atmospheric effect.

Soup tonight is spicy noodle, not sure what flavour, but it's good anyway and I have a second bowl as well, then it's rice with curried vegetables and cheese sauce and I add some chilli sauce too from the condiment bottles and there is green and red chilli sauce but I only ever risk the milder green stuff. As there seems to

133

be no sweet coming tonight, Marguerite produces some Drambuie and I have a wee mouthful but two minutes later, hot fruit salad arrives and the remaining Drambuie is added making it taste even better. To finish, the cooking staff bring in the big Chinese vacuum flasks with boiling water for tea, coffee or hot chocolate and the water bottles are filled and I nip down to my jungle tent to throw it into the bottom of the sleeping bag. No gorillas spotted. Although someone produces cards, no one seems in the mood so it's back to journal writing and pitch-black outside now. Steve and Dave are playing chess and a couple of people are looking at maps. When the guys come in about 8:00pm to clear the stuff, it's our prompt to depart. Today was hard after the easy day previously and we're all tired, so head-torches on and we head to our tents. The porters' fires are still burning brightly in the cave entrances and it looks prehistoric and I have prehistoric dreams, but not of Tarzan nor, sadly, of Jane.

Friday 19th October.

I have had a great sleep, only woke up once but it took ages though to get over last night but since I went to bed at 8:20pm it's not a problem and I woke again at 5:30am, so I was dressed and packed before the bed tea and washing bowl arrived at 6:30am. I'm first up to the dining tent but the place is busy with our porters getting packed and waiting for the tents next, then the dining tent is coming down so it's breakfast outside again, but the sun hasn't penetrated here yet and it's quite cool. The rest arrive and we sit down for jungle breakfast. I feel good this morning too and quite cheery but not everyone looks the same. I scoffed the breakfast of muesli, then bread and fried eggs and lots of black tea. No aches or pains at all this morning. But Davy has been really ill during the night.

We leave at exactly 7:30am and we climb steadily for an hour, up and out of the valley at an easy pace almost forced on us by the steepness of the track and some big stone steps and still in the trees though and out of the sun. Lots of ups and downs again and we don't really seem to gain much height, but we have a view of distant Mera through the undergrowth and it looks very white. After almost four hours we stop for lunch at Takthok and this is where we will join the main trail again and will come back this way and over the Zatra La. It's windy now that we're out of the valley, but we have a sheltered spot for lunch and no knee problems today. In fact, I feel really fit and ready for the lemon tea on arrival.

Lunch is warm chips, cold pasta and cold, tinned sardines in tomato sauce and more black tea and just hanging about on the blue tarpaulin in the sunshine and really relaxing. From here we meet the main track coming from a couple of directions, including the track to the Zatra La, the high pass we will return over, dropping us back into Lukla but the recent snow might have made it impassable for a day or so. The trail from here leads to Kote, which Dave reckons to be just over 11,500' and that means that Tagnac, the village we will reach the day after that will be at least a 1,500' increase. The track, despite being used more, doesn't really improve and we go down for some time to the waters of the Hinku Khola. Our Sirdar, Lhakpa leads just now, swinging beads and chanting Buddhist mantras all the time. We get another view of Mera Peak through the woods. The path from here is even rougher and it takes us a full hour to reach Kote. We had a really tricky bit to descend as there must have been an avalanche that covered the trail in mud and rock. The porters just forced their way through the bamboo jungle rather than risk it.

Just as we are a few hundred yards away from the edge of the village the rain starts and it gets heavier so we get our waterproofs on and just as we are walking in, unbelievably, I see a Sherpa I recognise and it's Som, our climbing Sherpa from our Chulu expedition in Annapurna and the same red tartan shirt as well! As we pass some shops, Som comes out a doorway and it's him all right and we give him a hug and he can't believe seeing us either. He's here with three American clients and climbing Mera peak with them and he says last year he took the same guys up Island Peak, which we climbed four years ago. We have a big flat area in the village, next to the river but it's cold and it's wet and the first priority is to get the dining tent up. A table is produced, not ours but our seats are brought out and we have tea and biscuits but it's only marginally warmer in here and outside the rain has turned to hail and then back to really persistent heavy rain.

No chance of getting anything dried tonight, so as the tents are now up, although stretched out a fair bit, the only way to keep warm is to get some hot water into a water bottle and go to our tents to lie in a sleeping bag and I actually get quite comfortable and nod off till 5:30pm when I wake up and the light is fading fast. The only toilet is a fair walk away from my tent, just a wooden shack perched on rocks in the middle of the river. The toilet is the usual hole in the floor with the river right below it - which is why you don't drink out of streams here. Later I get out of the tent to head up for dinner as the hurricane lamp is being tied up in the dining tent and then the gong goes. It's so cold we all have hats on and some, including me have gloves on too. If it's this cold here, what will it be like at nearly twice this altitude? At least the rain is off and the purple sky is clear and a few stars out already and no wind at all. Dinner starts with a tureen of vegetable soup, which, when it's opened, fills the entire tent with steam. The main course is pizza with spaghetti, cauliflower with cheese sauce. Marguerite has bought three expensive bottles of Everest beer but I actually struggle to drink it, but of course, force myself. It's freezing in the tent and not much appetite for cards and everyone is quiet tonight, either reading or writing. I think we all got to the stage where we just wanted to be warm and soon the water bottles are being filled to heat our sleeping bags - and toes and fingers. As we get to the tents we realise they are frozen rigid and quite white as the dampness has frozen on them, so it's a quick pee then into both bags and the water bottle too of course and I get slowly warmed up but I'm still awake from before eight till after eleven and only slowly thawing out.

Saturday 20th October.

I slept well and woke at 5:15am to find the inside of the tent frozen white but I needed to get to the loo and as I got out the tent, I saw that all the tents were white with frost on the outsides and the ground too. There is wood-smoke rising straight into the air from a few shacks in the village and some porters and locals walking about, their breath white in the freezing air. It's a strangely beautiful sight and like an Indian camp from the wild-west. Back to the tent and inside the bag to wait for bed tea and washing water and the cooking team are as cheerful as ever going from tent to tent, making tea or coffee outside each tent. After tea I get packed up and no shaving on this trip. If the tents were uncomfortable yesterday to take down because they were damp, it's a nightmare today with the canvas on the dining tent especially, being almost rigid with ice as we help the porters try to fold and stuff the thing into its bag. My fingers are frozen after this of course and no source of heat.

As the porters are a bit behind, we firstly have to stand at our table for breakfast and then sit as the chairs arrive. No sun up yet so it's porridge and tea this morning but everyone is anxious to get moving and get some heat. We will follow the river for most of the day and because we are in a deep valley, we have no sunshine for the first hour of walking but apart from the penetrating cold, I feel fine. The riverbanks have been scoured on either side and there is flood debris everywhere. The scouring must be twenty to thirty feet high caused by the natural dam above Tagnag bursting a few years ago when a huge chunk of glacier ice fell into the glacial lake. It caused this devastation and wiped out everything downstream, which meant for us, some hard going today.

We head up all the time, soon walking on scrubland beside the glacial melt-waters of the Hinku Khola and wee, blue Gentians are everywhere, just coming out in the morning sunshine and lots of juniper bushes too but sadly no gin with us. As happened yesterday, a helicopter flies up the valley. Our guide today is called Phuri but sounds something like 'cheery' and he is too. He points out to a sort of sheiling away ahead of us, and that is exactly what they are, summer pastures for the farmers from lower down the valley. We see another helicopter above us as if heading to Tagnag or Mera. We have good views of Kyshar in front of us.

There are some yaks here and there and the cooking team has gone ahead of us and are preparing lunch and when we stop we have orange 'tea' to start. On the way up someone spots some Edelweiss and Marguerite starts singing the sound of music. The porters have set up the blue tarpaulin again, but there is some debate about stopping here with Dave who thinks it's too windy where it is so it's moved to a more sheltered spot, or so we thought but I think it's windier but it's closer to the cooking area I suppose. Lovely views all around us with snow-capped mountains and I think this place is called Gondishung. We have cold tinned salmon, cold beans and fried potato, and something that looks like a warm Cornish pasty, and freshly cooked. All good though and Palden and his team are stars. It is just lovely sitting outside in these surroundings in the sunshine and from here we will continue to walk up the broad valley to our camping spot for tonight. Just as

137

we finish, someone shouts 'avalanche!' and away ahead of us is a huge cloud of snow powder from the avalanche, which has come from the west face of Mera. We all grab cameras and I film the aftermath. The powder cloud must have reached the path we will be on soon and it makes you think that after all that snow you would hesitate being on any mountain.

From here we have another two hours trek to Tagnag and it's different walking today as it's just up and quite gentle with none of the ups and downs from the last few days. I feel really relaxed and fit again today and it's great being out in the sun but behind us, clouds and mist are sneaking up the valley from away down in Kote. On the way, we take a bit of a detour to have a look at a wee sort of monastery and apparently just one monk lives here. It is pretty remote and a bit of a climb up to it from the path. Lhakpa, our Buddhist Sirdar, calls us together to show us something special. The something special is up a steep track to the wee monastery almost built into the hillside. It takes us a good ten minutes to get up. In a wee cave next to the monastery, carved out of rock is a 3-D image of all the surrounding mountains. Nawang points them all out, including Mera of course, and its three main peaks. How could you do that without being able to read a map?! Presumably the monk could, but he's not here to confirm or deny. Away partying maybe?

There is still snow powder in the air and we complete the walk in less than an hour from here. Tagnag, surprisingly, is bigger than Kote but still just a wee village and most of our tents are already up. There is a wood and stone lodge next to where we are camped and we are in here for our tea and biscuits and will eat our meals here too. As we go in the low door, I notice the sign above the door says 'dinnig room' but it's now quite cool and none of us are looking forward to 'dinnig' in the cold dining room. When we come out into the light, it's snowing so our planned afternoon walk up to the glacial loch called Sabal Tsho is cancelled. There is nothing else for it but to retreat to our tents, get into a sleeping bag and stay warm. It was good news that our guys got us into the lodge to eat dinner and there was a stove in there, of course it's not lit in the afternoon but hopefully it will be tonight. I didn't expect it to be so cold so low down and we are all in our tents the rest of the afternoon and we are quite distinctive with our mainly yellow tents.

We will be here for two nights to acclimatise, and I'm pleased we will have the lodge to eat in. We are at just over 13,000 feet here and I spend an hour looking out warm clothes for the next two days and although I feel fine, as a precaution, I have my first Diamox tablet. We are all out milling about before dinner and snow is lying on the ground with no sun at all now and it's quite misty too. We watch some trekkers come into camp from the direction of Mera and it turns out they are the returning Himalayan Kingdoms group. Dave has a chat with their leader but it's not good news. One of their group was rescued by helicopter with cerebral oedema, which is serious altitude sickness, lethal without getting to lower levels and he is in a Kathmandu hospital now. Another guy with them has third-degree frostbite and he shows us his blue toes and even the trek leader has a frostbitten thumb and he had four pairs of trousers on against the cold! The trek leader reckoned it was maybe as cold as minus thirty and of course that was one of their helicopters we had seen. I think we were a bit taken aback to say the least but it all figures.

This is far colder than I've been at these heights before and probably like everywhere else, the weather patterns are changing and it certainly gives us all something to think about. We will heed the warning about having to wear really warm clothing by the team going down. So we are in the lodge for dinner and the lodge has lots of gaps where the wind gets through but the stove is lit and the big lantern gives us enough light and before dinner comes, Dave announces a proposed change of plan. After our acclimatisation day tomorrow, we will head up to camp at Khare, effectively our base camp, and we will stay there for three days. During the days there we will take longish walks higher, even to the Mera glacier, to help acclimatise.

This will give us a chance to use our plastic boots and have some crampon and ice axe practice so the plan then is to climb directly up the glacier to high camp, missing out intermediate camp, but reducing our time at high altitude and of course the extreme cold associated with it. It will mean two really hard days at the highest altitude and we all agree with the plan. No one else has mentioned Diamox, which is odd as I know Dave has ample supplies but I say to Marguerite for her and Davy to start taking it too. Dinner is really good tonight with vegetable soup then rice and vegetables with a sort of meat stew and I suppose it might be yak rather than cow, but it tastes great anyway. The stove produces some warmth too and plenty smoke as well. After dinner we discuss plans again so on Friday morning we will trek to the summit of Mera all roped up and that will be a long day as we will then trek right back down to Khare, missing high camp.

Later, Dave then goes to talk with our Sherpa guides who will lead us that day. So with the fire now going strong, we stay and play cards and chess and the mood is good now that we have a plan agreed. It seems like a late night but at eight, we get our hot water bottles and head for our tents. Our guys have, as always, set up two toilet tents over a hole in the ground and in the mornings and at meal times there is also a small barrel of warm water with a tap and liquid soap to wash. I make sure I wash as many times as possible and always use antibacterial gels on my hands before meals. So off to my tent after a quick loo visit and right into my sleeping bags and a waterproof sheet I have over the bag as well to try and reduce condensation soaking the outer bag. With just underpants on and quite warm with the hot water bottle, I fall asleep quickly but am up for a pee at midnight and again at three. It's a side effect of Diamox and the sky is full of stars again and very peaceful although there has been the odd faraway crump and roar of an avalanche somewhere.

Sunday 21st October.

Probably the best sleep I've had so far but it's a cold morning and still some snow on the tents. My outer sleeping bag is soaked and this is a problem, as it will freeze at higher levels. Bed tea is late today - but no rush to get going and at 7:30am I get warm water to wash too. Breakfast is in the wee lodge, which is freezing and its hat and gloves and breakfast is rice pudding with raisins. Hazel has a trick of breaking a biscuit into it and it's a good idea, adopted by us all, then just a hot, boiled egg and black tea by the gallon. The sun takes another hour to reach us but before this we get hot water for washing clothes and some of the porters sort out a rope to hang the clothes on. Everyone has a sleeping bag out to dry and I wash a fleece top, which is frozen rigid ten minutes later on the rope. The plan this morning is to walk steeply up the left hand side of the valley to see what's left of the glacial lake. This is the lake that burst when some of the glacier above, fell into it and the scouring right down the valley is reminiscent of where a glacier has been. I'm glad to get moving this morning and feel fit. I have another half tab of Diamox and said to Marguerite to take some as well, so she took the other half but says Davy is on steroids so can't take Diamox and I don't think that is good news. I will make sure we will share a tablet morning and night. The trek only takes an hour but it's up all the time, so this will help us acclimatise. The sun is out but the wind is bitter up here. Even so lots of photos are taken. The lake is a dirty turquoise below us and we can see the level it was once at before the walls burst. The younger Nawang climbs a big rock to set a good pose for our photographs of Kyshar behind and the Sabal glacier.

We take our time ambling down and as we get lower the wind gets up a bit and this will be a pattern as it blows clouds up the valley. It's too cold just now to sit outside back at the camp so we all go to our tents and I sort out some gear and read my book for the first time. I have some nuts as well and drink a pint of water and soon the gong goes for afternoon tea. The wind has dropped a good bit and it's warm in the sunshine so we sit outside with tea and custard cream biscuits. Later I walk about a bit and stop where a woman has lots of jars of nuts and red and green chillies out drying and there are other fruits in jars. I ask what some are but I could only make out chilli and she laughs when I just shrug.

A big yellow dog appeared and with Nawang the younger as interpreter, I asked the woman who belongs to it but it appears it came up with another trekking party and stayed on. Although you are not supposed to touch any dogs in Nepal because of the deadly risk of rabies, I give him a custard cream biscuit and have a friend for the next hour. He's really friendly but his face shows evidence of being in a few wars and reminds me of my Gordon Setter Dana. During this time everyone had disappeared back to their tents as the mist has now obscured the sun and it's suddenly cold again and this time it looks as if it will stay cold, so, back to my tent again. More gear sorting, with warmer stuff now at the top of my bag and I can't find my head-torch and fear I must have dropped it this morning so empty my rucksack just as I remember where I put it. Typical! I lie wrapped up in the single sleeping bag for the next hour thinking about the days to come. I feel quite confident but it's the cold that is the enemy and especially hearing about frostbite. Soon it's 5:30pm and I get my fleece bootees on to go for dinner and hands washed first of course.

The room is really smokey and the stove door is open and a bit of rough wood about three feet long is half hanging out - hence the smoke. We're all early so we get a game of cards going and everyone seems relaxed tonight now that we have a plan. The soup is indeterminate but has plenty of garlic in it, which is beneficial at altitude I am told. The main course is mashed potato with cheese and more garlic and also with this is cabbage and steamed momos. I prefer them fried, but eat them all, in fact have a second helping. Again, a half Diamox for me but no one else seems to be taking it. Dessert is a brilliant looking banana tart, again with criss-crossed pastry. Dave is given the knife to ceremoniously cut it and we give the head cook, Palden, a big round of applause and a great atmosphere. We sit playing cards and then watch Dave and Steve play a game of chess and it turns out to be an epic game. It is really fine and warm in here tonight and that is the first time I've written that so far. When I take my hot water bottle to the tent, Marguerite follows me and she says Davy is ill and hasn't been good for three days and has taken more Imodium. I say that's crazy as he needs to be taking a broad-spectrum antibiotic as well, but there is worse, he has miscalculated on the steroids he needs to take and hasn't enough and he can't take Diamox either with steroids so not good. I think Dave or Val should know about this because you can't just stop a course of steroids without problems, but I don't think I was much help.

This shack is where the porters will sleep so we get ourselves packed up and I'm off for a last pee and meet Marguerite on the way back quite upset about things. I give her a wee cuddle and suggest she has a word with Val in the morning. The sky is full of stars and all the mist and cloud gone and Mera looms grey before me and menacing in the starlight. Someone somewhere is having a party tonight and there is a thump-thump drumbeat and singing and probably the HK porters who have come down today. It's not going to keep me awake though but then a loud crump of an avalanche somewhere. Safe here, although we were told the snow powder from the one we saw before reached here that day. I fell asleep OK but in the morning some said the party went on till 2:30am.

Monday 22nd October.

Up early again at 5:30am and bursting for a pee but still dark and as I open the inner zip to get out I find a golden dog's sleepy face looking at me. He'd crept in here obviously to get some warmth and now I'm not sure if he'll let me out but a thump of his tail and he lies down again so no problems. When I come back I give him a couple of custard creams. He repays me later by drinking all my warm washing water as soon as it was delivered. When I'm getting packed up the dog comes out of the tent as Nawang the elder is passing. He says, smiling, 'Good Karma, the dog being with you. Good luck for the mountain'.

And no rabies either I hope. The dog must have sneaked under the outer compartment and made a bed on the groundsheet last night. I have a trek companion and someone to share the tent with at last! Breakfast is in the lodge and we are all now using Hazel's trick of crumbling a biscuit into our porridge and I might try it at home but we also have really good scrambled eggs and a slice of toast. And nothing but free range eggs here I suppose but it's bloody cold again this morning. We know the sun won't get us until about ten o'clock so we don't hang about and set off for

144

Khare and unbelievably, the dog comes too, due to custard cream addiction - but when we have an easy stream to cross the dog isn't happy about this and I have to help him across.

When we stop for a breather at the top of a hill, Marguerite gives him more biscuits and a clap and I christen him Mera and someone says that's a great name for a dog. I said I would call my next dog Mera, and I did too. Again I feel fine today and the half Diamox at breakfast and dinner seems to be helping and no headache at all and not as out of breath as I felt yesterday. Yet again this morning another helicopter goes over towards Mera and we now know it's not a tourist flight but someone else in trouble. It's a fair haul today and will take the whole morning to reach Khare. I'm aware too that the Jagged Globe crew and Som's clients will be heading here today as well so I hope there will be enough room for us all.

We meet a squad of six or seven Germans on their way down and have a chat but they all look knackered. I ask the first guy if he got to the top and he says yes, but four of their party got severe frostbite and had to be helicoptered out this morning. And he says it was minus thirty degrees, the coldest he's ever been. We are all quiet for a wee while after this but we stop for a rest on a big grassy slope dotted with wee blue Gentians. A beautiful place, like an alpine meadow with the steep, white, western side of Mera behind us almost reminding us about what is to come. A lot of photographs are taken and we spot a couple of avalanches, but they are very far away up on the mountain. Hazel takes a photo of Marguerite and I and it's probably one of the best shots taken on the trip as we look so small against the mountain. Lots of Gentians on these slopes. We troop into Khare at 12:30pm and it's a sprawled collection of camping terraces and huts and everything looks washed out and drab and it's like some frontier hamlet from a western, but bleak and a cold wind. There might be about thirty tents here and some going up some going down. It should be almost 16,000 feet here according to the expedition notes but I make it 15,166 feet so again there is this disparity in height. I have checked my altimeter with Steve and Chris and we all pretty much agree. This will make for two hard days when we go for it, as it's almost another thousand feet higher to the summit than we calculated in Tagnag and this not only will make the days harder, but we also risk altitude sickness.

There's a stone and wood hut next to where we will camp and we go in here for lunch. Some are concerned about the two climbing days but Dave, quite reasonably says that we'll see how we get on when we have a day walk to the Mera glacier tomorrow and he's quite laid back about it all and says there is no reason why we can't all get to the summit. Hazel though, has already said high camp is her chosen limit even though she is well acclimatised already. Lunch is spicy beans and mushrooms with chips, a slice of salami and a sort of pancake but none of it is very warm so a few cups of tea and we go to sit outside and enjoy the sun. Most of us just sit about or write our journals or read. The mist comes and goes but it's mostly warm. Quite a dramatic viewpoint as well with Mera Peak right in front of us. Its Nepalese name is Khongma Tse, just as Island Peak was Imja Tse. As we sit here facing our mountain, we all see another avalanche but too far away to know how big it is and so we sit here in the sun till afternoon tea appears at 3:15pm. Mera, the dog is lying in the sun asleep while we have tea outside and despite the presence of biscuits, he remains asleep (not like mine back home would be!) We are sitting outside the shack on our camp seats and I feel good again today. All our sleeping bags are drying in the strong sun and mostly we just hang about and I write up more notes. It's only later that I think I have grit in my eyes when I realise the sun here is fierce and I've burnt my eyes a bit, with no sun cream on and no glasses either. I've let myself slip as I am usually very careful, but this was careless.

When the cloud comes up the valley, I go into the tent to sort the gear for tomorrow. My plastic boots and crampons will be required. Dave reckons we can get up to the Mera La, which would have been intermediate camp, and back for a late lunch. Although we can see it from here, it's well up on the Mera glacier and involves a steep section to get up onto the glacier itself. Optimistic I think to myself. I go up early for dinner about 5:30 pm and the fire is just being lit in the shack. The big paraffin lantern is already lit but it is cold in here. I got talking to the couple who operate this wee campsite and they come up from Lukla in the spring and won't stay much longer after we depart as it is too cold and of course, no climbers come anyway as the season will end early December. It's a struggle to get this fire lit, despite fat being poured into cardboard. Dinner is chicken soup so called but tastes like the garlic stuff we had last night and the main course is potato cake with some bits of meat, and cheese sauce covered with bits of cauliflower and a sort of pureed vegetable. We have warm fruit salad for our sweet. Mera the dog has snuck in and spends all the time here at my feet, but isn't a problem. During the meal, we have the usual fire pantomime - it went out twice - it's a top-loader and it's just a couple of branches shoved in with no real kindling. We play cards till about eight when we get our water bottles filled with very hot water and it's off to bed. Of course, just as I get really snuggled in and feel quite warm, I need a pee. It's the Diamox side effect, or one of them.

Tuesday 23rd October.

I woke just after five and slept well and the Diamox is a real help. I feel good and glad to see there is no condensation on the outside of the sleeping bag only to realise it's frozen. This is a big risk for high camp but despite it being freezing this morning, I have everything ready for today before bed tea arrives. No dog in my tent last night. At some point I heard a big crack of an avalanche again last night. No sign of the dog at breakfast. The porridge is very runny this morning, but good - and of course with crumbled biscuit to firm it up. Then after that, scrambled egg and a slice of toast and of course, loads of black tea. Outside the shack Marguerite says to me that Davy isn't well again. Val has said to half the steroid dose but not to continue to take full doses then just stop as that could be dangerous. But the fact is that it gets serious from here, or rather, from tomorrow. You wouldn't want not to be 100% fit and he probably shouldn't have come here being experienced enough to know doing anything at high altitude is really hard even being fully fit. This morning we watch a rescue helicopter coming up the valley, land and quickly take off back to a hospital in Kathmandu with other casualties.

I'm not used to wearing plastic boots but they really are fine today and we leave after breakfast and head up a small steep slope to the track, which takes us eventually to the foot of the glacier. At one point Davy goes past me to be in front, then takes a different track to be in front again but the wrong way. It was a bit strange as there is no rush today and we should be going at a slow, steady pace. Very erratic behaviour and he seems a bit unsteady too. This is what I was scared of happening and why I had suggested he should give this trip a miss.

It's steep going in places and my heart is pounding and I'm breathing hard. We have a rope with us to practise abseils and the use of a jumar, but I think it's only us three that have them and we shouldn't need them except as a help at the very top. We pass a stone shack with a tarpaulin roof and a guy selling beers and soft drinks which is amazing, away up here and really isolated but good passing traffic though. As we get closer to the glacier, after about three and a half hours, it's time to put crampons on. I think Dave realised at this point there is no way we would make the Mera La. We meet some French climbers coming down, looking exhausted and as we talk we learn that none of their party made it to the summit as they were either too exhausted or turned back in the extreme cold, scared of getting frostbite. However none of them had plastic boots I noticed. But it's another warning of the extreme cold.

We stop a fair bit away from the glacier and this is as far as we will go. I feel OK, in fact, really fit. Davy looks ill and sits with his head in his hands. Dave and I quietly discussed the steroid situation and Dave's noticed Davy was stumbling a bit on the way up. Marguerite says he's been struggling too and the next two days will be a lot harder than this. Even coming down will be a long hard day as we have to get back to base camp at Khare in one long trek from the summit. He shouldn't be here, simple as that and could put us all at risk or else prevent us from getting to the summit. But it will be his call, not mine. Dave gives him 800mg of ibuprofen but that's not the answer but it'll help the sore head. It's not cold here at all in the sun and in fact I take my jacket off but my sunglasses have been on all day today. Davy actually falls on the way back down, but nothing serious. I only realise how steep we've climbed up to the glacier base on the way down when we look back and this is where we will need plastic boots from tomorrow. I still plan to just wear mine from the start as they're OK today.

Steve, just back from altitude in South America, seems very well acclimatised and forges on downhill. I wish I were that acclimatised, although I feel OK. Hazel is fine too but Val and Chris have been slow but Colin and Sheila slower still. We stop across from the big snow-slope coming down from the glacier. Steve says he's OK with everything and heads down to sort out our later than expected lunch. There is some ice axe braking and jumar use but I don't bother and after half an hour or so, we all head back as well and it's a careful plod, as you wouldn't want to fall and be out for tomorrow. It's really slippery in places. We get a good view of base camp going down and it looks a busy wee place with wood-smoke rising and people milling about. Back at camp, my plastics are off and lunch is ready but it doesn't look great. Fried potato slices, coleslaw, some pasta and a cold sardine each, in tomato sauce. It goes down alright but that's some combination. We're sitting outside again as there is still sunshine. As ever, though, the mist is coming up towards us. My sunglasses are on all the time today.

Chris isn't up for lunch and has to go for a lie down and Davy eats a bit and then he's away too. The dog is here too and looks like he slept on a wee pile of straw behind our tents last night. Up on a rise above us there is a group of people hanging about in obvious anticipation. The woman from the shack says to Lhakpa, that they expect a rescue helicopter to get some people out but it will be too cloudy until tomorrow. I hope I won't be in that queue. A few of us sit outside in the sun again and as a treat, I buy a bottle of coke and write my notes as the woman from the lodge sits beside me and, smiling, says, 'writing'. I say yes and ask if she can write, 'no school' she says, then she asks, 'you have children'? I say four and she's impressed, and all of them boys I say and I get the photo of them out to show her and it turns out she has two sons who live in Lukla, and go to school there. I show her a postcard of the hills around Lanark and at this, some of the porters gather round and I feel like David Attenborough and all sorts of questions are asked and it's quite intense for about twenty minutes but interesting and good fun. As the gong goes for afternoon tea, it starts to bloody snow, so it's a quick brew and back to the tent and the mist has reached us earlier this afternoon. Everything to be sorted for tomorrow and I tidy up the interior a bit and lie in my bag and think about the next two days. I've got my down bootees on tonight for extra warmth and lying here I have a look in the mirror at my right eye and still very red and really stupid of me. Hopefully it was just the sun and not an infection but I have some drops for it, which seems to help. So, lying here alone and a sudden feeling of dread about the next few days because it just seems such a big haul compared with what we've done. I fear we could be taking on too much and it's not as planned. On the plus side our walk will have helped and we reached almost 17,000 feet today. I can't help thinking that just acclimatises you for that height, not for where we are going, however another day here will help.

The dinner gong gets us all together and this time the fire has been lit early and it's quite warm, so we have garlic-free chicken soup. Then there is some chicken with roast potatoes, carrots and a cold sauce which tastes like tomato soup and the sweet is only a choice of an apple or an orange. I take the orange, but it's green! We play cards for a while, enjoying the relative warmth and watch the couple make their own dinner, crushing garlic and red chilli and adding grated ginger to make Sherpa stew and it looks and smells good too. Off to our tents just before 8:30pm and I notice the sky has cleared again and stars are starting to show. Very cold again tonight. Off to sleep thinking that only Dave and Steve were 100% today and Hazel I suppose but the rest of us found it hard going. Tomorrow we can do what we want and I plan to climb up the long ridge behind the camp. Dave went up there the first day here himself and says it's a good

150

viewpoint. So we all have agreed to get a bit higher than our next camp.

Wednesday 24th October.

I must have slept from about nine last night until three, when I needed a pee but happily have no sore head yet, although I did get a wee hint earlier, nothing much. Inside the tent is frosted up already and for the first time, my feet are not cold, just very cool and a foretaste of things to come? A long lie this morning, no rush to go anywhere as a group and bed tea arrives at 7:30am and by this time the sun is hitting my tent making it lovely and warm in here. I get dressed and go outside to see the cooking squad setting up the breakfast table outside, which will be great this morning. I have a look at the worrying high cirrus cloud. Which is not usually a sign of good weather and we need good weather for at least the next two days. No dog though this morning and looks like he's deserted us I think for better rations. Everyone else appears after ten minutes or so and we are all pleased to be in the sunshine to be having breakfast, which is muesli, then fried eggs with chapati, and black tea. The plan for us is to do the ridge behind the camp and Davy and Marguerite say they'll be ready at ten, so I go back to the tent to get sorted for the walk.

So, at ten, I'm ready to roll and I have both cameras and water and my poles. Steve is going up too and heads off on his own and he says he'll just go slowly so I hang about for another ten minutes and see Marguerite come out her tent with her journal and sits with her back to me so looks like they have changed their minds so I set off on my own. The walk up is brilliant and I'm quite happy to walk on my own. Steve is way ahead but the views are spectacular and away below me I can see a figure coming up slowly. It's Chris and that is good as he's not been too well, so I'm glad he's up for the walk today. When I reach Steve, we're three quarters way up. And I only catch him because he's taking lots of photographs but I take a few as well and then we press on to the top. It's not difficult and there is a sort of path and at the top we shelter behind a big rock. We are up in an amphitheatre of high, white peaks and absolutely fantastic so I shoot some film as well and just finish as Chris joins us.

After a chat for about twenty minutes, as we move out of our rock shelter I can feel the wind has got up and is freezing but this is good as it makes me re-think about what to wear against the risk of frostbite tomorrow. Steve goes down a different way but I know lunch is planned for one o'clock so there's plenty of time and Chris and I head down the way we came up. Back at camp is warmer and being so sunny, it's a pleasure to have a relaxed lunch outside and we have one tinned sausage each and potato cake and beans. We have orange tea to start and then black to finish. After lunch, we sit on our 'sun veranda' at the side of the shack and either read or write. What a place to sit with the white, western, bulk of Mera in front of us and the odd Lammergeier flying in high circles above us. As I look up at the cloud pattern I notice, it keeps changing. As usual the valley cloud blows up to us and it gets really cold again so we all retreat to the relative warmth of our tents and I sort my gear out for the next two days. Only one kit bag between two will go to high camp and I will share a tent with Chris. Dave will share with Steve and Hazel and Val also will share. Not sure at this point if Davy will even attempt high camp.

We all go up to the shack early for dinner and again, the stove is already lit and there is a big pot of water on top of it. So, dinner starts with mushroom soup but it's just garlic soup with mushrooms I'm quite sure. Marguerite can't take it and some others struggle and after this of course, everything else still tastes of bloody garlic. We have chicken on the bone next with rice and there are lovely green beans and mixed vegetables in some sort of sauce, maybe garlic, but anyway it's all good and for a sweet we have apple fritters which are lovely. We have lots of tea again but a hot chocolate as well for me for a change, and extra calories. It's the quietest dinner we've had and everyone is a bit apprehensive about tomorrow. There is some discussion about how wise it is to have two hard days, are we properly acclimatised, etc., but Dave is very optimistic and he agrees that for those who don't want to wear their plastic boots over the initial rocky parts for about a mile or so, a porter will take the plastics and the crampons to the start of the snow line, below the glacier. I'm going to just wear mine from the start.

Thursday 25th October.

I sleep surprisingly well and the plan is for bed tea at 6:00am and to be away at 7:00am but in reality because of all the re-packing it's a bit later when we leave. The plan is that only the minimum of the porters will come up, the cooking team and the Sherpa guides and then when the tents are up at high camp, the porters will come back down. So we have a packed lunch for today. As we leave the village, Davy is off on his own so fast he misses the path we take and is even in front of the Sherpa guides at one point. At this altitude you need a steady but slow pace. Arriving at the snowline, we get our crampons on or at least those of us who are already wearing our plastic boots. Then we have a problem. The porter who has the others boots and crampons has gone on ahead instead of waiting here and is probably at or even on the glacier by now so another porter without a pack is dispatched to find him and bring the gear back but that could take maybe an hour. Davy and Marguerite are taking ages sorting their crampons out and Steve says to Dave he'd like to go on alone and off he goes. After standing about for another ten minutes I say to Dave that I'll go on too as it's too cold hanging about.

153

So for the steepest part of the climb today, up onto the Mera glacier, I'm on my own and it's fantastic and I take my time. Just an ice axe now, no poles, just in case of a slip and when I'm nearly at the top, there is Som and his three American clients and they all have down jackets, hats and gloves. I have a light fleece and my sleeves are rolled up as it's pretty warm climbing up here, but they just think Scotsmen are hardy - or stupid, and we have some good craic together. At the top of the glacier, I take their photographs for them all with Som and the summit of Mera in the background.

The top of the glacier here is fairly flat so the crampons are off now for the next mile to the Mera La where, ordinarily, we would camp tonight. I take off my rucksack and wait for Dave coming up next and I find this a bit strange as he's the leader but the rest of the team down below I suppose have all the Sherpa guides, so they're fine. Dave shares his flask of tea with me and some chocolate and we head up to the Mera La. Here Dave takes a lot of photographs and points out the first planned camp area, which is well down from where we are, but still on the glacier. He takes a few shots of me and one will appear in next year's HK brochure. I take a few shots as well but still no sign of anyone else up on the glacier yet and no sign of Steve either, but he's pretty fit and might even be at high camp now. Looking down now I can see a few groups heading up on the glacier and they could be ours.

Dave says just to go on myself and he will wait on the rest, so on the final part of the walk to high camp, I'm on my own again but at one point I catch up with Som and he turns round and starts to name all the mountains in the distance, Everest, Lhotse, Makalu, Baruntse, Changabang and away in the distance, in Bengal, Kanchenjunga.

It's only when I turn around that I realise how high and how far I've come and still not cold with the sun out, but there is a wind and it's blowing spindrift and it's slippery too here, OK going up but I'll need crampons coming down. Looking away down on the glacier I can see some small figures, maybe our party and it looks as if someone is lying down, but might be a porter's big pack and too far away to tell but no one moves for ages. My own preoccupation is not to miss high camp and walk on past it. Dave says it's at a big rocky outcrop and I won't miss it, but when you're on your own you do think about these things, however, it's not a problem and as I walk round the rocks, there are our tents, and a couple of others. It's a very precarious site with a very steep drop on one side and the tents are balanced on a narrow rocky shelf. I'm a bit worried when I notice the tents are roped to the rocks! I spot my bag outside the tent Chris and I will share and I see Steve is eating his packed lunch outside and is quite cheery and talks away to me, but all I can manage from the cook is a cup of tea. I couldn't face food at the moment and feel really tired and have to go and lie down in the tent. Since we left this morning it's taken me five and a half hours to get here and I haven't hung about much.

Another cup of tea is brought into my tent. I feel as if I could just go to bed now but it's only mid-afternoon and just over an hour and a half later, the others arrive. I only see Chris who is one of the first to arrive and he looks shattered. I know Dave's been giving him some medication but I don't know, or ask, what for. Marguerite pops in to say Davy isn't well and it had been him lying down on the glacier. He has chest pains next and I'm surprised Dave isn't getting him back down but maybe he doesn't know. Anyway, there's not much I can do about it but I feel he shouldn't be here. Dinner is going to be at 4:30pm so we can get enough sleep before leaving at 4:30am and breakfast will be at 4:00am. At this moment, neither Chris nor I feel like eating but we can hear the paraffin burners hissing cooking the meal while we're both still lying on our sleeping bags. The soup doesn't help as it's garlic and ginger with Rara noodles and I really have to try and force some down. Next is Sherpa stew and although Chris has some, I couldn't look at it, never mind eat it. I manage the warm fruit salad and get a row from the cook for not eating the stew. He says I have to eat for the mountain. I know he's right. I have two mugs of sugared black tea and a couple of biscuits. Marguerite comes in to tell us Davy can't eat and I say that neither can I. I feel that she wants me to do something, but I'm too exhausted and feel really tired and a bit worried for my own health. I'm even too scared to use the toilet tent as a slip getting to it would be scary. I sleep badly and despite the Diamox, my pulse is racing and I wonder how long your heart can take this or is it pre-programmed to stop after so many beats? If so, I'm using up a lot and such are the pleasures of high altitude thoughts and sleeplessness.

Friday 26th October.

The cook's burners hissing loudly wake me at 3:00am and I feel a bit better but take another 125mg of Diamox with the bed tea and I share some chocolate from the packed lunch with Chris. Breakfast is in our tents and its rice pudding and I ask for sugar on it and have more sugary black tea and manage to eat OK. I will need the calories today. All my gear is ready and I have a set routine of top half clothes on first while the bottom half are still in the sleeping bag, then Paramo trousers and then the inner boots for the plastic boots which have been in the sleeping bag all night to keep warm, then the big boots on. It only takes me ten minutes. Outside I talk to Dave and Steve over a cup of tea and it's not as cold as I would have thought and I feel pretty good but there's no sign of anyone else. Hazel has already said she won't be going higher and now Steve says I should go with him and Dave as I am one of the fittest, but I point out that I only got here before the others because I left earlier and I don't want to take chances today pushing myself too hard. Dave says Davy is too ill to go and will have to head down later. Dave also mentions some drug for high altitude illness that he has with him and I wonder then what good it will do us if he's away first. Anyway, enough to think about and we get another packed lunch. I am quite chuffed these two guys think I'm as fit as them. We are waiting on the others and again I'm surprised it's not colder and certainly not colder than minus ten or fifteen, certainly not minus thirty and no wind at all.

We will be roped up for the ascent of the next part of the glacier and I ask who is on what rope. Chris and Marguerite will share a rope and I ask to go with them and so it is all agreed. We will get crampons and ropes on around the rocky outcrop and on the actual glacier. This is where we get our harnesses on and then our crampons. Mine are my trusted semi-step-ins, which are quick to put on even with gloves on. I'm pleased to see our Sirdar, Lhakpa will be our guide. I'm ready to be roped up first and only Colin and Sheila are behind us getting their harnesses on. There is no sunrise yet at 4:45am, but a good moon and already we can

157

see head-torches away up the mountain in front of us. But we have a problem. Marguerite yesterday apparently had a problem with her right crampon and she can't get it on her boot. I try to help but neither can I. With hesitation, I try to get it on even with bare hands though I'm worried about bare hands on freezing metal so quite a fraught moment. This is taking too long and Colin and Sheila are away before us. She says she'll walk with only one, but this is the Himalayas and although there are no severe slopes, It's easy to slip, but she's determined and as we are getting later and later Lhakpa says not to bother with the rope either. Maybe we just jump the crevasses.

So, at nearly five o'clock and last away we begin the long ascent in freezing darkness. Just a big snow slope really but it's a struggle at this altitude. Marguerite is also coughing badly this morning and we are walking so slowly that Chris asks if he can go on alone as our pace makes him think he will never get to the top. So we walk slowly on using our walking poles and our ice-axes still on our rucksacks. We walk in a line, with me in front, then Marguerite and Lhakpa. I'm confident now that we're moving that I'll get there even if it is very slowly. As the first early rays of the sun come over the mountains away towards the Bay of Bengal, the light is piercing yellow and it's spectacular and we just have to look around. Everything is pristine, crystal white and now we have a big pink and orange sky with no clouds, and still no wind. The moon is still huge hanging in this glorious sky. I just think that it is certainly not minus thirty today. I can see Chris pulling ahead and Val is ahead of him with her own guide and is slowly pulling away from us. We have passed Colin and Sheila but when we stop for a prolonged rest they catch us up. Colin and Sheila have had enough and say that they are going back down. They've got to almost 20,000 feet now and that's their highest they have ever been and say that yesterday just sapped their energy, so we wish them well to get down safely. We plod on very slowly and at one point when we stop again we can see Chris and he's not much faster than we are. I look at Lhakpa for some support and he just says, 'bistari', which means 'slowly'. We have no option I think. At this point I'm thinking Marguerite might turn back, which would be awkward as the guide can only go with one of us and she's not well and has only one crampon. Looking up ahead we notice that the two other parties are going really slowly and although the sun is up it's not warm. We stop regularly for a sip from my water bottle, which I had filled with warm water before we left. Lhakpa patiently waits and says nothing but stops when we stop and starts when we start. Ahead, one of the groups has stopped for ages and even now we are managing only thirty paces and stopping to rest, hanging on my walking poles, and I'm in front and stop and start when Marguerite is ready.

Increasingly the sun is now strong and to save her time I let her use my factor 10 sun-block stick on her lips, forgetting factor 10 isn't much good for a blonde girl, especially at this altitude. I use it too as we will be out in this for potentially seven or more hours. After about an hour and a half, I try to convince her and myself maybe, that the slope is getting easier. In the distance someone is coming down and it's Steve and he's been to the top and says it's less than an hour away from here. He gives me his technical ice axe and takes my heavier axe down with him. And he takes our climbing harnesses too as we won't need them if we're not roped up and just having a wee bit less weight really helps us.

We plod on, still thirty steps then a rest and I get used to Marguerite's voice saying, 'OK, Jim' when we rest to get us going again. Now when we stop I just rest on my poles but as we go slowly on, we soon come over a rise and can see the top. More to drink for the last push and we get there and meet the others. Marguerite has done exceptionally well getting here on one crampon and not feeling well and it's hugs all round and with only 44% of the oxygen at sea level at this height it feels like it too! We have not been too far behind the others and they are still here and no wonder. The views are the best I've ever had in the Himalayas and in perfect weather conditions. Mera stands quite separate and we can see many of the highest mountains in the world, Everest, Kangchenjunga, Lhotse, Makalu and Cho Oyu. I take a lot of photos and some film but, eventually my camcorder batteries go in the cold. However I get photos of Lhakpa and me taken, some with the Saltire flying, as it has on so many mountains, for the third time out here in the Himalayas.

The rest are going on to see other views but I know it's best we head down now and Lhakpa, as ever, is ready when we are. Marguerite asks for another drink but I've hardly any left so she says to get her bottle out of her rucksack. But there is no bottle! She'd left it in the tent. So here we are at almost 22,000 feet in the Himalayas with no water. I ask Lhakpa and of course he says to use his full bottle but it just goes to show how easy it is to get into trouble. The reality is we need to have drunk at least four litres today. So we are ready now after maybe only half an hour on top of the mountain that we came all this way to climb, to go back down with exalted feelings, and generally elated.

It's on the way down we realise how hard the pull up here has been. I ask Lhakpa if the high camp tents will be gone and he says yes, but a couple of the cooking team will wait for us with warm drinks and that is brilliant news. At one point he stops, and points out Khare, our base camp that we left two days ago. It must be at least 6,000 feet below us. We have to get there today so we plod on down to high camp. Eventually we can see the rocky outcrop of high camp and all of the tents have gone. But the cooks have a shelter made and they have a big kettle of hot orange. Lhakpa says we must eat too to have strength for going down. However, the thought of two cold boiled eggs and a cold samosa doesn't appeal. There is another chocolate bar and I eat that, but Marguerite looks shattered. Sitting in the now warm sunshine I give her a cup of warm orange but she's coughing hard and has a sore chest. We wait till Dave, Chris and Val come down and get another drink.

After about half an hour or so we head down the glacier and Marguerite keeps her one crampon on. Dave and I take ours off and at one point, on a steeper part of the glacier, we both slip and fall, so we all take it a bit slower and use the poles for balance. Soon the glacier levels out and we can see teams of porters heading up with their loads. More sun-block on my nose and lips and it's now so warm, all our jackets are off and there is still no wind. More chance of sunstroke than frostbite! It's a wonderful feeling knowing that all the planning, the training and of course the expense, has been worth it. We came halfway around the world to the most amazing mountains in the world and got to the top of Mera Peak and our highest ever. As I lead us down the glacier, I think what might have been with illness in the party and it could have been us waiting on a helicopter. Anyway, soon we are at the steep part, heading off the glacier and it's even warmer. So it's time for crampons back on. The lower altitude is helping us all, and I am amazed how the snow is really soft and just slush on the way down compared to yesterday. We have been really lucky with perfect weather and certainly never minus thirty.

We stop at the stone and tarpaulin shack for some drinks but the guy only has one sprite and three cokes left. More coming, he says. Marguerite gets the sprite, the rest of us share the cokes and never tasted better. This is when I realise that apart from tea and some orange, I've hardly drunk enough and realise later how dehydrated I was as I don't pee from the very early breakfast this morning till 8:30pm at night!

Then it's a slippery downhill walk in slush, semi-frozen scree and rock till we reach the stone ridge above base camp, a very welcome sight. It's now 3:00pm and I've been awake for twelve hours and walking more or less for ten hours. We walk into camp tired heroes and the cooks have left tea out for us and biscuits so afternoon tea is made no matter how many or few there is and my appetite now returning and I eat a few crackers with peanut butter. I've seen my dog but he didn't bother with congratulating me except for a half-hearted whack of his scrawny tail. It seems Davy was given some sort of medication at high camp from Dave and now he's given him anti-nausea pills to add to his daily intake of drugs. He certainly doesn't look great.

It is still warm as I get into my tent and with some warm water I have as good a wash as I can, use some wipes as well, then wash a couple of vests, and so eventually sit alone in this yellow tent to contemplate the last hard two days. I am quite elated that the job's done. Som and his American party arrive back whooping and shouting that they got to the summit and they go on for ages. I'm first into the dining shack and the fire is on but it's hardly warm with all the gaps in wood and stone and plastic sheeting windows, and a door, which can't close somehow. No building control here. Marguerite comes up to say Davy's worse so they won't be having dinner as she wants to keep an eye on him. I ask her to take a photograph as I remember that I have a wagon-wheel biscuit, given to me by my pal Sandy in Fife as a challenge to get it here. I get my photograph taken holding it and when I get back, will show Sandy the length I went to get his biscuit to the Himalayas. Crazy bringing it all this way, but it will be a good laugh back home. When I go out I talk to Som who says they camped even higher than us and he's pleased of course that it was successful. His American clients are still giving each other high fives and talking loudly about their day. Compared with these guys we were pretty quiet about the whole thing.

Dinner tonight is chicken soup, remarkably garlic-free then we have potatoes and vegetables with, surprisingly, meat, and a chunk of it too. The cook says it's a buffalo burger and it's so good, I have two. Then someone says they haven't seen the dog tonight. Hmm, makes you think! The mood is great tonight and there is an atmosphere of celebration and the highlight is the cook's special cake. It's a sort of cherry cake and has a lovely golden-brown crust and it's great washed down with copious amounts of tea. I've brought the whisky up tonight and this is what it was being kept for of course. It's cask strength single malt and can take a bit of diluting. So Steve, Colin, Dave and I have a large cup each and we have a toast to the mountain and the good company that we've shared. Dave is pleased I think because he got five out of nine of us to the summit and everyone to high camp. But the real heroes are the porters, cooks and Sherpas who made it possible. We toast them as well! So, with everyone very tired, we all retire about eight and Dave says no rush tomorrow, so there will be a long lie and bed tea at 8:00am. It feels a bit of an anti-climax going to bed now but I've still taken Diamox as we are still high and I feel high too tonight.

Saturday 27th October.

I sleep for an unbelievable ten hours apart from a pee break at midnight and my legs are surprisingly, only slightly sore. I feel pretty good this morning, lying here with a mug of tea, all packed up before the tea came. Looking out the tent door and there is Mera in the early morning sunlight. Life feels good this morning. To let the team get packed up, we just sit on the grassy terrace for breakfast and there is muesli, which I don't bother with, then scrambled eggs with chapati, which is great and more tea as well, lovely and relaxed here in the sunshine. We can see another group getting ready to head off for the glacier and a high camp somewhere. No dog at all this morning and I still think about those burgers. Today we are to head down to Kote for lunch and then straight on to our campsite near where we had lunch on the way up. The walk down is easy and a relaxed pace and the last photos are taken of Mera's summit dome, pure white in plenty of sunshine this morning. We stop at a very makeshift stone stall and I buy a bottle of sprite and take my tee shirt off quickly. This propels my sunglasses, which were on my head, into the distance. I never found them and they were good ones too! We set off again over grassy moorland on a good path above the river, and we can hear a helicopter and it appears round the mountains, heading up towards Mera. I realise that it's only been the two days we were on the actual mountain, that I haven't heard a helicopter. We have been lucky with the weather. I mention this to Dave and he points back up to Mera at the high spindrift coming off. Very strong winds today he reckons. We were very lucky with the weather and temperature.

It takes us longer than expected to get to Kote and as usual, around midday, the mist is starting to form and blow up the valley. As we head down we lose the sun and it gets cooler. As we walk into the wooden shacks of Kote, I pass a guy walking out and instinctively say 'Hi', and I think he looks familiar, which is a strange feeling here in the middle of nowhere. Lunch is on the wooden veranda of a teahouse but it's our cooks who have prepared the lunch and we have potatoes with cabbage and cold tinned sausages with mushrooms. Oh, yes and a slice of very hard cheese and a sort of potato cake. Another strange combination, but I eat it all. Dave is talking about going over the river to a Buddhist shrine, actually a huge standing rock, which has been cleft in two. You can just about squeeze from one side to another, so Steve and I go with him and there are plenty of prayer flags and coins tucked into a smaller shrine. Apart from that, it's just a very big boulder. Back over with the others, the guy I said hello to coming into the village is sitting with our group and I recognise now the Jagged Globe jacket. It's Mungo Ross, a guy we've been up Tinto with back home on the Wednesday training nights in the summer when a few of us from the club walk up the hill! His wife, Helen has been up there with us as well. He says he is off to Paraguay next.

From here it's generally up again and it's very misty. Marguerite, Val and Davy are up front with our guide for the day and I'm a bit behind but quite happy today to plod along with my own thoughts. As we will be back in Lukla in a couple of days I think back to two years ago in Annapurna, getting into Pokhara to hear the news my mum had died. I still have to phone home again from Kathmandu. I take the last photo of snow-capped Mera behind us and it looks really far away. Eventually we stop on the very rough track along the riverbank and the trail here is badly eroded and we have to carefully clamber up and down some sections. Steve catches us up to say to hold back as Sheila has gone over on her ankle quite badly. When they all catch up, I can see that Dave has her ankle well strapped up but she is limping badly and no doubt treated with a high dose of ibuprofen. From here it's a hard slog through bamboo canes and rhododendrons and it's almost 4:00pm by the time we reach our campsite. It's very bleak and cold and there is a big wooden shack and our cooks have made afternoon tea in here but a strange misty atmosphere. Inside it's a bit dark as there are no lights at all but there are two teenage girls and a couple of guys sleeping on benches either side of a long, home-made, clay oven. The girls are quite giggly sitting beside the fire but there is no heat coming from it though and there are lots of draughty gaps too. We are sitting at wooden tables on benches at the other side. I notice a couple of empty glasses and think these two guys have passed out with too much drink. It's not only cold, but the hanging mist is making everything damp as well. As we head for our tents, the cooks have started a fire near the shack but this just seems a miserable place, even if we are eating in the shack. I decided that we will finish the whisky tonight. So, after a couple of hours in the sleeping bag, I get ready and go up for dinner. It's still freezing in the shack and only one of the guides, Nawang the elder, is here so I decide to have a whisky and ask if there is water. My water is treated with iodine, not an ideal mixer. He gives me water in a wee teapot and suddenly he offers me a glass of rakshi so I give him a wee taste of 'Scottish rakshi' and he really likes it (and so it should be at £60 a bottle!). I wish I could reciprocate but I prefer the malt to the firewater!

The rest soon arrive and Marguerite has brought her remaining Southern Comfort. It is only marginally warmer and dinner is to be inside here for us and for the entire crew. We are all having dal bhat, but it's OK as there is some sort of meat in it as well. The cooks are using umpteen kilos of rice tonight. It's really crowded with us all together but maybe marginally warmer because of that. It certainly isn't because of the fire. Everything is being cooked outside which seems a bit odd but as usual Milan insists on setting all the plates and cutlery in his exact fashion and just shoves our stuff out of his way. He's a perfectionist and quite funny and everything has a certain place.

Talking to the cook, Palden, he said this is a big challenge for him to cook for everyone at the same time. It's a good atmosphere with us all crammed in here but there's still no heat from the stove. After dinner, I offer round the whisky and this time Sheila takes some for 'medicinal reasons' for her sore ankle. There is also rakshi on the go and the two teenage girls have got music playing on a wee cassette machine. As the night progresses, or deteriorates, some of the porters are up dancing and haul up some of us too and it's party time. To the tape music, I start to play the drums with a teaspoon on the kettle and the plastic lip of the powdered milk. Marguerite plays the spoon on the Chinese vacuum flask and Dave, who played in a jazz-band, plays the kettle lid like a triangle. It turns out a great night and we all forgot about the cold as the whisky and Southern Comfort rations were depleted.

Sunday 28th October.

Naturally I slept like a log and woke up to a brilliant clear morning, all the mist has disappeared although it's still quite cold. Today will be a long hard slog to near the top of the Zatra La, a high pass which might have snow and this is what the porters were concerned about at the start of the trek. Normally it would be three days walking but we've agreed to have the extra day in Lukla and we will camp close to the top of the pass. At least we know today that all the height gains are positive with less up and down. The scenery is reminiscent of the West Highlands and the weather is really fine with plenty of sunshine.

At one point, today's guide, Nawang the elder, stops to pick leaves from an aromatic plant, juniper I think, and puts the leaves into a bag. It's a plant they dry and burn in temples and we smell the leaves and almost all of us pick some too. The leaves smell lovely but I picture me being stopped in Gatwick with this bag of dodgy leaves and an excuse of collecting them for Scottish temples. As usual, as the day progresses, the mist appears and it soon cools down. We have trekked quite hard today and when we are about three quarters of an hour away from our next camp, a porter appears with a big kettle of lemon 'tea' and we all have some biscuits left. We have a seat and a wee picnic.

Our plans for a hard push, followed by an early lunch and then a beer or two in the sun at Tuli Kharka, are dashed. It's now misty and very cold and our camp is a collection of stone and wood shacks, maybe eight or nine of them. Our tents will be in a grassy flat area close to a couple of the shacks. But there are no tents here yet, so lunch is outside on the blue tarpaulin and not exactly the weather we thought we would have. Lunch is chips and coleslaw with a warmish cheese pasty and a slice of salami and we go and watch the tents go up, glad to have a hot cup of tea to hold. After that, there's not much else for it but to get into our tents and sleeping bags and get warm and wait.

Afternoon tea is a couple of hours later and after some negotiation we have our tea in the shack next to us, which is really big. It has a sort of shop - well just some shelves and a selection of some soft drinks and Mars bars and other such stuff and I buy a bottle of coke. There is a stove in the eating area, which is not lit as its daylight. Dave says he'll ask for it to be lit for tonight as we will have dinner here but it's freezing just now and we all sit in gloves and hats. After tea, nothing else for it but to get back to the tents and get into our sleeping bags and wait for dinner. I do a bit of reading with my head-torch on and at one point Dave asks if I'm OK with tipping the porters the amount he'd suggested earlier. I say no problem, and say we need to tip the Sherpas and the cooks too but he's thought of that.

I'm in for dinner just behind Colin and Sheila and it's 5:45pm. The stove isn't lit and we can see each other's breath. We all have hats and gloves on again and some have their down jackets on. We protest to Dave who goes off to see the owner. So for the next half hour there is a pantomime act of various people trying to get the fire to light, including someone with an amazing Chinese hand operated blower, which produces sparks but no fire. Eventually with cardboard, fat and a few twigs we have a poor fire.

There is a smidge of whisky and Southern Comfort left and it helps on a miserable night like this. I can't remember what we had to eat. It was so freezing cold. I think this must be the worst night we have had or maybe we were able to put up with more on the way up. Glad to be back into my sleeping bag with my bottle of hot water, which is the only comfort in this place.

Monday 29th October.

Despite everything I slept well again but I'm still on 125mg of Diamox and make sure Marguerite is taking hers too and it really seems to be working. Today is quite a pull and the pass is very steep, over 15,000 feet so higher than Mont Blanc. We stop on the way up at a shrine with lots of prayer flags blowing in the wind and lots of photos are taken. As Dave puts his hand on a shrine of layered rocks they start falling off like in a cartoon and he can't stop them. We say we will report him for desecration. It is a very long plod up but at the top of the pass and the views were just incredible, and Dave and Steve can name a few distant peaks. As this is another high point, the Saltire is unfurled for a Scottish contingent team photo. Someone commented that we are the only ones with alcohol and a flag with us - like a mountaineering Tartan Army.

If getting up was a hard slog, going down is really hard on the knees and the poles really help here but it would be terribly hard with snow on it. It's all cleared for us by milder weather but still the porters take it really easy with their huge loads. After nearly two hours we stop for lunch at a dump of a village called Chutenga I think. It's quite untidy with litter and stuff lying about and we are in a wooden shack again but the weather is warmer though as we are down in a valley. The cooks have gone ahead from breakfast this morning and prepared lunch and we have tables and chairs. Lunch is Spam with chips and coleslaw and a slice of bread and some dodgy, watery tomato sauce is produced and it helps it all go down. There is plenty of tea as usual but no heat or much light in the shack. I'm glad to get moving again, and for the last time on the trek, my big rucksack is hauled onto my back and by now the porters have mostly passed us and we will eventually pass them. There is still a fair distance to go but at least we know it's a mostly downhill plod and the thoughts of a warm shower and a cold beer keep us going, and of course, chance to sleep in a real bed again.

About twenty minutes after we start walking again, Val goes over on her ankle and it appears serious. Initially she can't put her weight on it but Dave straps her up and it worked for Sheila. Dave suggests 1200mg of Ibuprofen but she'll only take 800mg - she's a doctor after all - but he is the man for recommending heavy doses - hit the pain hard as he says. We still have a couple of thousand feet to get down to Lukla and the path is increasingly slippery. We also have to cross a river over two tree trunks which gives us some good photos, but is not as bad as the single log bridge earlier on the trek. After this the path improves and soon we can see far-off Lukla hospital, just above the village. More people are about now and I give some kids we meet some wee Scottish flags I brought with me and Sheila gives out pens.

At just after 4:00pm, we entered Lukla and we left this morning at 7:15am, so it's been a long enough day. I can't believe I'll be in a real bed tonight and a heated dining room. But a shower first I think, then plenty of beer and so with these thoughts we march through the streets to our teahouse and where this all began and we are starting to lose the light now. There's the usual delay in getting rooms sorted and we sit having tea. Dave appears to say the place is really busy and they are short of rooms and I'm sharing again with Chris. But at least this time we have a really big room and plenty of room for our kit and we will be here for two nights. The priority is the first shower in two and a half weeks and it's warm and great. Dinner is at 6:30pm and I'm upstairs to the room quickly to get changed and down to the dining room. Again tonight, all the guys will be in to eat with us. This will be our last night all together. The downside is that it's dal bhat, never my favourite but there's apple pie to follow and a few Everest beers to wash it all down. Someone produces a kettle of chang and I have a couple of milky glasses which all helped me have a great sleep.

Tuesday 30th October.

In the morning, after breakfast, Dave takes us up to the big field at the rear of the tea-house where we came on the first day getting the loads sorted with the porters and this is where, Lhakpa, as

Sirdar, is paying off the porters. They are finished today and what we do here is put any unwanted gear or gifts onto an area of ground behind the teahouse and then Dave and Lhakpa get involved in deciding who gets what. It's hard to be completely fair but everyone gets something and they are all smiles as usual. And of course they get their tips from us.

I pull Lhakpa aside and get him to sign my Mera peak map and then give him the watch I brought with me as a gift and Dave takes the photos of the two of us.

It's a good friendly end to the trek and none of it would be possible without the crew we had and we say our goodbyes to them all. Most of them will be looking for more trekking work almost immediately I guess but it's not an easy life. Today, the plan is an easy walk, leaving about half ten, to a small gompa outside Lukla that Steve seems to know about up on a hillside. We have a packed lunch made for us of a boiled egg, a marmalade sandwich and one of peanut butter, some biscuits and two slices of salami with some cheese. The monastery is on my map, but there is no trail shown. On the way out of the village we stop at the Maoist 'shop' or 'Prachanda Office' and try to get a free postcard and I say I'll buy a tee-shirt on the way back and the guys in the place are really friendly. From here, it's all downhill to start with and we pass hundreds it seems, of trekkers heading back to Lukla and porters too and yaks. No wonder the flights are always full and amazing that there are enough rooms never mind planes. I'm so glad that we weren't on the main routes from here. We stop after an hour at a tea shop and it's really relaxing just sitting watching the world go by. Amazing too the shapes of people on this trail and from all over the world when you hear the voices. I'm glad it wasn't as busy when we went to Island Peak but that was during the Maoist troubles. Now they run the place it seems.

When we head off, after about half an hour Steve stops at a sign in Nepalese and there is a track going uphill. We're not sure if this is our route but we press on and take another track going up past stone dykes and fields and still not sure but we can see the gompa away up ahead. Suddenly an elderly looking woman is shouting at us and comes down through a field and clambers over a six-foot dyke, hoisting her skirts and she's pointing the right way up and appoints a child to walk some of the way with us. "The best guide we've had so far" someone jokes. I have been disappointed that I'm never that impressed with Buddhist stuff but this is a unique setting as the monastery is set high up into the mountainside with cracking views down the valley towards Lukla, although mist prevents us seeing any mountains.

It appears the monk is away but there is an elderly caretaker who shows us inside and we donate some rupees and Dave gets a shot of one of the trumpets. This amazingly extends from about four feet to eight feet and as Dave always likes to say, it makes an 'awesome' sound. There seem to be a couple of trumpets at almost every monastery. The flowers in the garden are lovely. We have our packed lunch in the garden among the flowers and when the old boy comes down to us, we give him some of our food and he seems very grateful - but probably gets carry out meals from Lukla.

This must bring us good fortune surely, and the views down the valley towards Lukla are impaired by mist and low clouds and this is why almost all the flights stop mid-afternoon. Although we can hear the drone of aircraft engines, we can't see any planes in the mist but one seems to be circling for ages. I'm wondering about tomorrow and whether the weather will affect us. After a few photographs we head back the same way, only hitting the main track where we first thought we might go up. Dave sets a cracking pace on the way back and it's a struggle to keep up with him. But we are all only carrying light packs and it must be the combination of this and the lower altitude, but we pass every other trekker. Maybe we're just fitter.

On the way back, we stop at the same tea shop and outside the shop across the road from us is a giant pumpkin. I remind Dave it's Halloween and he goes across to haggle for it because we want to impress the team with it later. After some haggling Dave buys it for 300r, only for the cook to say later he could have got it at half the price. However, Dave accepts responsibility for explaining to the Sherpas and porters about Halloween. Back at the teahouse I get a quick shower and a few of us are heading up the road to the 'Waves' pub as it's our last night after all. So Marguerite, Davy, Sheila and Colin and I - the Scottish contingent, have a few Everest beers.

There is music as well and at one point Dylan is singing that 'it ain't dark yet, but it's getting there' and that always reminds me of my Dad's death and at one point I nearly have to leave. It is always quite emotional thinking about him when I'm out here. Sadly, this will be another story he will never hear, or my mum now. The cook has done an excellent job with the pumpkin and he's made pumpkin soup and really carved the pumpkin face well which has pride of place on our table, suitably lit with candles. Not only pumpkin soup but really good, garlic free, chicken soup as well. Then we have chicken and potatoes followed by chocolate cake and a few beers are consumed. Steve, Dave and I help to empty a gallon kettle of chang as we debate the future of China and sort out the world.

Wednesday 1st November.

We're on one of the first flights out and the 5:30am alarm call wasn't welcome as I have a very sore head and I have to resort to two of Dave's pink 400mg Ibuprofen to ease the pain. I then have a quick wash, some porridge and then omelette. Plenty of tea inside me and off to the airport. We're on Yeti airlines again and Yeti 4 is our plane and we take off just after eight. Not feeling great until, from my fourth row seat, I can see the black-stockings of the female pilot - quite sexy, all in black with shiny black hair. I watch as she pulls the throttle back and that thought stays with me till we land back in Kathmandu. I've felt better, even with some breakfast and pots and pots of tea inside me.

For the first time though, we circle for ages before landing and this is just like Heathrow on my early morning flights in, holding because it's so busy. We get a very smooth landing and are through getting our bags ten minutes later. Then onto the waiting bus and back to the Shangri-la hotel and it's still just mid-morning and an oasis of calm. At the hotel desk, I get my airline tickets back and check that Marguerite's and my return flights have been confirmed so then I get my stuff out of the safe, keep some cash out and put the remaining cash and passport back in and then I head to my room, a different one and on the ground floor. I'm in the bath when Dave knocks and when I answer he says he's got us better rooms in a quieter part of the hotel on the third floor. So back into the bath for a long soak, then up, dressed and back to reception. I change £250 into rupees and leave the airline tickets in the safe and ask for my bags to be moved to my new room. Then off to the bellboy and order a taxi to take me into Thamel on my own. I have a plan to buy souvenirs today and get the shopping out of the way. I tell the taxi driver to take me to the Pilgrim Bookstore.

He doesn't look confident but off we go into the traffic mayhem and eventually we are stopped by traffic in a street I recognise and I pay him about £1.20 and get out and it feels great being back here, and on my own which is different. I soon realise it was the wrong book shop I gave to the driver as I recognise the 'Walden Bookstore', that I meant but in the space of less than two hours I've ordered the obligatory t-shirt embroidered with 'Mera Peak', been to the kukuri shop and ordered four Skean Dhus if possible from the brother of the guy I bought mine from two years ago. I've to come back tomorrow at ten but I bought lots of other stuff too. And now back into a taxi and heading back to the hotel. I get the stuff up to the room and phone home but no one in so leave a message. I grab my journal and head down to the extensive and beautiful Shambala garden to have a beer. At lunchtime I ordered tandoori chicken with naan and a litre of Everest beer for only 400r. So, here on my own now with a brilliant lunch, sitting in the sunshine in lovely surroundings and all the shopping done, well almost, and it now feels as if the trip is over. Job done and looking forward to getting home, but it's so good here I stay all afternoon and have another two Everest beers. This hotel garden is a great wee oasis for journal writing.

The plan is that we are going out for a meal tonight and we are to meet in the bar about 5:30pm, so after a shower and change of clothes, I head down and have, funnily enough, another Everest beer and also have a cigarette with Dave. Then, after half an hour we get into a couple of cabs and head off to Thamel and to the 'Third Eye' restaurant for our team dinner. By the time we get there I'm bursting for a pee and I'm last to the table. We're out on a roof terrace, which is lovely and the place is packed and the service is slow. The food is fine but isn't as hot as it might be either so Dave complains and we get a few main courses knocked off the bill. To finish the outing we have a drink at the famous 'Rum Doodle' bar for tradition then back to the hotel. We all sit in a group at the bar on big sofas and after a few rounds I buy a bottle of champagne and get flutes for everyone. Marguerite, Chris and Davy are away for a more sensible night. Dave and I get through a few more fags and a nice end to the day and our last night with us all together. I use the room phone to speak to Cameron, my youngest son, and I hope he passes the message that I'm fine and leave for home the day after tomorrow.

Thursday 2nd November.

I start the day with a bottle of chilled water from the fridge, then a shower. And this certainly beats camping and down to breakfast, served on the lawn, at 8:30am. I joined Dave, Steve and Hazel. Chris joins us later and Colin and Sheila are at another table. The breakfast set-up is fantastic with lots of yoghurts and juices and the buffet has everything. Tea is served at the table. So plans are made by everyone and my plan is to get back into town and collect the t-shirt and hopefully, the knives. Last night I agreed to share a cab with Sheila and Colin and to take them to the gem shop where I was yesterday. It's a lovely morning again and quite warm already. Despite yesterday's purchases, I buy more stuff and then go to the kukuri shop and I recognise the guy right away and he recognises me so we shake hands and he has four knives as promised and he asks if I can remember the price last time. I can't, so he opens a big ledger and after a couple of minutes he finds my transaction from two years ago. The price of silver has gone up, he says, so I say maybe, but I bought one knife then, now I'm buying four and we agree on the same price and we part on good terms.

I meet Sheila and Colin by accident in the street and I show Colin the Skean Dhus and he wants one but I say he might have to wait a day. We leave tomorrow, but I go back to the shop with him but it's just the brother again and he says he will try to get a knife in the next couple of hours. From here it's a bit of a walk for me back to the gem shop I've discovered to buy a few more things, then it's a few more streets to find the t-shirt shop and I buy more stuff here too. Finally get a taxi outside the 'Rum Doodle' and back to the Shangri la. Back up to the room to do some provisional packing, then, as it's lunchtime, down for lunch - the same tandoori chicken and naan and a beer. Again, I sit here for most of the afternoon with people appearing for a drink or lunch and talk of the purchases made. I also finish the Rebus book, which I've hauled all the way to the mountain and back again. Sometimes monkeys come into the garden.

This morning we have all seen signs for a barbeque in the gardens tonight with live music and we ask Dave to check it out and see if we can attend. He comes back to say he's booked a table and we can all pay separately later and we will plan to kick-off at 7:30pm. So, all arranged and back to the room for more packing. A bit worried about the weight of my hold bag. The barbeque was unbelievable with tables and tables of food around the middle of the gardens with about thirty people serving and cooking. There is every type of cooked food and we all make a few trips up for food to see what's on offer and there are singers and musicians as well. Big flares are burning and the whole thing is very atmospheric and great for our last night. Dave and I are on the fags again and all very relaxed tonight. Still a relatively early night and again I sleep well.

Friday 3rd November.

Another early rise as I need to get into Thamel to pay a last visit to the ring and gem shop to get Margaret's present. However, breakfast first as I have all morning and it's only gone eight when I have breakfast, sitting on my own on the lawn with tea and reading the Kathmandu Times. After all the days trekking and climbing this feels so civilised. I can see Marguerite and Davy at another table a bit away deep in conversation. I have a selection of fresh fruit and some cooked food too and it's really warm again this morning. So after my quick dash into town it's time to check out and get all packed, as the bags will be left downstairs for collection later in the afternoon. I settled my bill and got the passport and airline tickets from the safe. As always, I've spent a bit more at the bar than I thought and the champagne was over £50, Nepal or not, but it's imported, and I did have something to celebrate. So, back outside to sit in the sun with my big and heavy, rucksack with me. Davy has already left to catch his flight to Delhi but we don't leave till four so plenty of time for lunch and a beer and some reading. Some more of our party will be leaving earlier and some are staying on. I sit thinking about the bus and go and order a taxi for Marguerite and I, as I remember how busy everything was at check-in and it will do no harm to be there earlier.

After lunch, same tandoori chicken, we say our farewells and swap email addresses and promise to keep in touch and swap photographs and all that stuff. Soon it's my turn to leave. I went to find our taxi to take us to the airport and we told the rest we were meeting a friend from last time there. Now through the hot and dusty streets to the airport and I can't see anything that's changed here since last time and as we turn into the airport, there are crowds of people and some armed guards at the doors. The building has been locked for 'security reasons'. This is crazy because anyone with a car bomb or whatever will have all the targets they want with hundreds of us stuck outside! Despite trying to ask the guards we have to wait for almost an hour outside and inside the building is totally empty. Our plan is to run when we get in, to the Qatar check-in desks but we still have to pay our exit visa fee first and then checking-in is our priority. We do run, but we aren't first and we're in a queue and a lot of flights were cancelled yesterday. In front of us a Swedish couple who couldn't fly yesterday are told there is no reservation for them today. Then it's the same with a German couple. Then our turn and we're relieved to get sorted out OK.

I notice that we are both over the weight limit, but no one bothers and the seat allocation is limited. Although we have a window seat to Doha we are in a middle row of four to Heathrow, but, hey, we're going home so it isn't a big deal. Then we have to fill out the emigration slip and go through passport control and then on to security. Every bag is always searched and the guard asks if I like his country and I say yes, it's my third visit and he just hands me the rucksack back after a cursory look. A bit of hanging about again but we have rupees to spend so I buy a couple of beers while we count what we have left. This time it's a box of six vodka miniatures and a couple of bottles of orange we can buy from our change. I don't think I've drank vodka and orange since I was at school but anyway a few sips pass the time nicely and I haven't really spoken a lot to Marguerite about the trek back from Mera so we catch up. We are of course almost first on when the flight is called and we're settled in well to the back of the plane. Once we are airborne I get the video camera out and we watch my film of the trek for a good half hour until dinner is served. This flight only takes about four and a half hours and we are landing in the dark in Doha.

Saturday 4th November.

We have almost four hours to kill before the Gatwick flight and we will get a sleep on this flight, about seven hours to London. As we wander about I spot the Qatar executive lounge or the 'Oryx lounge' as it is called. It costs to get in and you need a Qatar ticket of course so I ask how much and it's only about ten pounds each for four hours. Naturally it's lovely inside and really huge and we look around at all the snacks and all the soft drinks and juices. No beer. No alcohol at all in fact, so we eat fruit and nuts and drink bloody mango juice until our flight is called. Both feeling really tired now. I only learn later that there is alcohol but you have to ask for it. It's a big plane and we are in the middle of it, in a row of four but plenty of room though and we are quite comfortable. Drinks are served before and after dinner and we manage a nightcap then I get my blanket around me and fall asleep.

Sunday 5th November.

I wake up feeling cold as the pilot announces we are over Frankfurt with just over an hour to land in Gatwick. I always think it's funny how he takes twice as long to say where we are in Arabic than in English and maybe he tells them more. Breakfast is served and coffee, the first for weeks and it tastes great. Then there is the hassle of Gatwick and walking miles to collect our bags where we meet Colin and Sheila who travelled back business class and they looked better rested than we do. Marguerite goes to get a trolley as the bags start to appear but you need a £1 coin. How stupid is that with people arriving from all over the bloody world?! Anyway, we get sorted and say cheerio to Sheila and Colin who are heading to Glasgow later but are off shopping. Colin and I agree to share our video footage. We have a couple of hours too but have to get the train to the domestic terminal first and decide to have a mini-breakfast at a coffee pod place before we head over. No feelings of tea withdrawal.

The Easyjet check-in is open but there is already a big queue and at the front a few people away from us some guy has three pieces of hand luggage. You can only have one, so we watch the pantomime of him trying to get everything into one bag. We must have waited half an hour. Anyway, when our turn comes, both our hold bags are a bit over, as we knew but this time it costs just over £30 but worse, you have to go to another desk to pay it, bring the receipt back to the check-in desk before you get the boarding cards. Even worse still, there are fourteen people in front of me in this next queue and my temper is not good at this point. This takes another half hour as there is only one person at the desk. We are now tight for time and head straight to the security check and we think we might manage a seat and a pint before we board but the checks take ages, shoes and belts off. As I grab my rucksack, Marguerite's is stopped and searched after going through the scanner. They found a couple of the vodka miniatures we forgot about and took some delight chucking them into the bin in front of us. As we walk about the lounge area I notice on the screen that our flight says final boarding and we have to run down the corridor to the gate. The flight doesn't leave for half an hour but there are no passengers at the gate as everyone has boarded and we're lucky to get a couple of seats together at the back.

So, for the third time in twenty-four hours we're taking off again and after the stress of Gatwick we have a couple of glasses of white wine to take the edge of reality and an hour later we are landing into a rainy Edinburgh. Rickie and Margaret are there to meet us, and there's hugs all round. Another big trip all over but the memories are great. The highest I've ever been, the fittest I've ever felt and I had no illness at all on the trip. A superb three-week adventure in the Himalayas and probably the last time we will be there.

Book Four

The North Col Of Everest And Lhakpa Ri 2010

Saturday 10th April – Scotland.

And so, after months of serious planning and years of dreaming, I leave to join the 2010 Australian Everest expedition in two days time to climb with them to the North Col of Everest. But, it's Saturday and I have a toothache and although I always get a check up and an X-ray of my fillings, this is sudden and my dentist can't see me till Monday, which is when I fly out. A phone call to dentist and climbing club member, Tom Colquhoun, sorts it out and after a quick examination, he gives me a couple of packets of antibiotics. The first lot... "are OK to have a beer with, but if you need to take the second lot you absolutely can't, but you won't feel like climbing a mountain either - you can start the first lot now or wait till you get there". So with Sarah-Jayne's (daughter-in-law) special lucky stone with me and with Tom's drugs I feel ready for the challenge ahead. So, here I go, off to climb on Everest with Marguerite, my climbing partner again in the Himalayas. I am now sixty and I want to do this and finish the Munros too this year. I have loved all my previous trips to the Himalayas but they don't come bigger than this, for me at least. And this time, my wife Margaret, also a club member will be trekking in Tibet about the same time and we will meet up somewhere there depending on how things pan out!

Monday 12th April – Scotland.

At Glasgow airport on Monday afternoon I have toothache again so I take the first pills - a double dose as Tom recommended and then a pint because Tom said it was OK. In fact I had two pints waiting here with Rickie and Margaret and Marguerite. This is the most complex trip ever for either of us and for Margaret too in terms of planning. We are about to leave on the daily Emirates flight to Dubai and then onto Beijing. From here, after a couple of days with the team, we will travel by sleeper train for forty-seven hours through China and into Tibet. At Lhasa we have another two days acclimatising and then overland for three more days to Everest base camp. Then the climbing starts and that's for another couple of weeks. We will be away for almost five weeks. The tricky bit, apart from being on the highest mountain in the world is getting back as we will not return to China but go out through Nepal. And of course the summit team and the leaders and Sherpas won't be coming back with us - they might be on the mountain another couple of weeks after we leave. Margaret will be travelling slightly behind me in Tibet - to some of the same places but she will fly from London to Bahrain then Kathmandu and after a few days, she will fly to Lhasa. We plan to meet up on the Tibet/Nepal border in a town called Zhangmu in about four weeks' time, on her birthday, but if it all goes wrong, then we will meet up in Kathmandu - eventually. As well as complex, it's also the most expensive as all our flights and travelling are all one way. Added to that is the cost of the North Col climbing permit alone at $2500 each ($10,000 for the summit climbers). This trip is funded by early retirement money as Marguerite and I have both chosen that route. As always, there is a lot that can go wrong. And so as our flight is called, I give Margaret a cuddle and whisper, "see you in Tibet" and we go through security. I've already booked our seats and they are in front of the wings on this huge Boeing 777. Seatback screens of course and it is a seven-hour flight but by the time we are over Frankfurt, my toothache is gone and I can enjoy the food and wine. I also watched a few different movies.

The flight is good and we land ahead of time in Dubai - that always happens when you aren't in a rush, but we taxi for ages. The airport here was always huge but now it has an enormous extension, almost completed. Every airport I think I've been to in the world is being extended - what do they know about oil that we don't? We will have about two and a bit hours here so we walk through the shopping mall with our rucksacks, but we don't need to buy anything and we head to what seems the only open bar in the airport, only it's a seafood bar. However, we manage to get two beers at £5 each. At least we have a seat to watch the world go by.

Tuesday 13th April – Dubai.

Soon we are on another Boeing 777 headed to Beijing and again it's a seven-hour flight. The plan is to try to sleep on this stretch of our journey and after dinner and a couple of glasses of wine, we do just that and it's a pretty quiet cabin with no screaming kids. It's daylight when I wake up. I think I slept for a good few hours. Not what I thought I would see over this part of China as it is very mountainous and there is snow on the tops. As we descend it gets really bumpy and remains that way for an hour - almost until we land. Not good seeing these big wings shaking up and down. This is supposed to be the world's biggest airport, but from the taxi in it doesn't look it and even inside it doesn't look like it as we queue at passport control. There is one queue for Chinese nationals and ours which is signed, "Foreigners". Hmm, welcome to China. Passport checking is something these guys take seriously. Ahead of me, there's two people in uniform at every desk. As I watch, some people are asked to remove their glasses, some to give a side profile. I have a new beard and longer hair than normal so when Marguerite in front of me is asked to tie her hair back as in her passport photograph, I burst out laughing knowing I will get sent home for not looking anything like the guy in the shirt and tie in my passport. But, they let me in.

So, we are ready to collect the luggage and follow the signs. The building is no bigger than Glasgow Airport. The signs lead to a station platform where we take seven minutes on an automated train to reach the baggage halls. All the airport terminals feed into here and it is really huge. We were just in one of many terminal buildings. We get our bags OK and that is a relief but the next challenge is to find the Chinese Expedition Liaison Officer who will take us to our hotel. He is appointed by the Chinese Mountaineering Association (CMA) and every expedition here must have one and pay for him of course, all the way to base camp and back. He will sort everything from garbage disposal to all the army checks and be our general fixer. I have of course, no idea what Mr Kong looks like. Presumably Chinese though. As we go out through arrivals we see him. Amazing, but he's carrying a sign from Chessell Adventures, our expedition company and he has organised a taxi for us and soon we are on a six-lane highway leaving the airport and this joins one of six ring roads around Beijing. It's just so, so big and congested. Around seventeen million people live in this city and they all seem to be driving today. This is what happens when people change from bicycles to cars. I ask Mr Kong lots of questions which he answers carefully and slowly in reasonable English. Better than my Mandarin. We are staying at the Tiantan Hotel in downtown Beijing. It's a four star and looks pretty good as we drive up. The hotel is in the Chongwen District on the Tiyuguan Road. It takes ages to get our rooms organised but eventually Mr Kong sorts it out and says we should be down here at 6:00pm to meet the others and go for dinner. Now, the deal is that we are on B&B rates at all the hotels so we pay for dinner and lunch ourselves. He might take us to the most expensive restaurant in town! It's now after 5:00pm so we head to our rooms on the fifth floor. It's great to get a shower and unpack some stuff and we are here for a couple of nights, which is good. Every other Himalayan trip has meant an early rise the very next day after travelling halfway around the world. I have a great room and my big window shows the sky darkening and in the fog, or smog, everything looks a bit other-worldly with Beijing's lights coming on. I could be in any city anywhere on earth. All the aesthetic charm of Cumbernauld town centre on a wet afternoon I'm thinking. I went down to meet the others for the first time. Katy, the Expedition's number two (Duncan, the leader, is already at Base Camp) introduces us and we say hello to everyone - well, not everyone as more will arrive over the next two days. Looks like mostly Australians and some Brits and Swiss, German, Canadian and New Zealand climbers too. We walk to the restaurant behind the intrepid Mr Kong who I think looks about eighteen years old. The restaurant is only ten minutes away down Xingfu Street - and Chinese of course. As we enter the restaurant there are big aerated tanks with live fish and shellfish too. So it looks like we are having seafood. We are taken upstairs to a private room and sit round the usual revolving table and green tea is brought out to us and beer ordered too from our smiling waitress.

There are a lot of plates brought to us, all of them delicious, but not one of them has seafood in it or meat. Marguerite eats slowly - only because of her wayward chopsticks. The green tea is continually topped up. I get to talk to Richard from London who is a summit climber - and a runner. We have both brought our running gear and Richard has already been running about the city but warns of the pollution levels. He's already climbed Cho Oyu, arguably I'm told, harder than Everest and well out of my league. I like the guy. There is news coming through about a devastating earthquake in Tibet with thousands dead and It seems it may be near where the railway goes to Lhasa which might alter our plans. However there is not much detail. At the end of the meal we are offered raw oysters and I down mine no problem. Then I am brought another - well, it'd be impolite to refuse, so down the hatch too. I refuse the third though. Now the awkward bit as we are told that if Kong offers to pay we must let him - to save face. He pays, so we keep quiet and there is no mention of sharing the cost either. Should have ordered champagne! So we walk back, talk to our new companions, none of whom mention a night-cap, so we all head to our rooms. It's only when I get in that I realise how tired I am but I didn't get a great sleep on the plane. It's brilliant that there is no early rise tomorrow as the other times I've been to the Himalayas I've been up at four in the bloody morning to catch a plane or a bus. Agree to meet Marguerite for breakfast at 9:30am.

Wednesday 14th April – Beijing – China.

Today is a free day and we plan to wander about and maybe have a picnic in a park somewhere, as you might in Glasgow or London. The weather is overcast or that could just be the smog but It's only a fifteen-minute walk to The Temple of Heaven or to the famous Pearl Market, and we intend to visit both. As we seem to be first down we make the most of this to collect enough from the buffet for our lunch later. There are cheeses, meats and watermelon going into Marguerite's bag as we have breakfast and there's Chinese and Western food in abundance. We met Katy with our, just arrived, Expedition Doctor, Torrey. She's from Hawaii and although a bit loud, she has a great sense of humour. I suspect she doesn't suffer fools gladly either. More people will be arriving today says Katy. At reception, I get a map and a couple of hotel cards, in case we need to get a taxi back. It's a pleasant morning and we walk to the Pearl Market. The reality is that the 'market' is a huge warehouse- like a building of three or four storeys and although they do sell pearls, they sell electrical goods, handbags, you name it.

The sales pressure on the bag floor is ridiculous, with girls tugging at your clothes, offering you a seat, tea, anything for you to stop, that we have to get out. However, I got a pair of sunglasses and also bought a chop for stamping letters with my four boy's names - in Chinese allegedly - how would you know? Anyway, they look good and come with a wee ceramic bowl of red stamping paste and a nice presentation case. Outside we have a couple of cups of expensive green tea. Almost £2 a cup but we are in the tourist area. No Chinese people in the cafe. After this we go round the back of the building looking for a shop selling hopefully, chilled beer. We do find one, but also notice an even bigger building advertising jewellery. It was great - all small stalls where stuff was being made and no hard sell. A girl approached us and asked if we were buyers. So we said yes and we're looking for samples to take home. We ended up with stacks of really nice things like earrings and bangles and bracelets for very, very little and all wrapped in wee silk bags. Some of the girls point and laugh at me carrying beer. I suppose we aren't a common sight. So, now to find a park and we can see it on the map but can't find how to get to it. Before we go much further we pass a bakery and buy, with much pointing, some pastries and breads. I am brave enough to ask directions eventually from a guard at, I think some sort of barracks. He motions for us to follow him so it can't be far, but he only takes us to a bus stop and points to number 43. Too risky for us to get a bus, so I thank him and leave him puzzled as we walk away. And as we walk around a corner, there is a park. It costs about 20p to get in and there is someone to sell you the ticket and at the gate, someone else to check it. And that is how you keep 10 million people or whatever, employed. So, in the now hazy sunshine of a Beijing afternoon we have our stolen picnic and a couple of cans of beer in this lovely park with a woman hugging trees over the pond from us and singing in a beautiful voice. Bet she's employed to do that too.

At just after 4:00pm we head back, not that far either and we have our first 'team brief' at five. However, in my room is a note from Katy to say the meeting will now be at six. This will become a pattern on the trip. So, plenty of time to wash some clothes, have a shower and charge phone and cameras. This will be a pattern too. Still not much of a view as the mist thickens. I call Mags back home to update her. Downstairs on time and goodness, a lot more people - this is beginning to feel like an expedition. There is Linda, Australian, Meerie, also Australian, Grant from New Zealand, Simon from England, Stefan, a German Accountant, Phil, from England and Lawrence, a French girl living in Switzerland and Damien from Essex. We will catch up with another two members in Lhasa or base camp. Some others are only going to Advanced Base Camp and a couple are only going to Base Camp. But the North Col Team is almost complete. We have a drink and Katy tells us what will be happening over the next couple of days. We are warned not to have any pro-Tibet literature on us or in our bags. And no drugs as there are apparently mobile execution vans for serious drug offences. She again warns us that we will probably have to pay for dinner. A bus is waiting outside to take us to this evening's restaurant and we meet and greet the newcomers. Mr Kong is in charge and gets us onto a waiting coach. We have to take our shoes off at the restaurant door. The place is quite tight and we sit very low on benches. Beers are brought and of course, green tea. Lots of dishes appeared but raw eel was the only odd one. There are bowls with various sauces and Marguerite nearly dies after trying a big teaspoonful of green wasabi paste before anyone could stop her but it's quite funny. We sit with Torrey, the doctor, and Richard and James, from London, who is just back from rowing the Atlantic and Travis, a personal trainer guru from New Zealand. A good laugh and good to get to know our teammates and no bill was produced, so a great night out.

Thursday 15th April – Beijing – China.

I head down for an early breakfast and a great sleep again last night. The plan was to run this morning but on Richard's advice, I don't. Too much smog he says and he isn't going to risk infection. And certainly lots of people are wearing masks and even some of our people, including, this morning, Richard. The benefit of being early is that there is more food and it's hotter. A cook will do your eggs any way you like, but we have lots of fruit with us and take a few snacks too. Today the Chinese Mountaineering Association, will take us to the Great Wall and the Ming Tombs, although it's not only Mr Kong who will be with us. The smog is bad again but the traffic is worse. Michael, our smiling Chinese guide says this is normal and we sit in lots of queues for over an hour before heading out of the city. It's still misty here and as we arrive at a very busy bus park at this part of the Great Wall, it is disappearing into the mist higher up. However, despite this, we are all heading up as far as we can go - it stops apparently? First is the team photo which Katy will put onto the website tonight. We attract a lot of interest and some Chinese people want to be photographed with us, which is odd, but I suppose we look odd to them.

It takes us almost an hour to get to where the wall hasn't been renovated. It is still a fair height with really uneven steps. No views of course but not many people at the top either, except an Everest Team showing off. After lunch a short drive to the Ming

Tombs - or one in particular - Chang Ling I think - but that could be the name of a beer. It's impressive but not that impressive and although it takes a couple of hours to get round, it isn't the most wonderful sight in the world. So, back in the coach and back to Beijing and past the Olympic Village we see the big blue cube swimming pool and the birds nest football stadium, but it's too misty to take photographs. The coach gets parked and we will now walk to tonight's choice of restaurant which is high risk as no one pays attention to pedestrian crossings and you can turn right on a red light. It's rush hour again and also dark now too as we follow the intrepid Mr Kong. We get in and are shown into a private dining room. A long table, with seats on each side and four huge copper bowls set into and along the table. Green tea is served, then before the beers, some clear firewater stuff, which is only drinkable if you down it in one and there is good-humoured pressure on everyone from the waiting staff to have another.

Eventually these double cauldrons arrive and are set into the copper bowls. They are full of boiling liquids and there is a flame under the copper bowls to keep them roasting hot. The top layer of soup stuff is very fiery and the bottom two layers less so. Raw meat, raw fish strips and vegetables are laid out and with chopsticks, you cook your own food in the liquid of your choice by holding the raw food in it with chopsticks. At my first attempt my raw ham sticks to the side and is eventually vaporised but we all get the hang of it eventually and it's really quite good fun and good food. That is, except the very roughly cut and raw looking sheep's stomach. No one attempts it. I have some very black slimy mushrooms, which are great and sea cucumber. Spinach is good too, quickly cooked. We all thank the staff and leave, again, without us paying.

As we walk back to the coach there is some talk about catering on the train, someone is sure that it is a hit or a miss and that they can run out of food. We have planned another raid on the breakfast buffet and also to get back to the bakery where we bought stuff for our picnic. So, no panic for us, but for some, it's like the end of the world as they buy crisps, rolls, chocolate and other snacks, and of course lots of water. We buy more beer, although Marguerite has asked Mr Kong jokingly to buy us a case for the train. We will pay for it, she says. We are early back at the hotel at 8:30pm through a dark and foggy Beijing and on still very busy roads. We go into the bar for a nightcap and to discuss our plans for tomorrow but have an early night as we need to be packed, ready to go tomorrow morning. I get all my packing done but my rucksack feels a lot heavier. Our bags will go onto the coach in the morning, but we don't need to check out until lunchtime.

Friday 16th April – Beijing – China.

My alarm call wakes me at 5:30am. I fall over again until 6:15am, so it's a bit of a rush to get down to meet the others at 6:30am for the breakfast buffet. We're first here, but the doors are locked and there was quite a queue ten minutes later when the doors were opened. I had a great breakfast too, including four cups of tea and a couple of wee bottles of orange juice for later. I have some snacks saved in my room minibar fridge till we leave. It takes ages to get organised although we have our kit bags down in time, all are heavy and we give some others a hand from the lift. I check out and pay for two beers and six bottles of water from the mini-bar. However, as I walk to our coach to stash my rucksack a girl from reception chases me across the car park, shouting. A bill to pay she says - I show her the receipt her colleague has just given me and she is very apologetic. I don't think she had a gun though! We leave late at 9:00am for Tiananmen Square, again, courtesy of the CMA. It's very cold and misty when we arrive and we are wearing our fleeces. The Square is impressive. It can hold a million people we are told. There are queues to visit Mao's tomb and I would like to have gone but there is no time. We are going this afternoon to the Imperial Palace. As I take a last photo of me with the Chairman's portrait at the entrance to the square, a Chinese guy grabs me and is talking quickly and I assume he wants me out of the shot his pal is trying to take. No, they want to take his photograph with me!

The Palace is fascinating and all of the massive doors we pass through are original. There are quite a few Palaces and although it is busy, we pass through from one to another quite smoothly. A lot of restoration work has been done and the place is huge. Everyone takes lots of photographs. But, time is tight today and soon we are off for more food and after about ten minutes driving we stop at a less than impressive building where, upstairs, is our lunchtime restaurant. It doesn't look much but it is big. I'm sure the sign outside translates as 'coaches welcome'. We have three tables in a private area and they are organised better here than anywhere. Drinks are ready and we have tea and beer served as the food comes. It's the usual stuff but really good and more than enough for lunch. Especially as we now know 'dinner' will be at 5.00pm with the officials from the CMA at a Beijing Roast Duck restaurant. We'll be seriously overweight by the time we get to Everest!

The panic over the chance of no food on the train has heightened. No bakers near here though, although we are promised a couple of hours for last minute shopping. It's the Temple of Heaven next, and we have walked here ourselves previously as it's close to the Pearl Market. Although we are close to it, the coach has to take a long way round. Michael, our guide, talks us through the history and it's really interesting hearing about it. Now, people come to exercise, play music and generally hang out. It's a lot warmer now as we follow him around. From a viewpoint we can see down to Tiananmen Square and the government buildings. The park is huge and we have a good wander around before heading back to the coach. I ask Michael if we can just meet up with the coach at the Pearl Market as we know our way and want to shop elsewhere. He's apologetic but it's 'not advised'. So, we have to wait ages on people taking more photos and going to the toilet. When we park, we are first out the coach and off to 'our' bakery to stock up. On the way back we buy ten cold cans of beer from the wee shop we found a couple of days ago and then we go to 'our' jewellery store. As we come off the escalator on the second floor we are spotted by one of the girls we bought stuff from last time, she runs to us shouting, 'I recognise you, I recognise you'. This isn't that impressive as there aren't many Western looking people in Beijing. Anyway it was a nice touch and she was lovely. Inevitably we buy lots more stuff. The girls are amused that I'm carrying a big bag of beer - just like the last time I was here, they mention. We are first back to the bus which is now locked. The road is really busy and it's also a lot warmer so we have a cold beer while we wait. So, late, at 5:15pm, we head to the last restaurant visit in Beijing. The train to Tibet leaves at 9:30pm, but the station is reasonably close to the restaurant apparently. The coach has to park a couple of blocks away but the restaurant is lovely. The top brass from the CMA are hosting this dinner and again they have really looked after us well and we have paid for nothing.

It may specialise in roast duck but we have other things first - vanilla mashed potato, the slimy black fungus, fish, chicken and lots of vegetables, and all delicious. To drink, we have tea of course but also beer and red wine. The two big, browned and glazed ducks are carved with some flourish in front of us - cut, not shredded and the usual spring onions, plum sauce and pancakes are produced. I manage two. It's a very relaxing occasion. The alcohol helped no doubt. Relaxing until the CMA President speaks. He talks of the high risks, our preparation and how they all wish us well for such a difficult endeavour and he hopes we will have good luck on Everest. I hope so too and we all shake hands with him and we all receive a gift as we leave. Mr Kong gets us onto the coach again. So, we are now off to catch the World's highest train. I've been trying to get out of Katy what our accommodation is on the train. Even back home I emailed her to say we would pay extra for a four-berth compartment - the six berth is cramped and has no door onto the corridor. Even now she remains vague about it and I fear the worst. At the station, the coach can't get us to the entrance so porters have to be fetched with trolleys to take our heavy bags into the station. It's a pantomime as it's a steep incline. They drop bags, slide back and generally act like it's a slapstick comedy. This continues inside the terminal and in front of us is now a big escalator, maybe 80 feet high - no sign of lifts. So, they rush a fully loaded trolley onto the moving stairs with five of them holding the trolley from hurtling back down onto us. It worked but health and safety wouldn't like it. All our rucksacks get X-rayed. We have been warned not to have any pro-Dalai Lama or 'Free Tibet' literature with us - we were also told hotel staff will search our bags while we are out to find anything anti-Chinese.

Our train, T27, is waiting at platform 30 as we walk along a big corridor and below us, lit up in the gloom, is the train. No escalators so it's another pantomime as the porters bang the trolleys down the metal stairs. Amazingly, there are no casualties. There is something romantic and exciting about a train all lit-up in the darkness, ready to take you somewhere mysterious, but this isn't the Orient Express and we will be on it for two days. No one is saying much and I ask Katy again about our berths, 'just let's get on the train, then we can sort ourselves out'. Fine by me, so I'm first on Car 2 and the first berths are for six, then the next, and the next and I'm nearly at the end of the coach. Obviously, there are no four berths on this coach, so plan 'b' and I get us into a compartment to share with two Aussie couples we have got to know, Barbara and Steven and John and Karen - they are going to Advanced Base Camp only for a day visit. So, sorted, but not ideal and I can't say I'm happy about the subterfuge about all this. We have a door-less compartment with bunks in three tiers. Blankets and pillows are provided. The top bunks are the cheapest and look very high up.

Worse to come as the kit bags are coming on and there is no room for all of them. We manage to get ours right up to the top of the compartment and we volunteer to sleep in the very high top bunks. The 'summit' guys have huge bags and mostly have two to our one so there is no room and they are left in the corridor. So here we are, cramped in here for forty-seven hours. I feel pissed off. To calm me down, I take a walk along the train corridors. There is a restaurant car with maybe forty seats and its five cars along from ours. The toilets seem to be all squat types. On the other side of the restaurant car are the cheap seats - just a semi-reclining seat and the train is full. Hopefully full of food too! To cheer me further, as we get back to our compartment, Mr Kong arrives with a big box of twenty-four cans of beer! As people pass, we offer free beer and share a few with the Aussies and the craic is good. At exactly 9:30pm we leave Beijing on another stretch of this big adventure. In our bunks at 10:10pm and I have a wee Southern Comfort nightcap above a 20-foot drop. The lights go out at 10:30pm. Like the French sleeper trains I can remember as a wee boy, there are soft blue lights on all night. I shut my eyes as we thunder through the China darkness.

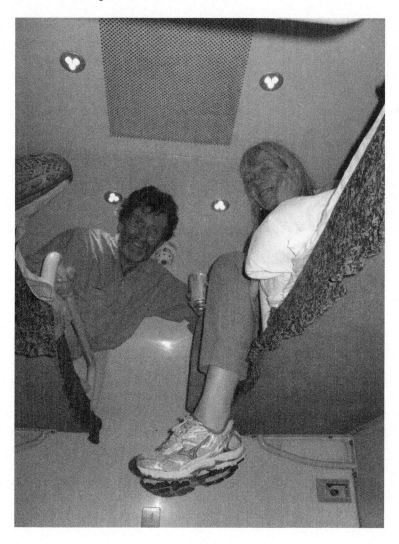

Saturday 17th April – the Train.

I slept really well and I can remember when I was really young and travelling across France, Spain and Austria in sleeper trains. I can still remember the excitement and looking out as we flew through the night past level crossings, hearing their bells ringing and passing through big lit-up towns. The top berth is too high here to see out the window. So, at 6:30am, we climb carefully down and go through to car 4 to brush our teeth at the sinks installed there. Only for us both to panic that we had used taps labelled 'no drinking'. Ah, well says Torrey, our doctor, you'll know in twenty-four hours if it's a problem. So, at just after eight we head to the dining car. Now, having experienced many times the expensive nature of dining on British and French trains, I was a bit apprehensive and the car is packed and there are no seats but the Head Waitress or whatever she is, wakes up two Chinese guys and moves them to give us a seat. She brings us green tea - serious stuff with leaves and stems in it. It's just great to get a seat and a view and we also get five top-ups for our tea. So I try to figure out how this all works, when we are moved by her - politely - to another seat to allow some railway workers to have their breakfast. I like her. I'm starting to enjoy this journey and at 10:30am, order two beers and we write up our journals as we fly past pretty barren countryside. All the shades of barren desert are here, tan and brown hills, some sheep and goats here and there. There is no effort to move us so at midday we go back and get the food we have stolen from yesterday's breakfast buffet. We have another couple of beers and the dining car is empty. Why would you want to stay cramped up?

Later I share a beer with Meerie, the Australian woman - she has ten kids and is taking custody soon of two grandchildren. No wonder she's away for five weeks! Outside the sky is clear blue but the landscape is lunar. I have spotted a fox and lots of antelopes. There are some white mountaintops in the far distance. We trundle on across the vast Chinese plain. The scenery is impressive in scale rather than being beautiful. As we travel we see big developments everywhere, new roads - motorways I think and stretching maybe a hundred miles. Big office blocks too and lots of new houses. This is a country on a mission. We pass lots of new looking rolling stock and diesel and electric locomotives. I nip back to get some of our own beers while Marguerite orders more green tea. In car 5 the toilet is overflowing onto the corridor carpet. Not good - this is the first day. We have been in the dining car almost all day and at 6:30pm, we order dinner. A couple of our team are in now and have already ordered so we ask them what they're having. This afternoon we counted lots and lots of army trucks spread out on the road for miles.

We have two bowls of rice and one bowl of spicy chicken and green peppers. More than enough and it cost the equivalent of £2.50! Marguerite has mastered the one-use chopsticks by not separating the pair at the base and using them like tweezers. It works. We have a couple of bottles of water to help rehydrate. At eight, our Aussie friends come in so we head back to get the compartment to ourselves and sort out our gear to be more comfortable. We also have some beer and invite all passers-by to have one as well, and get into conversation with a few people, including Torrey. She's really funny with her ascetic Jewish wit but you wouldn't want to cross her. Before ten, we are again perched high in our bunks. Tonight, one of our Aussie girls took our oxygen saturation readings - all fine and high nineties, but we will get to 16,000 feet on the train tomorrow. Oxygen is piped through the train and there are O_2 ports at every bunk. I wonder about the probability of this though. Again, we share a nightcap in the blue lit darkness above the void.

Sunday 18th April – the Train.

I took a while to get to sleep and slept until 7:00am this morning. The train has stopped for half an hour at this point and as it gets moving, we get up, or get down rather. I head off to car 3, which has real toilets. Brush my teeth with bottled water this time. We both head to the restaurant car for breakfast, now we know it's affordable. We share two slices of toast, two fried eggs, two slices of tinned meat and slices of tomato and this is also served with butter and jam and of course, green tea. At 11:30am, I have my last green tea top-up. If I could, I think I would travel the world on a train. We are now high on the Tibetan plain at over 15,000 feet. It's pretty grey and desolate outside and in places a bit like Scotland. Soon we will get to over 16,000 feet. As the line is so high, and lies on the permafrost, a cooling system of pipes driven into the ground keeps it frozen all year round to prevent the track buckling in summer. At some point today, we go through the world's highest tunnel. Around 100,000 workers were involved in creating the railway, few of them Tibetans.

As I head back to our compartment to get a book, there is one of the summit team guys sitting on a corridor fold down seat, with oxygen pipes connected and also Steven and Barbara, the older of our Aussie friends are also on it through the tubes in the compartment. I feel fine, not even light headed but walk slower on the way back. Can't help thinking that if you need oxygen now, what will you be like higher up? As I head into the restaurant car there is a catering trolley with stuff out of the store. I have to photograph the packet of 'spiced donkey'. I wonder now about the spiced 'chicken' last night. Hmm. We've been travelling now for over forty hours on the train and it feels like home. We have a conversation with some others about our arrival time - some say 5:00pm but the book says 9:00pm. There is no information on the train itself, except to tell you elevation in metres. We stop at Tang Bei and Joan, another Australian who is only going as far as Base Camp, is sitting with me now and I share some Yanjing beer with her. We have changed engines three times now I think but you can't get out at the station and wander about or take photographs. Joan says she saw a few people smoking and Marguerite saw a guy with a pipe going in between cars. It's supposed to be non-smoking. Quite a few toilets are now locked.

At 3:30pm we reach Na Qa where a lot of people get off. We are in the middle of nowhere with lots of new buildings and a big, new marshalling yard. Why here? Maybe a nuclear plant or a prison but no one can tell us. We order lunch of rice and shredded pork (or donkey?) in garlic sauce and I get some more beers from our compartment. Outside we are seeing more and more yaks and goats. We are descending slowly and are now at 14,800 feet but going slowly and our ETA looks like going back all the time. Eventually the word comes through that we will be in Lhasa in less than an hour. We head back to do some packing and somehow we need to get our big kit bags down from the top bunks. We have to carry our own gear off the train through the corridor, which is already filled with bags. We clatter across a big river, the Tsang Po, which flows to India and becomes the Brahmaputra, and enter into the 'forbidden city' of Lhasa. The station looks brand new - and totally empty. I nearly get arrested by a policeman in a big black coat for approaching the engine to take a photograph who strongly seems to be suggesting I don't. There are no porters here - and no trolleys, so we have to manhandle everything out of the station and I can feel the 11,000 feet altitude now, suddenly having to exert myself. Worse, the buses can't get close to the station - security no doubt - and we all help to lift or drag our collective bags to the waiting buses, which look too small. I'm not impressed. So, not happy that porters weren't sorted, I make sure we are on a bus at least. As we drive through the city it's obvious the station has been built on the outskirts, like you would with an airport, but not a railway station? As we head past some new, shiny big hotels my heart sinks a bit but when we draw up at the Himalayan Hotel, I realise this is where Michael Palin stayed on his Himalaya programme and that cheers me up as he is one of my heroes. Then I remember he didn't like it as it was freezing cold inside.

As usual, I am amongst the first in the queue. We all get rooms on the same floor - the sixth floor, and I'm sharing with Richard which is fine. The room is really big and if I stand on a seat, I have a brilliant view of the incredibly white, Potala Palace high on Mount Marpori, now lit up as it's after eight and getting quite dark. Dinner has been arranged for half past but I need a shower after two days on the train and don't get down till after nine. Worryingly, there is an oxygen machine in the room, but with only 68% of the oxygen at sea level, it might be useful for some. It's not warm either. I turn the heating dial up full with little expectation it works. Dinner is a big buffet and a lot of the team have eaten first and have left, but there is plenty of food and we both have a big bottle of Lhasa Green Leaf beer to wash it down. We get talking to some new team members who have flown into Lhasa. One of them, Frank, is on our North Col Team and he's been on Everest before. Frank is a gadget man. We are now a big team and another woman, Diane, will arrive tomorrow as well to join us. She has her own adventure company and is out here in Tibet already with clients. Her company is called 'Wild Women on Top'. I'm not making this up. There is talk about going downtown but someone says there is a curfew and so at just after 10:00pm, I head to bed, to avoid being shot.

Monday 19th April – Lhasa – Tibet.

I took ages to get to sleep and I can feel the altitude but no headache. Up early and on the seat to look at the Palace again. It's very impressive and we will visit it tomorrow. At 8:30am, Richard and I meet the others for breakfast. The carpet in the lift has the day of the week printed on it. I don't know why either. Damien, a North Col climber like us, appears and has shared a room with the French Canadian Summit climber, Lobuche and is cracking up as he has been using the oxygen machine off and on all through the night. He was the guy using oxygen on the train - not a good sign if you're off to climb the highest mountain in the world. Anyway it was his choice to share but Katy has sorted him with his own room. Nothing planned until midday so we can have a wander about on our own. We walk out into bright sunshine and head into the city, passing lots of market stalls selling vegetables which look as good as you might see at Tesco.

At the corner of the market a vendor is selling saffron, heaped stamens in a big orange, conical pile and we will definitely buy some on the way back. And big cubic lumps of yak butter on a cart is pulled by a bike. There's lots of army around everywhere as well, marching about in small groups. On the way back, the saffron seller has gone, which is typical. We meet some of our group and go for a coffee near the hotel. Within minutes of us sitting down, the sky darkens and there is a big hailstorm for half an hour. We still get to the hotel on time but the hills around the city are now white. The plan for today, Katy tells us, is to visit a lesser monastery or just do your own thing and I opt for the latter. Lunch has been laid on though, so we are all together for that and it all seems free as well. After lunch I head into town and further than we were earlier, to the Bhaktor Market.

In the square are fountains and two huge, stone, pot-bellied incense burners at the entrance to the Jo-khang Temple - it means 'Temple of the Buddha'. It dates from the mid-7th century AD, so older than the Potala Palace. I think there is a solid gold Buddha figure here 1200 years old. It's like the Mecca of the Buddhist world and very ancient looking. The smoke from the incense burners is, to Buddhists, a conduit between heaven and earth, down which the Buddha can travel. The clouds of incense smoke are a bit overwhelming! You can bring your own juniper bush to burn apparently. The Dalai Lama took his final exams here. Chairman Mao wanted to bomb the Palace but relented. It's a lovely sunny day and I take a few photos, being careful not to photograph the numerous army and armed policemen around me. I also notice soldiers with rifles on some rooftops - what are they expecting to happen? I haggle with some stallholders and buy some souvenir stuff on the way back- all friendly though - and we are at the hotel easily for 5:00pm. I feel comfortable here in Lhasa somehow, with its serious looking soldiers and tall Lhasa girls with lovely smiles and shiny black hair, some monks in yellow and saffron coloured robes but I don't know who is who. There are older looking people dressed in furs and traditional clothes and of course, the surrounding, snow-capped mountains. Like Kathmandu, it could be my spiritual home.

I arrive on time at the hotel only to be told, we are now meeting at 6:00pm. Ah, well, up to the room to see if I can figure out the heating system. Failing, although I've moved the thermostat, I've time to send texts home and get some clothes ready for the next few days, and get some clothes laundered by the hotel too. Back in the room Richard is wearing his mask, which is a worry. We will go by coach tonight and the same format - Mr Kong and his Tibetan pals are in charge and we end up right back in the square I was in this afternoon. We walk through some market stalls and follow Mr Kong up the stairs of a restaurant you would walk past - not great looking. We are all sat in the main area on a long table and, unusually, we can order anything we like. The food is really good and a change from constant Chinese food, I have pakora and tandoori chicken and we all have Lhasa beer, which is very weak but ideal for all of us. It's a good atmosphere tonight and the last of the Summit Team have now arrived. Katy announces that we can get the bus back or walk - I know the way and have no problem with that - I feel safe here and the same in Beijing, even if we really stick out as 'foreigners'. And it was worth it with the Temple really busy and incense smoke everywhere and pilgrims prostrating themselves. Apparently you can pay someone to do the prostrating trip for you round the Temple and it still counts. The perambulation is called the 'Kora'. When Chris Bonington was here, he reckoned there were 3,000 people inside the temple. At the Temple entrance, in the smoky gloom is a wee building full of hundreds of lit candles and you can feel the heat on your hands through the windows. So, through very dimly lit side streets, with lots of stares, we get ourselves back to the hotel and a quick talk about tomorrow which is a morning visit to the Potala Palace and a walk up a local hill in the afternoon. It's a nice early but cold night and Richard got the bus back and is already asleep as I sneak in.

Tuesday 20th April – Lhasa – Tibet.

I slept really well and better than last night. Marguerite says she had a bit of a sore head but recovers over breakfast and we sit with Richard, the summit guy. Now, he and others have masks on all the time and I suppose you would want to minimise any risk of infection. It's a lovely sunny morning as we depart on time to the Potala Palace. The deal is that you have an hour to get in, see everything and get out. However, we have to queue for almost an hour to get in, but it's an interesting place even so. Apparently it has 10,000 rooms. It is also thirteen storeys high - about 1,200 feet. Before there were skyscrapers, this was reckoned to be the highest building in the world. Now it's really just a museum.

We are searched as we go in but cameras are OK and

soon we begin the inevitable climb, floor to floor. For the record, I counted 380 steps from where I came into the top open area - or at least as far as we are allowed to go. And at the top you can't film or take photos. And there are guards - in plain clothes - to make sure you don't - as some of our group found out. The views over the city and mountains are however, wonderful. On the one-way system down we pass all the ornate - some solid gold - coffins of past Dalai Lamas and lots of statues. There is also some really dodgy wiring which dimly light up the dingy interiors of the chambers we pass through. Everywhere there are yak butter candles sputtering away adding some light but also adding to the fire risk. Up to a third of Tibet's Yak butter production goes to providing fuel for monastery candles and lamps apparently. Pilgrims stuff money into the shrines and coffin masks. There is no bar.

Suddenly we are out in sunshine and going down a different way but with excellent views of Lhasa again. The Palace is certainly interesting and without any Army presence and it seems the Chinese have accepted that they can't change things like this. Like Nepal, it seems like the last signs of some lost ancient world, long since gone, leaving only these religious fragments, and the people clinging on to their way of life in these high places against the power of so-called progress. For how much longer I wonder? Already there are plans to extend the railway.

We go back to the hotel for lunch, served downstairs today in a private room. Usual stuff but fresh and hot and of course tea and beer are provided and the plan is to go to a hill on the outskirts of the city but you can't just go and walk anywhere. We need permission from the authorities. Makes you appreciate our freedom to roam in Scotland. So after lunch, I go upstairs to get my boots on after a week of being a tourist and head down for the coach, which leaves at 2:00pm. We drive in sunshine for about forty minutes and the driver gets off the bus with one of our Tibetan 'guides' and goes to a house. Permission is refused for the planned hill so it's plan 'b' again. I think this is the least fit I've felt in weeks. We drive back the way we came earlier and stop at a gate house where the guide talks to an old man at another house. It's OK this time. But, he says no photographs to be taken on the hill. Maybe it's a secret hill. Some of our party are going to see another temple instead of the walk and they stay on the coach, the rest of us are off up a dusty path. It's also very warm. Despite this we set off at a pace I think is too fast. No guidance from Katy, so I settle at our own pace. Sweat is lashing off me and I stop to drink every fifteen minutes. The summit guys are here and as expected are faster than us as they should be.

It only takes an hour to get to the top so it's a bit like a Tibetan Tinto, my local hill, but the views are amazing and we spend about half an hour up here. Marguerite takes the rucksack on the way down and neither of us brought poles, which was a mistake. The coach is waiting to take us back to the hotel. Dinner tonight is at 7:00pm and the same place as last night, which is fine by me. Upstairs for a shower and discover the toilet won't flush so have a look inside the cistern - broken chain from the handle. I fix it with a safety pin and it works OK. With John and Karen, we decide to walk to the restaurant as we know our way about now. It's still warm in the evening sun and we take the back streets to arrive early at 6.45pm. We have been given 'window seats' tonight the smiling Tibetan waitress tells us. After a beer I go to the toilet for a pee and through the open window realise I am looking at an army guy with a gun on the rooftop opposite. He's also looking at me, which is a bit disconcerting. I resist the urge to wave. The rest eventually arrive, with Katy last, as she's been to the supermarket - I assume to buy stuff for base camp. It's back to a set menu tonight and the one beer allowance we've had so we have to buy more and it's 10 Yen, about a pound for a big bottle of Lhasa beer. Everyone will walk back, including us.

Back outside in the square, Karen spots a rickshaw and says why don't we get one of these back? Why not? We agreed to the price first - it's Y10 - a pound again. So they get theirs, we get ours and into the darkness of Lhasa we go. And in the dark streets I notice our driver is using his mobile phone while pedalling into the busy main street and no lights on these things either. A couple of times in back streets we have to get out and push the rickshaw over rubble. Sometimes some locals had to help us so it's quite an adventure. We never meant it to be a race but I'm sure they started it. Quite light hearted but becomes serious as we near the hotel and both these guys are going mad to be first on the forecourt. We beat them by seconds and give the winning driver Y18 for the journey and he's laughing too. Maybe that was just hysteria. As we are leaving Lhasa tomorrow, it's final packing and after twenty minutes I go to Marguerite's room to see if she's struggling like me. Both our kit bags are at bursting point and we can't get our walking boots in even though we came with them packed! I don't know how many times that happens but after that, it's an early night for me.

Wednesday 23rd April – Lhasa – Tibet.

I had a great sleep and could have slept on but needed to get down for breakfast and arrangements for checking out and to pay my laundry bill, which is only Y25. We will be travelling in two small coaches as there are lots of us now, about thirty I think - and even at this the back seats are full of luggage. Marguerite has acquired grapes, nuts, wee cookies and even orange juice from the breakfast buffet, so we won't go hungry. We get a seat at the back with the only opening window. Today we will travel overland on the 'Friendship Highway' to Shigatse, which is Tibet's second largest city. I don't know what to expect but reason that the hotels will get poorer the further we go. We're a bit too used with nice big hotels with free drinks and meals of great quality. We leave at 9:00am under a cloudless, intensely blue sky. Mr Kong is joined by a Tibetan guide called Kusang. Today we will cross the high passes of Kamba La, 15,700 feet and then Karo La at 16,500 feet. Later we will climb over the Simi La and down to the plains of Gyantse.

I will remember that this is a good seat on the coach, as you miss the sun - as well as having an opening window. The road is really good and as we leave Lhasa and its comforts behind, we get a panorama of mountains in front of us as we drive fast on the surprisingly busy road. I notice that all the summit guys have masks on, including Richard who I chat to about his gear. It is really expensive looking and I ask him if he has sponsorship but he says he's tried but got nowhere. We slow to a halt at some shantytown type buildings in the middle of nowhere and immediately some good looking, black haired girls appear to try to sell us beads and bangles. We are having lunch here. It's ultra basic with plastic seats and dodgy tables. No glass in the windows, just dirty plastic. Someone comes back from the toilet and says don't go because it's horrible. No menus but I can hear the hissing of a paraffin stove. We will get what we will get. We eventually get jasmine tea. Then we have beers. And rice is served first, then some vegetables and fungus - the black, slimy kind followed by a green salad and a bowl of fish stew with a whole fish in it. And then a big dish of chicken chopped up and I helpfully pointed out the chicken's feet sticking out. They must just have chopped the whole of the bird up. Anyway, it was all freshly cooked.

After nearly two hours we are heading off again. Still a few hours travelling to Shigatse and the sky still pale blue. At some point I fell asleep but as we drew close I woke up and we passed a few big, newish looking hotels but we turned left and were almost out of the town as we turned into a really unimposing driveway. Welcome to the Gyan-Gan Hotel a sign says, and my heart sinks. As we hang about reception in some confusion, Mr Kong gets the rooms sorted. I am expecting dormitories but he hands me a key card. The hotel is so big we all have a room to ourselves again. My room, which is on the second floor overlooks the bend in the main street and a sort of park and I can see a big monastery as well. It's the Tashi Lumpo and the home of the Panchen Lama, the Chinese approved Lama. The guy who the Dalai Lama nominated in his absence was taken to Beijing years ago and hasn't been seen since. Boys are sent to monasteries from the age of five and can only come home once a year. I should have brought my boys up as Buddhist! However, it was the only monastery left untouched in the Cultural Revolution. Before the Cultural Revolution there were 2,000 monasteries in Tibet, now, under a dozen remain, the rest destroyed. There are juniper bushes everywhere despite their daily burning in the incense burners. There is a giant Buddha statue here made from 280kg of pure gold. And I have a knife with me.

I have a bathroom with a shower over the bath as well and two single beds and a big vacuum flask and tea bags. No heating at all. So, first I need a shower but it's not looking good, just a trickle - and cold. Eventually I got the trickle to run hot and then the handle fell off. However, this let me use my multi-tool thing to sort the flow and had a really good shower. Also ran the bath and washed some clothes, pleased with the facilities, although a radiator would have been good. I go downstairs and get talking to Damien - a nice guy and he tells me about the fundraising he's done. Reckons he'll raise £50,000 and I'm amazed. Also tells me he has been sponsored by The North Face and I notice that everything he's wearing is North Face stuff. He's going to the North Col, just like us. Yet Richard, an accomplished climber, got no sponsorship. Dinner will be at 7:00pm in the hotel so I have a few hours. I walk up into the park, which is overlooked by both our rooms. There is what looks like an outside big-screen, but for what? Certainly not a drive-in movie place I think. I get stared at a lot and I'm getting used to it. Shigatse is the second largest town in Tibet and the capital of the province of Tsang, with a population of around 60,000. We are at an altitude of 13,500 feet here. It's a sprawling town, but quite pleasant to walk about it's tree-lined, wide roads. However, I hear of plans to extend the railway here from Lhasa. Shigatse sits at the junction of two big rivers, the Ngang and the Yarlung Tsang Po, which becomes the Bramaputra in India.

It's really warm as we wander among shops and market traders so we think it's time for a beer. No pubs of course, and we want a change from our hotel so we set off to find a 'western' type hotel. And we do, only we seem to have gone through the wrong door and we are in a bar - full of men playing cards - they all stop to stare at us so we sit down to hear the giggles of the waitresses who all come to our table. They come over and say 'hello'. I ask for two beers. The three of them giggle so I give a pouring demonstration. More giggles but an old Tibetan man at a nearby table says something to them and I'm led by the arm by all of them to behind the bar and they point at boxes of bottles. I lift out what must be the oldest two bottles of Lhasa beer in Tibet, with peeling, faded, green labels and hand them to a girl. They are brought to us with more giggles and two bowls of nuts - like pistachio, but harder and round. All the men have resumed their card games and it's then I realise that the room is full of smoke. Everyone is smoking - no ban here. On the way up the street, children stop to ask in their best English. 'How are you' and we always reply. I'm getting used to being stared at by now and we cross the road to look at a big Tibetan mastiff in a cage in a shop-front. In another cage are two mastiff pups, looking, as lots of Tibetan dogs do, as if they've been knitted. No idea why these dogs are in a shop-front. Back to the hotel and get ready for dinner and meet Karen at reception and offer to buy her a beer. Ask at reception but it's really confusing - I only want two bottles of beer but eventually it seems they have only one can. So we share it. Asking for two glasses could have taken another fifteen minutes to sort.

Dinner isn't in the hotel itself but across the car park in another building and a cold barn of a place. Usual format of revolving tables, a selection of food brought to the tables, green tea and beer. We sit with some of the summit guys and am interested to hear them talk about what they think the climb will be like. They are all individuals though, not much team talk - reminds me of a saying in a book - which I have with me - by Andrew Greig, called Kingdoms of Experience about climbing Everest's unclimbed ridge. He says something about an Everest team being like a choir composed of soloists. Off early to bed at 9:30pm. The decorative, iron framed windows cast lovely shadows from the car headlamps turning the corner and as I sit writing this journal with a wee Southern Comfort, it's quite psychedelic. So, writing finished, teeth brushed, bed-sheets checked for beasties, Margaret texted with an update and into bed. This feels good tonight, maybe too good.

Thursday 22nd April – Shigatse – Tibet.

I think the dogs started barking before midnight and went on all night. Eventually got up and put earplugs in which helped a bit. Breakfast was a shock as we've been spoiled by big buffet breakfasts of fresh fruit, meat, cheese, hot dishes and cold but here we are served a tray with two slices of bread, some yak butter and jam - and a cold boiled egg. Still have green tea though. The plan is to leave later at 11:00am to allow Katy to buy fresh fruit and vegetables to take to Base Camp. I made a short film about the hotel and the town and to take in the monastery as well. Some of the team are going to visit it this morning. I also walk down to film the big mastiff but its mood is no better. Later on, we searched for the barking dogs. Fortunately, no animal was injured making this film - only because we didn't find them!

At half past ten we are loading our bags and generally

helping. Lots of bags in the back seats again and some are coming through the open window. We end up with a huge kitbag right behind our heads, I try to stabilise it with the other bags but it's a bit precarious. Just before we leave Katy is looking for Marguerite. She may have left something in her room and she goes with Katy to see what the cleaner has found. Not clothing, but a plastic bag with £200 of Chinese money in it. Must be a couple of month's wages at least for the very honest cleaner and she gets Y100 from Marguerite in thanks. At just after 11:00am we leave - a convoy now as we have hired a small pick-up to carry the vegetables. We are off to Xegar or Shegar today, a smaller town than here in Shigatse. I have a look at the map but it's hopeless trying to guess distance on it. I'd be happy to drive straight there if possible. However, after two hours on a deteriorating road we stop at a shanty town for lunch. The place is called Lhatse I think and the road into Western Tibet starts here. The place looks like a run-down frontier town - the wild west of Tibet. We get out of the coach and everyone on the dusty street stares at us as we go through a restaurant doorway into - well, a big dusty courtyard, and are directed to another shack at the back which looks like another eating place. Inside, there are tables set out and we are given menus from young Tibetan girls with the head woman watching over all this. Orders are taken. Nothing is written down. We are sitting with another couple. Our order is two chicken fried rice, one tomato soup and an apple pancake. Tea is brought and beers and soft drinks. All of this carried from yet another building on the courtyard. The fried rice arrives, but pretty cool, after fifteen minutes. The soup arrives one hour later and Marguerite's apple pancake is an amazing one and a half hours after my rice. It's chaotic with missing and wrong orders, though entertaining for a wee while. We go for a walk, with some people still not having their food after nearly two hours. The whole lunch stop takes three hours. Katy, I notice, doesn't take any responsibility for this fiasco. A Tibetan Fawlty Towers. We are on the coach again for a relatively short drive to Shegar. After half an hour the driver hits a bump and swerves violently. This brings down the big kitbag and I only just manage to stop it hitting us but a rucksack hits Damien hard on his head. It could have been worse.

We are, again, in bleak grey countryside with some primitive farming here and there. Nothing is green and it looks very barren. Some fields are being ploughed by donkeys, some other fields are being sown with seeds by women and girls and old men carrying baskets of yak dung. White washed houses, bright in the afternoon sun. And a new railway coming their way soon - it will change all of this and maybe not for the better. We pull off the main road for half a mile from the main town and along a dirt track and into a courtyard and in front of us a sprawling concrete 'Qomolangma Hotel'. As we queue at reception, I notice that it brags it has 100 rooms, but so does Greenock prison. Good thing is we all have our own room. I'm on the second floor and it's a very small room, but with en-suite. Really dodgy wiring but there is electricity so a last chance to get everything charged. Dinner will be at 7:30pm, which is fine and we are eating here. I meet Marguerite and Karen in the bar and catch up on journals. John joins us and I think this is as busy as the bar gets when more of the team comes in. Dinner is at the usual revolving tables and the food is much the same, although they will bring another plate of any dish if you ask. Have five cups of green tea and we discuss the plan for tomorrow, which is to visit the Dzong, or Fort at Shegar. Tonight we hear that Damien isn't feeling well. It is an early night for the rest of us and hopefully no barking dogs here. Apparently, you can buy a Chinese Kalashnikov cheaply, I'm told.

Friday 23rd April – Shegar – Tibet.

I consider taking Diamox this morning, but I'll see how I cope with the climb up to the fort. Breakfast for me is a banana, a boiled egg and plenty of green tea and I feel really good this morning and we set off - without Damien, to the old town at 9:40am. To start with we go to the wrong hill but we have a guide hired and he gets us sorted. It's a clear, cool morning with no wind and cloudless skies again. We nearly didn't climb at all. Since Katy was last here in 2007, it has become a restricted area but Kusang got us special permission this morning. The Dzong is actually a combination of monastery, fort and safe retreat, a relic from Tibet's turbulent past when Tibetan chiefs were regularly at war with each other. Chris Bonington describes it as the most spectacular fort in Central Asia. It looks really steep but our guide takes us round the back of the fort and we have a bit of scrambling to get to the top. Some imposing rocks to clamber over and we have done well and are up there with the others, although we take it easy too. Just after an hour we're at the top and highest yet at almost 14,000 feet.

We are surrounded by bright prayer flags and in the
distance, I can see Everest. This is my first sight of its north face
but it looks very far away. We drink lots of water and soak up the
sunshine and views. We still have Beijing cookies and eat some of
these too. We go down a different way, less steep and with great
views of the white-washed houses in the town and men ploughing
and women sowing, almost biblical. I photograph piles of bricks
made from mud and straw and baked in the sun. As we pass a
man ploughing with a horse, one of our guys asks for a go and he

gets a good photograph. So, in the warm sunshine we leave to go back to the hotel for lunch. Not hungry at all. It's the usual stuff. I never thought I'd get fed up eating Chinese meals but I am. Drink plenty of green tea to rehydrate. No problems with altitude at all. We go for a walk after lunch. Our hotel is in a sort of compound and we walk out to the dirt track road heading into town. School must have just come out and there are lots of kids about. The usual 'hello' and 'how are you', to which we reply amid giggles from them. At one point three older girl's come up to us and one touches Marguerite's blonde hair and shoulder as if she wasn't real. We must look odd to them.

On the outskirts of the town, we head back. I've lots of repacking to do and tomorrow we leave for Base Camp so we need to get things sorted for a different kind of life for the next few weeks. And it's taken nearly two weeks to get here as well. But we're tourists just now, not climbers and that will be a hard transformation. This is so unlike previous trips out here. I meet John and Karen in the bar before we all go into dinner. They walked into the town and Karen has a cracking silver bracelet she bought very cheaply. John says he can feel the altitude here but so far so good for me. Dinner is the usual selection and green tea, and a beer, but an early night as we will be having an early breakfast at 7:30am. In my room I consider getting a wake-up call, only to realise there is no phone.

Saturday 24th April – Shegar – Tibet.

I'm not really hungry so a light breakfast for me and surprisingly, we set off on time at 8:30am on another sunny day. I make sure the bags behind us are better packed. Damien says he feels better but it means he's done no walks since he came. It was a good confidence boost to me being able to do them OK, but really we have done next to nothing since we arrived in China. As we leave Shegar, the tarmac stops and we are on dirt. I can hardly believe we are doing this journey in coaches rather than 4X4's. Everything we pass is a Toyota Land Cruiser. No doubt it's cheaper but what this is doing to the suspension horrifies me. After another Army checkpoint we start to climb and I can see the road away ahead and with clouds of dust from the odd vehicle making its way up or down. This is the road the Chinese built to support their Everest Expedition and for taking the Olympic Flame to the summit. The bends are like Alpine passes I've driven over from Italy into Switzerland and sometimes we almost have to stop to get round them. The engine is straining now as we get to the top of the Pang La pass at 17,000 feet. As we get there, our coach catches in the wind a load of prayer flags and drags them down. Bad Karma I think and even the driver looks apprehensive.

The views are spectacular and of course we can see Everest pretty close now with white plumes coming off it horizontally which means hurricane winds up there. Also in front of us is Makalu, 27,594', Lhotse, 27,883' and Cho Oyu at 26,928' and of course, Pumori, 22,864', lurking in the background looking scary. Everyone is filming or taking photographs and, of course, there are vendors selling the usual beads and bangles even up here. Soon we were rattling and banging down to 13,700 feet and at one point as we drove over this rough road, there was a bang louder than usual. We stop for the driver and his pal to have a look. The suspension must get wrecked doing this. Another checkpoint, this time just to show the drivers papers, not our passports. From here we have to climb again to 17,000 feet and it's hard on the coach - and the driver - to get us up here. It takes almost an hour to get to 16,400 feet and we stop for a toilet break at some concrete buildings. They are really disgusting. Soon we passed 'tent city', which used to be at Base camp, but the Chinese moved them miles back to here. You can stay here and share a room, or a bed with locals. It's cheap but has its obvious risks of hookers and dodgy alcohol.

Then it must be just over ten minutes and we can see Base camp and what must be a hundred tents across a frozen river. The first coach crashes through the ice and into the river but keeps going and they make it OK. Our driver won't do it so we have to walk - with our kit. Soon there are guys appearing to say don't lift any bags we will do it, go and get coffee. So we do and meet Duncan Chessell, the Expedition leader, who shows us sleeping bags, down jackets and says do nothing just now, be aware of the altitude, we will have a briefing at 2:00pm after lunch. We can choose our individual own tents, which are all big, yellow maybe three-man types. We grab a down jacket each - no smalls - and even the mediums look huge. The Base Camp here was first used by the 1924 British Everest expedition. The site has a couple of permanent structures and a small Chinese Army post. The first thing I notice is the cold wind coming from the direction of Everest. So, we go and pick our tents. We are next to John and Karen and we are at the extremity of the tents with the tent doors facing away from the wind. I have to tighten some ropes and the tents are held down by piles of rocks. Sleeping bags are brought to us and insulated sleeping mats. I get my gear sorted as best I can. There are a lot of other tents dotted about from other groups.

Lunch is in the larger of two mess tents. We are told the teams will split, with the summit team and the people only going to Advanced Base Camp (ABC) in here and us, the North Col team, in the smaller mess tent. Lunch is freshly baked rolls with chopped tomato and cucumber and cheese. All with black tea for a change and I have five cups. There is a flat screen TV hitched up to a laptop and a lot of charging points for our stuff. The electricity is from solar panels and a generator runs for a few hours each day too. We have access to the best, paid-for weather reports it seems. And we are here four nights.

We are introduced to our Sherpa guides, Prem and Dawa. There are a couple of changes to the published itinerary we need to know about. We will now go to interim camp for an overnight stay and come back here the next day. At ABC we will have two rest days after climbing Lhakpa Ri, before attempting the North Col. On the way down we can stay a night at interim camp if we don't want to do it in one long day. Duncan says the maximum we can do today is a short walk to the blue lakes or to the memorial cairns. No uphill walking today as we have to acclimatise carefully. We all have to change our watches to Nepalese time as that's what they are using here as Expedition time.

On the way to my tent I talk to Dawa, one of the two North Col Sherpas. He is wearing trainers and I remark that they will be good on glaciers. He laughs and says he has been up at ABC putting up our tents and even up on the North Col and says conditions were so warm that he could have worn his trainers. He also says this year Lhakpa Ri will be easier as it is all blue ice with no snow covering at all, so no problem with hidden crevasses. That's great news for us all and I mention how clean Base Camp is after all I've read and he says it's all down to the Chinese being very strict. And there are no oxygen canisters lying about now - they are now all made of spun carbon fibre and are very expensive so they are collected and shipped overland to Poisk, the manufacturer, in North-West Russia to be refilled by that company. They have to go overland as no airline will carry them, empty or not. High altitude Sherpas can earn up to $1000 a day collecting them above 24,000 feet right to the summit, but it's very high-risk work. In my yellow tent I sit and think that here I am, fulfilling a long held ambition. And this cold afternoon in southern Tibet I'm here to climb on the world's highest mountain on its northern side in the next few weeks. I feel very small against its enormity, which looms in the distance. And I feel a bit scared too.

The paid for weather reports from a Swiss company, Geostat, have come in and Duncan says that the forecast isn't looking good with high winds for the next few days and a snowstorm predicted for Sunday. It may miss us, but it looks like it will drop a lot of snow on the mountains, particularly on Everest and the North Col. We are told there are two toilets, basically big, draughty, wooden boxes with a door and a flushing system using jugs of water, from a big drum inside. It's a sort of western type with a makeshift seat, only we are asked not to pee into it as it fills the tank quickly and all of the waste has to be collected and disposed of by the Chinese and paid for of course. There is toilet paper and hand washing gel too. There are two showers which are just canvas sheets round an aluminium frame with a battery pump to a shower head. The cook will boil a jug of water for it. I'm not tempted today. Amazingly there is no litter anywhere, nor the stacks of broken glass that Bonington found here. Back in my tent I feel a bit dizzy from moving about too fast but otherwise OK. I get my stuff sorted for sleeping tonight although I feel I could sleep right now. Marguerite and I are going to walk to the 'blue lakes', which are up the valley and walk with the remains of the Rongbuk glacier on our right and try out the down jackets too.

We walk slowly and it's easy to get out of breath. It's really windy and dusty and we have our facemasks and sunglasses on, but that doesn't stop the dust getting into our hair and eyes. It takes an hour to get there and we have left the path a couple of times to look for them. This time we are right at them and yes, they are incredibly blue. They are formed from the glaciers melt-water. In the far distance we can see the blue ice pinnacles of the Rongbuk glacier at the foot of Everest, some ten miles away from us, but looking closer. To the Tibetans it is Qomolangma, the Goddess Mother of the World, to the Nepalese, Sagamartha. On early British maps it was just Peak 15 before it was named after George Everest in 1865. We have only ascended a couple of hundred feet coming up here and it's good to have the wind on our backs and the track is slightly downhill. As we approach the flat barren area of the camp, we pass the Chinese Army Expedition base, which is huge. Their teams are already at ABC or the North Col. This year, they have been nominated to put up the fixed ropes - from the base of the North Col to almost the top - or rather, their Sherpas have done it. The team that does it then charges the other teams at $200 per person for using them apparently. They have a noisy generator, which we will get used to hearing as the freezing wind is blowing the sound to our camp. As Palin said in 'Himalaya', Everest base camp is nowhere as romantic as it sounds. Not that it's any better at the other base camp in Nepal, which I visited eight years ago.

At nearly 6:00pm, we get back to the tents and grab our journals and water bottles - they will be filled with hot water each night for us to put into our sleeping bags. It gives you heat during the cold nights and you have a drink ready next morning before the 'bed-tea' comes to the tent. Duncan has advised against going to bed too early as you just wake up earlier, since we've changed our watches, we are operating two and half hours ahead. The mess tent slowly fills with ten of us. Damien joins us but he's not well and no Diane either as she hasn't arrived yet. Dinner is indeterminate soup, but hot and OK. The main course, my least favourite meal of dhal bat, but this one has real meat in it and good vegetables and this is followed by boiled apple slices and warm custard and stacks of black tea which you prepare yourself from three or four big Chinese two-litre vacuum flasks. Torrey, the doctor, comes in to say that tonight is important - if we survive tonight good and well, but we must expect to feel bad tomorrow too and I'm still wondering about starting the Diamox. The cook comes in with a pad and asks for breakfast orders - no choice, you get what he cooks or you can just get cereal. There will be porridge for everyone too. I go for a cooked breakfast. Outside the black, Himalayan sky is filled with amazing stars and I remember Andrew Greig's description when he was here about the clear night sky being like a big smashed chandelier. We will follow his footsteps much of the way.

It's really cold, so not much hanging about star gazing and I'm soon glad to be out of the wind. I take a half Diamox tablet to Marguerite's tent and I take half as well. We both agree we need all the help we can get, especially tonight. So, although it's only 8:30pm, it's still later on the Chinese time we got up with today. I sleep OK but need a pee three times due to black tea and Diamox doing its work. A pee bottle is a necessity here. It's a stormy night and I can hear other tents flapping like mad in the wind. Feel good being warm and secure against it. In previous expeditions you would be writing letters home from here but now, thanks to China Telecom, I can phone and text home as easily as being at home. In fact, the signal is better here in remote Tibet than it is at home in Lanark.

Sunday 25th April – Everest Base Camp – Tibet.

I wake up as it gets light and it's great to know I can just lie here as breakfast isn't till eight. I'm up and dressed before the tea will arrive at each tent with a couple of smiling assistant cooks - just boys. You have to ask for black tea, with no sugar. Tea arrives and we have it outside our tents. Anyway, it turns out Marguerite has two sleeping bags and has used the spare as an extra layer - she also has two down jackets. That's because before the briefing we threw all the stuff we were given into my tent and someone has put the extra things into the empty tent. Going to the toilet only to find being first there in the morning means that to get the flushing water, you need to break the ice on the water barrel with your bare hand. I then go to the mess tent for my cooked breakfast, which is, this morning, two slices of toast, two slices of warm tomato and a sort of chopped warm Spam. A lot of tea for me as well and sweet digestive biscuits. And another half tablet of Diamox. No Damien this morning and Linda and Meerie don't feel good and Simon has been sick. Most people didn't sleep well and some were too cold. And this is just base camp. Everyone is moving slowly this morning as if they were wading through treacle. Everest is clear and trailing its 100 miles an hour white plume of ice crystals towards Bengal.

We plan to walk back to the blue lakes this morning and film some shots of Everest as it's very clear, but windy. Our get up is a down jacket, sunglasses and face mask and a hat - we look like terrorists. We go maybe a bit faster today and I film a yak train coming back from ABC. The herders with their long black plaited hair and turquoise stones in their ears and knives on their hips stare at us. They ask for money but I try to tell them I've been filming Everest, not them. The two Rongbuk glaciers meet not far from here to form the central Rongbuk glacier and come down to 300 yards from base camp under a grey covering of stones and dirt. We walk back a bit quicker today and it's so good to get out of the constant wind and dust and nice to have your own space. And so, I put my life in order - head-torch, water bottle, socks, pee bottle, pens, journal, gloves, lip salve, etc., all the things you need to have to hand. I suppose the tent is a sanctuary or a prison depending on how you feel. I'm feeling fine inside this yellow glow. Reflecting on how long it's taken to get here but also thinking of the first Everest expeditions who came by ship to India and then overland from Darjeeling - as did Mallory and Irvine, whose footsteps we will follow from here. Apparently, Mallory hated Tibet and its people. I lay thinking about what is ahead for us as we follow in their tracks, for over an hour. At lunch, Frank can't eat anything and Linda can only take hot water and dozes off from time to time. Meerie, who has a special diet, is struggling to eat it. The news is that Mr Kong is really sick and both him and Damien have suspected cerebral oedema and have to be taken to lower heights as soon as possible - a Land Cruiser is on its way. Torrey has said there is no other option and only quick action will work. So, suddenly, we have quite a serious situation.

Lunch is a quiet affair with two team members down and out already. We have a hot roll with cheese and tuna with coleslaw and a few hard potatoes. The talk of course is about Damien and the money he was raising for charity. It turns out he's never climbed outside the UK, so has no experience of altitude and not a lot of hills in Essex, which is all a bit of a mystery. So, Mr Kong and Damien will be taken to the border town of Zhangmu to recover, and of course possibly return if they are able. They could have gone to hospital in Lhasa but it isn't free and you need to supply your own food, which complicates the logistics. There is no mountain rescue here. In fact, there are no rescue helicopters at all, unlike Nepal. No plans this afternoon, so I just sit in the mess tent, which with the sunshine is quite comfortable. We also have a couple of bottled gas fires for the evening but felt no effect from them last night. I sit here chatting, drinking tea and a couple of cans of coke. I got talking to Frank who has been here before in 2002. The weather was so bad they struggled to get to ABC, then got trapped there for a week by severe storms and had to abandon the North Col and come back here and go home, having used up all the time on their visas. He's a gadget man and has plotted our elevation on his Garmin since we left Lhasa. He has amazingly expensive gear and is quite laid back. I like him.

The plan tomorrow is to walk to the Rongbuk monastery - the highest monastery in the world - or to the Rongbuk caves where the monks hid when the Chinese bombed the monastery. We won't have time to do both and I think I'd rather see the caves, but a decision will be made by our guides in the morning. We all gave our best wishes to the not very well looking Mr Kong and Damien. Then we go back to the still-warm tent to tidy up and prepare for tomorrow and I go back to the mess tent after a couple of hours and sit writing on my own which is quite nice. A boy brings fresh hot water for tea and has a look at what I'm writing and we try to chat for a bit. Still plenty of biscuits on the table and now in the routine of having my money with me, my passport, a head-torch, water bottle and Diamox. The wind is now rattling this big tent hard. So I write for a while, chat with others as they come in and out and soon we are all in here and dinner is served. I take a quick half Diamox first. Tonight we are having pumpkin soup, which is really good. However, next is cold pasta - it gets cold quickly on the stainless steel plates - with a spicy sauce and some, almost raw cauliflower. Not great. The sweet saved the meal as it was banana pie and warm custard and washed down with a gallon of weak tea. Then the routine of getting a water bottle filled with hot water and off to bed at 8:15pm. Outside my tent it is blowing a gale so check our guy-lines before we crawl into our respective tents.

Monday 26th April – Everest Base Camp – Tibet.

The wind has dropped overnight and for the first time I wake up to a quiet tent. I slept well last night and warm too. No sore head at all yet. As bed tea arrives I'm already outside in the early morning sunshine. It feels so great standing here drinking tea with Everest in the foreground and surrounded by all these yellow tents. And people appearing from their tents, shouting 'morning' and looking around themselves. Not so good is the fact that we both have flecks of blood around our noses, but I remember that happening before and it's not terminal I hope, just a wee bit of haemorrhaging.

We are off to the caves after breakfast and as I have ordered a cooked one, I get the same tomato, Spam and toast concoction as yesterday, but it's not that bad. So at 9:30am we all set off down past the army post and some of the summit guys are with us too. It's been decided that the Rongbuk Monastery, or what's left of it, is too far away so it will just be a visit to the caves. Dawa says we will be back for a late lunch. It's easy going downhill and the wind behind us and we reach the caves in just over an hour. Outside there is a smouldering juniper bush - a sign that someone is here and some monks do live here permanently. Dawa and Prem look everywhere but no monks are found. Gone to the monastery for chanting they reckon so we wander about aimlessly. The place is huge and there are passages and terraces everywhere. Dawa won't take us down into the cave system as he's scared he will get us lost. The monks hid down here when the Chinese Air-force bombed the monastery. At an outside altar he tells us about a 'sky burial' he witnessed. As the ground is either frozen or just too hard to dig - and the fact that there are no trees for wood to burn corpses, sky burials still take place but are frowned on by the Chinese. Basically, your body is placed on a remote altar-stone, the Lama or chief monk then chops you up, sprinkles you with millet seed and leaves you to the vultures. Oh yes, you have to be dead first. Environmentally sound too. I might go this way on my local hill, Tinto, myself.

So, instead of a religious day we head to tent city - the sprawling mass of tents the Chinese moved here from base camp as it was a shambles. We all go into a big tent for tea. Well, not real tea but sweet and salty tea made with yak's butter - it's called 'bo-cha'. It's been described as liquid gorgonzola. Outside are lots of stalls all selling much the same stuff you could get in any of the towns we passed through. Incredibly there is a post office so you can send a postcard with an Everest Base Camp postmark. I give the tea a miss and buy nothing. Heading back uphill is pretty hard going and the wind has got up too - and the dust. Everyone has masks and glasses on and it gives us a feel of what is to come. Everyone is taking it easy and it takes an extra half hour for the return journey. Get back in time for lunch, which turns out to be chickpeas, chopped tomato and cucumber with two chapatis and real tea. This afternoon we talked to our team about playing a DVD in the South African mess tent. They share our facilities but are at ABC and won't be back for a couple of days and they allow us to use their tent. Firstly, they have more beer and secondly, they have brought leather seats from Kathmandu and their mess tent is much posher than ours. We agree to meet at 4:30pm for those who want to watch the Local Hero DVD, which Marguerite has brought with her. We will watch it on their flat screen TV. Roughing it at Base Camp!

As we share a beer in the tent, we are told that someone has been killed today on the North Col. His partner and him were pulled off the fixed ropes by a falling ice pinnacle. They were Hungarians and part of the team led by Jamie McGuiness. The guy who survived braked with his axe, his partner didn't have his axe out and was swept into a crevasse with tons of snow, As there are no helicopters or rescue services in Tibet, unlike Nepal, his body has been left there. The Sherpas have carried the other guy out, badly injured, to base camp, then Land Cruiser to hospital in Lhasa. Makes us all think a bit. Watching the film is a bit odd with these other nationalities, but I guess it's a universal story and we all enjoy having a beer and a laugh together but I can't believe how emotional I feel seeing places I've been to in the film, having stayed in the Pennan Inn long before the film was made. Am I homesick? Me? Goodness, tears in my eyes!

After six we all head back to our tents to get stuff ready for the night ahead, especially the all-important water bottle for later. I grab my journal, give Marguerite a shout and we head down to our own mess tent. It's freezing already with the wind still strong and just a relentless freezing wind. Dinner tonight starts with chicken soup and Dawa and Prem join us - maybe for reassurance after today's news. The main course is yak steak and then some fresh fruit and a great dinner. Dawa tells us that Damien is leaving

Kathmandu for England tomorrow, so we won't see him again. Mr Kong has been summoned back to Beijing - presumably to be shot. A replacement will be sent out. It seems colder tonight so no one hangs about much and I'm heading to my tent at 8:30pm. Feels great to get into my sleeping bag and get my head on my son Finlay's wee black, fleece pillow he used at Scout camp. It's also the only fabric that doesn't catch my beard!

Tuesday 27th April – Everest Base Camp – Tibet.

The plan today is to trek to between 18,700 feet and 19,300 feet for serious acclimatisation. We will walk up the frozen river behind the camp and we leave after breakfast at 9:30am. I have just porridge this morning and a couple of biscuits with my tea. It feels fine though but it's cold and clear and not too windy. Funny how you just get used to getting out your tent and seeing Everest in front of you! We set off at a ridiculously fast pace. The summit team are doing this too but these guys are super-fit. We hang back with some others at our own pace and quite a few are behind us. The going is rough with no path at all and a risk of going over on an ankle. Dawa is at the head of the team and so far ahead I can't see him. Prem takes up the rear, but I can't see him either and we come to a point where we have to cross the river. It's semi-frozen but how thick is the ice? There is water flowing underneath. I don't fancy the prospect of crashing through the ice but we can't see where the others crossed safely. So we just take a chance and show others behind where we crossed. Eventually we catch up with Katy and the lead team. It's taken almost three hours to get here and we are only at 18,000 feet. No chance we can go higher in the timeframe. Why didn't we just get a packed lunch? So, we head back and it's just as precarious. This I think is poor planning, at least for the North Col team.

We do get back in time for a late lunch and as we sit through the salad and chips, there is a bit of discussion about today's trek. And about tomorrow when we climb to intermediate camp to sleep there one night. Today didn't boost anyone's confidence. We all have a bit of sorting out to do, deciding what to take up and as we will all have to share a tent, I decide I'll risk a shower. Now this consists of a canvas frame and no floor. You take all your clothes off and the cook brings the hot water, shoves in a small plastic hose, switches on a battery pump and you dance about trying to get the warmish trickles on your body, but I felt cleaner - if colder. My highest shower so far. Then back to the tent, thankfully heated by the dying sun and get the kit sorted for tomorrow and a supply of Diamox for us both.

I walked down with Stefan, the German accountant tonight for dinner. He asks about Diamox and I say to see Torrey who I know has a big supply. He's getting the reputation for always being last in for meals as he's always sleeping. Dinner tonight is garlicky, indeterminate soup then rice with vegetables and spicy chicken and almost everyone takes a second helping, which is always offered. We have cake afterwards, which is really good. All of us are a bit hyped up about going higher in the morning. So, the usual pattern, a bit of chit-chat while we wait on our now, hot, water bottles coming back from the cooking tent, a pee in the dark on the way back to the tent, inside out of the now strong wind, into the sleeping bag, head-torch on and try to heat up. Again, the wind pulls at the tent fabric all night.

Wednesday 28th April – Everest Base Camp – Tibet.

Bed tea is a bit early this morning and I hear Marguerite saying 'yes please', but forgetting to say 'no sugar' and then her expletive as she tastes the sugary tea. Even in Nepal the tea boys were amazed that someone would drink tea without sugar. Mine is straight black, as usual. Then some teeth-brushing in the early sunshine and down for breakfast which is omelette with toast for me. Stefan goes off to see the doc and comes back with a bag of Diamox. We leave on time at 9:00am. Porters will carry our sleeping bags and down jackets to intermediate camp and also rations for tonight. We are dressed for cold weather though and especially for protection against the wind. Although we are travelling light I still seem to have a lot of stuff with me and of course two litres of water. Intermediate camp is at 19,300 feet and it will test our acclimatisation. Still feel pretty good and no headaches, or even sleeplessness. We again set off too fast and again, some of us decide we will go at our own pace. There is no rush to get there as we are only going to sleep there. We have a packed lunch as well so no pressure on us to reach camp early. The team walked up past the blue lakes where we have been before and onto the old Chinese Camp 2 of their 60's expedition. Although there are a few ahead of us, there are more behind but we all catch up here. At this point, Frank points to the sky and something I've never seen before, a 'sunbow'. This happens when ice crystals in the air surround the sun and form a perfect circular rainbow around it. Very pretty and I photograph it without success. You would need a better camera than mine to capture it.

We all drink water or juice here but suddenly Simon is violently sick. I know he's not been feeling great for a few days but this doesn't look good. However, on the plus side it has stopped his over-loud laughter so not all bad. From here the track gets steep as we head over to the East Rongbuk Glacier. We keep to our own pace again and higher up we are met with a huge yak train coming from ABC. It's a narrow path on a mountainside but the guys divert the beasts away from us. Even so, the path is quite busy with people coming back from the higher camps. They all look very tired. You're supposed to enjoy this are you not? The yak train has held up those further behind but after about two and a half hours from Base Camp, Marguerite, Grant, Phil and I stop for lunch. These two guys seem very fit and have built up a good relationship with friendly rivalry between the Englishman and the Kiwi. We are at the old Mallory camp, although just a rickle of stone walls now. Packed lunch is two wee slices of Spam, a boiled egg, a cinnamon croissant and two slices of very hard cheese.

We all top up our fluid level but I've not had a pee since we left so already a bit dehydrated. We see some antelopes down at the glacier edge. We've now lost sight of Everest but behind us Pumori looks more frightening than Everest. And the darkening sky behind it, a bit worrying too. The 'path' from here is very rough and hard going. My altimeter says we still have 800 feet to go, so a bit of climbing yet. And the sky behind us is now black and there is snow in the air so we stop to put waterproofs on. The forecast was for snow tonight but it looks imminent from here. If this was Scotland, the snow would have been here in ten minutes I reckon, but we only get a few light flurries. This will be the only time we will put on our waterproof jackets. There are lots of ups and downs and the terrain a uniform grey of rock and rubble from the glacier. Away ahead we now see the dim yellow of the tents at the camp. The snow is getting heavier but the sting in the tail is the steep section up to the camp and we catch up with Stefan who has had to take a few rests. And so grateful to be up on the rocky plateau where there are ten tents and a big mess tent. Exhausted, and by now it's almost dark.

   We just chuck the rucksacks into an empty tent and head to the mess tent. The snow is heavy and horizontal. No heaters in here, just humans to heat the place up and we're not first in. Some others must be forty-five minutes behind us, caught in the blizzard but Prem is with them. And it's great to get hot tea, which the cook here has brought in and asks if we would like soup. It's snowing, we're cold and exhausted, it's over 19,000 feet - of course we would like soup! A hero though. We are all in there when the last people arrive. All as shattered looking as we were. Tea and soup partially revive us as the big tents flap and cracks in the snowy wind. A generator provides light for the mess tent but only one cook and an assistant up here. There is also a radio and our man radio's Base Camp to say we have all arrived and then to Advanced Base Camp to inform Duncan who says it's snowing hard there too. So, off to the shared tent to sort our stuff, unpack down jackets and sleeping bags and just lie there until dinner, trying to keep warm. We talk through the day and about going back down tomorrow. Marguerite says she thought you were supposed to climb high and sleep low. Good point and we're doing the opposite. There must be a plan.

At dinnertime the gong goes and normally I would be there already, writing or chatting but I have to drag myself. Marguerite can't get up and has a sore head and feels too tired so I go myself with our water bottles to get filled with hot water. I have two plates of soup but have no appetite for more. A bit worrying that everyone is feeling a bit poorly tonight. Phil hasn't come in for dinner either. And this is just a rehearsal. It's still snowing as I get back to the tent. I give Marguerite a full tablet of Diamox and 400mg of ibuprofen and the same for me. Not a great night with broken sleep and really weird dreams and the tent being battered with snow squalls.

Thursday 29th April – Intermediate Camp – Tibet.

I have no headache this morning but feel a bit woozy. Marguerite has had a bad night and she has had to take painkillers twice during the night. She's dehydrated too and bed tea at 7:30am is appreciated. So we sit up in our sleeping bags drinking steaming hot tea and both glad to be going back to the comparative comfort of base camp. The toilet tent is a big blue plastic drum with a makeshift seat. Different, but it works fine. In the mess tent at breakfast I'm hearing that no one has had a great night. Amazingly, Stefan hasn't even brought the Diamox he was given and feels ill. Breakfast is a wee bit of omelette with a croissant and runny porridge made from millet I think. So runny I have to crumble salty biscuits into it to get a consistency. The snow is already melting and the sun is shining again but still cold and windy. Away ahead of us we can see the blueness of a big ice wall - the East Rongbuk Glacier rising into huge ice fins to form an impenetrable wall.

We are all packed and ready to leave at 9:30am. The porters have already left with our gear. As usual, Dawa leads and Prem takes up the rear. No rush again today as we are only going back to base camp. The wind is behind us and the sun is warming up our world as we set an easy pace. My back is sore from a badly balanced rucksack but we make reasonable progress although we all stop for a drink from time to time. The plan is to be at Base Camp for lunch around 1:00pm. On the way down we meet the other teams heading up - the summit team going all the way to Advanced Base Camp and the ABC team only to intermediate camp. John is carrying a really heavy load I notice as we stop to chat and Stephen behind me is coughing badly. As usual, the women are coping better. Dawa walks with us for the last half of the trek back as the others ahead know the route from here. I'm positive that when we traverse the last hillside we will be half an hour away from camp. In fact it takes three times as long to get back, which is depressing. We meet Duncan as we go in who asks how we are feeling and we all lie that we're feeling good.

We get the gear to our tents - the porters have already put our jackets and sleeping bags in. I just sit back for ten minutes resting. Then go down for lunch although I don't feel hungry at all. However, as a treat we have yak-burgers on freshly baked rolls and there's even mustard to go with it. It lifts everyone's spirits and we all talk about how we felt coming down and what ABC will be like. Dawa comes in to talk about what will happen from here. Today and tomorrow we should just rest he says. I feel I need it and later I go to my tent, now heated by the afternoon sunshine and just lie there for a couple of hours thinking about what's ahead and how I'll cope. Snow is forecast tonight too. However, I have a lot of sorting out to do as well as my kitbag that will go to ABC can be no more than 20kg says Duncan as it will be weighed before going onto a yak's back. Phil and I go down for dinner about 6:00pm for us both to catch up with our journals. I'm not hungry tonight either and plan just to have soup. Unusually, it's Marguerite, not Stefan who is last in. Tonight we are in the big mess tent next to the cooking tent as both other teams are now away for a few days. As the main course arrives I suspect it's the dreaded dal bhat, but it turns out to be roasted chicken legs with mashed potatoes with French beans and a nice gravy. Great, then a pineapple slice with custard and I ate the lot. Despite this I don't feel 100%, which I put down to exhaustion and dehydration. So, as always here, an early night and I'm grateful to be in my tent. However, I must have peed nearly two litres during the night as I was up three times. Diamox side-effects I'm sure. I could hear snow blasting the tent and nice to be in here warm and dry, so warm, for the first time here, I took my socks off. I think Margaret leaves the UK today. I sent a text to her from this tent to confirm.

Friday 30th April – Everest Base Camp – Tibet.

I wake up at first light as usual, about 5:00am, but that's Nepal time I have to remind myself. My feet are freezing cold and I can't find my discarded socks of course. Fall asleep again until 7:00am when I hear the bed-tea gong. New socks on when I get up - the other pair somewhere in my sleeping bag. As I go out to brush my teeth, there is a whoosh of snow sliding off my tent and I give Marguerite a shout. She's slept well too and we stand in the new whiteness of base camp drinking our tea - without sugar. Just a sense now of us all here collectively preparing ourselves for the hardships to come and a sense of being very insignificant in this vast, white amphitheatre. There's only an inch of snow lying but it changes everything. There is no wind at all this morning - a first and it's actually quite mild. Everyone is feeling a bit better at breakfast except Meerie and Linda who said they were very cold last night. Anyway, breakfast is some scrambled eggs and a cinnamon bun. Last day here so, after breakfast I put my cameras on the chargers in the mess tent. I've already charged the video camera and our phones and the last chance for a few days.

It's too nice and sunny a day not to do something although we're still not to do anything too strenuous, I decided to walk to the memorials to climbers who have died on Everest. It's only about half a mile to most of them on an escarpment next to a river running from the glacier. The river is the Dzakar Chhu. The river flows, its name doesn't. Among the memorials are ones to Pete Boardman and Joe Tasker whose books I have read, their names scratched into slate. It was Charles Clark, a team member who chiselled this back in 1982 on a slate from the 1924 expedition memorial. The Tibetans built the cairn. With Marguerite's spare camera I take lots of shots here with Everest in the background, including a huge Chinese monument to Everest with the wrong height given. They've refused to acknowledge the American GPS height apparently. I suppose it's their mountain. In 2020 they actually agreed with everyone else. On the other side of the escarpment and out of the biting wind we saw a family of Marmot's running for cover. They have been sunbathing no doubt. I walk back to the tents knowing that we will be doing more walking soon and we are both keen to get moving after all the hanging about. We both take our sleeping bags out to air in the wind and I go down to the mess tent to charge my mobile and camcorder. Inside the tent is so hot that Phil is actually reading his book outside but out of the wind. This is the first day since we came here that it's been warm enough to do that.

I go back to the tent but sit outside on a rock contemplating the fact that we are soon to leave the relative comfort of base camp for the unknown, and most certainly a colder unknown. I also think about having a shower but the thought of being wet in this wind makes me shiver and then the gong goes for lunch. All my electronic gear is now fully charged and ready to last a week. Lunch is boiled potatoes with yak cheese melted over them with a spoonful of small tomatoes and chopped mushrooms in an indeterminate sauce but quite tasty too. After lunch I get my stuff packed into the yak kitbag. I intend on carrying the minimum so as to make it easier on me. I won't exceed the limit of 20kg either. Despite the afternoon getting cooler I go down to see the cook, Geylu, and order hot water for a shower. Ten minutes later I'm stripping off in a canvas shower carefully at over 17,000 feet up in the Himalayas. The battery pump isn't great and a jug would have helped but I felt better after it and it wasn't as bad as I had expected and I washed some clothes too. I pass Marguerite going to do some last minute clothes washing as I come back from the shower.

We will need to double check later that we have everything packed that we will need. However all our climbing gear is already in our kit-bags. We went down to the mess tent early for dinner and all packed and double-checked for tomorrow. We have a can of beer each diluted with a can of Sprite and catch up on our journals and we all have a discussion about tomorrow. Outside the wind is getting up and it's really cold. All four gas fires are on but it's not even warm in here tonight. Frank fixes the improvised door closing rope and weight contraption, which helps a bit. My experience in Nepal is that everyone leaves doors open. Just before dinner, Lawrence, the Swiss girl, appears with a load of wet clothes and proceeds to put them round a fire, thus blocking the little heat available. And without asking if it is OK. So the tent cools a bit more. A few looks exchanged around the table but no one says anything. A few people still are not feeling 100% with altitude.

Soup, totally unidentifiable is first on the menu and we all debate what it might have come from. We ask Geylu - 'vegetable' he says which clears things up. Next is a sort of spag-bol dish but with chunks of rapidly cooling cauliflower. Not too bad but cold pasta isn't great. It's the stainless steel plates that cool so quickly. Next is warm tinned mango with syrup so quite good and of course gallons of tea. So, with our water bottles full of very hot water we venture into the freezing darkness and a quick last pee into the blackness and I get into my welcome sleeping bag. I am keeping my socks on tonight. It's not even eight o'clock and I lie awake for ages which isn't a problem and after a couple of hours, the wind stops rattling the tent and I must have drifted off to sleep. Only to be woken by shouting somewhere. A few of the summit Sherpas had come down from ABC today and must be celebrating.

Saturday 1st May – Everest Base Camp – Tibet.

I wake at 5:30am and I feel good this morning. I lie long enough for someone else to break the ice in the toilet cubicle. During the night I peed one and a half litres so Diamox and too much tea no doubt. I can hear Marguerite moving about and shout good morning. She says I was snoring last night. That I say must have been the can of beer. The plan is to get our ABC gear loaded onto the yaks for 9:30am but we are ahead of the game with almost everything done so we stand in the morning sun drinking our 'bed tea'. For the first time there is no spindrift coming off the summit of Everest, meaning little wind up there. Duncan thinks the Chinese Army team might push for the summit today. The Sherpas collect our gear for the yaks and our tents are collapsed and taken away. It feels quite final. A guy arrives in the middle of the camp on a motorbike with a passenger. The passenger with cool looking shades is the top yak man who has a sort of scale and he weighs each bag before it goes onto the yak. It's something like $300 per yak load and all of our teams will need well over two hundred yak loads for supplying ABC. That means just to get all the expedition gear and regular food supplies up to ABC costs around $60,000 and that is why a big expedition from this side of Everest is so expensive.

We will go at our own pace this morning as everyone knows the way to Interim Camp. It's really quite warm as we set off behind the usual suspects. I feel much better than last time and we both feel we are moving a bit quicker with less breathlessness.

We both have plenty of sunscreen on today as we will walk into the sun for a few miles. As we did last time, we stopped at the old Chinese camp two for a rest and a drink. Then it's just a steady pull uphill but again, we both feel stronger this time and there are no yak trains to dodge. In fact the trail is really quite empty and we make good progress to stop for a longer break at the old Mallory camp. As we sit in the sunshine, a grey haired man, oddly with no sunglasses approaches us in the opposite direction. With him are a tall boy and a girl. We say hello and they stop not far from us. This boy is the thirteen-year-old who is here to climb Everest and his father was cut on the face when the ice pinnacle hit the Hungarians and killed one of them. The father and son were climbing on the North Col close to them. They are heading to BC to rest. The kid makes it to the summit we hear weeks later. The rest of the trek up the glacier was uneventful but the yak team overtook us before we got into the camp. We had taken almost an hour off our time, which we were pleased with. At the camp, our bags are already unloaded, and the yaks are being fed and watered. They will stay here tonight to take our gear to the temporary Changtse Camp tomorrow.

I was looking forward to a night with just our team but there are another four guys sharing the mess tent. One is Jamie McGuinness who is a well-known guide and I had corresponded with him before. His clients - they are all Everest summit bound - are a mixed bunch but a loud-mouthed American is dominating the conversation as we all go into the mess tent for tea and biscuits. We don't hang about as he is now telling everyone he is an ex-marine and of course was 'special forces'. What else? One of our group asks a question and we can still hear him answering ten minutes later. We get our stuff sorted into our now shared tent, which is still OK as the tents are big, but no option to be tidier than I usually am. We lie and talk and keep warm for a couple of hours. Later we go in early for dinner and I sit beside Grant, the Kiwi. The ex-marine is quieter now and Grant whispers to me, 'did he tell you he's been on the Moon too'? I maybe laughed too loud but it summed this guy up. He'd obviously bored everyone and no one was going to ask him anything again. Dinner was soup and dal bhat, which wasn't great but plenty of tea as well. After dinner Jamie McGuinness showed us some planned treks to remote areas in Nepal on his laptop, Dolpo and Mustang I think. Not sure if he was trying to drum up business from us but he's very enthusiastic. So an interesting night after all and with a full Diamox each, we head to the yellow tent. Good to be on our own and have some peace and quiet but I am a bit worried about Marguerite's health, in fact, very worried.

Sunday 2nd May – Interim Camp – Tibet.

I slept really well but Marguerite has a bit of a sore head but no painkillers. For some reason breakfast is early at 8:00am and we will be off at 9:00am and I don't know why as it can't be a full day walk to Changtse Camp. About three hours walk I think, anyway it's a fine morning again although there has been a powdering of snow in the night. I have the runny porridge with some crushed biscuits for breakfast. Have an awful desire for toast and jam. As we leave camp there is a big drop across a frozen river with a corresponding big rise on the other side but we take it easy up the snow slope on the other side. We passed the three women and Simon as we set our own pace. Simon isn't yet totally well but soldiers on at a slower pace. Ahead we can see the start of the spectacular ice fins of the now enlarged East Rongbuk Glacier. As yesterday, the route has lots of ups and downs and we have frequent water stops. Ahead is just ice and distant, white mountains, although we are generally walking on stones and rocks, however, under that it is still a glacier.

This is the famous 'magic highway' described by Mallory. At one point I say to Marguerite that she's slowing the pace, which she takes exception to, so she makes me go first and of course I am just as slow. It's just the altitude kicking in and I feel a bit guilty and just feeling the pressure. To show how slow we are our yak train passes us although we left well before them. As we walk I think about tonight's camp. No mess tent. No cooks. We will cook ourselves and melt what water we need from ice. And there is no shortage of that here. The yaks are carrying our dried food and sleeping bags as there will be two man tents already in place. It's beginning to feel like an expedition now. We have walked for a good two hours but nothing ahead but the ice fins of the glacier to our left and the incredible icy walls of Changtse on our right. In the middle of some rocks ahead is one of our porters from the camp with a big kettle of tea. I can hardly believe it, but he is real and the tea is brilliant. He's walked from the next camp and brewed up here for us. Incredible, but not the first time I've came across the same sort of thing. Black tea with sugar is the only option. I drink it anyway.

My feet are a bit cool too. We've been walking on snow for over an hour and we didn't expect to be on snow at this level. We have good enough boots but they are not new and I intend to leave them in Tibet for a porter. So our boots aren't as good for keeping out the cold and our plastic mountaineering boots are on a yaks back heading to ABC. We were told there would be no snow until ABC and there wasn't until a few days ago. The ice fins, now about thirty feet above us, start to drop into a tight small valley. We can see no signs of a camp although we are nearly four hours walking. As we turn left to follow the path down and really close to the glacier wall is a yellow tent. Our spirits rise and then another and another tent. It becomes quite steep and slippery going down and it starts to snow as we arrive at the camp which is about half a dozen yellow tents and a couple of other larger ones.

We have to share tents as we are at high altitude so I pick ours as the one closest to a gigantic forty-foot ice pinnacle. It is amazingly almost fluorescent icy blue - the ice fins form because of the intense sunlight and very dry air - the ice sublimates and passes straight from solid to vapour. We get our rucksacks in OK

233

but getting the yak packs down the slope towards our tent then up a short rise is a nightmare and I slip a lot. Dawa helps but he slips too - Sherpas are not immune to this! After sorting out the sleeping bags I go to meet Prem at his black tent to get our supplies. Basically it's dried stuff and I pick two bags of spicy Schewan dried noodles and some soup with a couple of packets of porridge for breakfast and of course tea bags. I also collect a stove and a couple of pans and two cups and cutlery. All of this stuff we have to re-wash with our limited water supply. There is a shortage of matches but I make sure I have a few in the box. Can you believe we're up here and short of matches? Jeez, this is an Everest expedition!

As we are short of water, we have to melt snow and ice and we get the stove going immediately for tea. We have our own biscuit supply and some nuts as well. It continues to snow and is so silent and weird with these big ice pinnacles around us. Quite magical it was and just a bit warmer. It must be forty minutes before the last of the team trek in and they look exhausted and they've been walking in the snow for at least an hour. The women are in the tent next to us and Frank is sharing with Torrey on the other side. We know this because Torrey gave him a loud bollocking for bringing snow into their tent on his boots. And, no, he didn't argue! Later he helped her climb a bit of the pinnacle using his technical ice axes to compensate.

As it's hardly mid-afternoon, we sit in the tent drinking tea with the stove working hard melting ice as we play chess. Amazingly we have not opened a book yet or listened to our iPods because there has always been company. Having said that, we realise now that we haven't played cards either, something we have always done on other expeditions in Nepal. After two bad defeats at the hands of a mercenary chess player, I go out to collect more ice. I also collect snow in a carrier bag to let it melt in the relative warmth of the tent. We are actually more comfortable in here than the mess tent because the wee stove has really warmed the place up and as it's full and we won't need it again, it's in constant use as we will need water for tomorrow's push to ABC. As the light fades, the snow gets heavier and it looks pretty serious stuff. This will have implications for everyone on the north side of Everest. However, our priority is now preparing dinner. The thought of having pot noodles at almost 20,000 feet in a blizzard isn't great but actually they are really good. The plates are too far gone for us to properly clean so we cook the noodles, add the sachet of spicy sauce and Marguerite eats from a waxed pot she had nuts in and I eat from the pot. We sit up against our yet unpacked sleeping bags on opposite sides of the tent. A beer would be good but we're too high to risk that now. It feels really good here.

The stove is still on and I've collected more snow and ice. It's stopped snowing so hard now and we are heating water for our bottles to put in our sleeping bags. It all takes ages at this altitude. We can feel the temperature drop although it's now only 7:00pm. A full Diamox each and a precautionary 5mg of Ciprofloxacin for me as my tummy has been a bit sore today. We are also using the 'spare' sleeping bag Marguerite has wangled and opened out; it gives us both some extra insulation. Our lights are out at 7:30pm but despite the hardships, this has been the best tent experience yet. Outside we can hear the faint friendly clang of yak bells above

235

the soft splatter of snow on the tent. Overall, a magical night in a unique situation I'll never forget.

Monday 4th May – Changtse Camp – Tibet.

During the night the creaks and muffled bangs from the glacier are quite worrying until you think it's been doing the same thing for thousands of years but I still think about the big ice pinnacle above us. I wake at exactly 5:30am and the inside of the tent is pure white with the frost from our condensed breath and wee ice particles dance in the light of my head-torch. Both of us have had a good night's sleep. It's too cold to go and chip ice so we make do with melting snow scooped from near the tent - avoiding any yellow stuff. Not as efficient as melting ice but it still works. Our day clothes are in our sleeping bags with us to heat up for ten minutes. At ABC we will be taking our plastic boot liners into the sleeping bags. Neither of us could be bothered with soup or porridge so we have tea and plain biscuits, some nuts and a bar each of the New Zealanders top chocolate biscuits called Tam-Tam. Not as good as a Penguin we agree. Time to get moving again and we plan to leave at 9:00am. It's a real effort to pack everything up. The cooking gear has to be handed back, sleeping bags - three of them - have to be rolled up and kit-bags packed again and water bottles filled from the pans. As I take the cooking stuff back up to Prem, I see that the yaks still have snow on their backs. They are hardy beasts. It is a fine clear morning with a light blue sky. No snow although the ice pinnacles are coated now and not so blue looking. The yaks get loaded up again.

So we head off and into the unknown a bit as we are heading to ABC which is higher than the highest 'trekking' peak' in Nepal. Three years ago we both got to the top of Mera Peak on a spectacular morning in perfect weather but it was a huge effort just to get there, take some photos and film and get down to BC. This time we will be sleeping higher than that summit for four nights, and quite a thought as we will be on the very flanks of Everest as well. So again we set our own pace still with the fangs of the glacier beside us. Their ghostly blue glow is now dampened by yesterday's snow coating. To our right is still Changtse and although it looked like a proposition on the map back in Lanark, it looks awesome from here. Very steep slopes of pure ice as far as you can see. All around the scenery is just awesome with distant white teeth of mountains appearing as we walk past valleys with other glaciers coming from them. No doubt lots of these mountains in deepest Tibet are unclimbed. As is the tradition, halfway to ABC, the yak-team overtook us. Coming down the other way, the team that only went to ABC for a few days passed us. I almost envy them going back to base camp eventually.

As happened yesterday, we are well into a three-hour walk before we see a tiny yellow tent in the distance. It's a lot higher than we are and a hard slog up to it. We get there only to be disappointed that it isn't ours. Not even nearly ours as the sprawl of summit teams goes on for about half a mile at least with some tents now below us next to the glacier we've climbed up from. There are much more tents here than at base camp. As we arrive at our clutch of tents in this city of tents, it starts to snow. Dawa is there as we arrive and gets us into a big mess tent. We're still segregated from the summit team, which is a pity but it's great to get some hot drinks. Dawa says he will sort out the tents as soon as he can. Our feet are now wet and cold and not good at 21,000 feet. The women and Simon are forty-five minutes behind us getting in and again have walked in the falling snow. When they arrive we have lunch, which is chickpeas with coleslaw, a chapati and a slice of Spam. I roll this into the chapatti but it's an effort to eat the chickpeas. Marguerite can't eat anything but a slice of spam and has a sore head. After lunch we find our tent. It has an extra layer of insulation mats. Get the sleeping bags looked out including the 'spare'. It is definitely colder up here. I go for a walk and watch some Sherpas hacking ice from the glacier wall and filling up sacks with it. It's the only source of water and all the teams here must consume huge amounts each day. Marguerite sleeps all afternoon and eventually I wrap myself in my sleeping bag and sit thinking of what's to come. Someone next to us has a wracking cough. I've never heard anyone worse.

At six the dinner gong sounded. I don't feel hungry but Marguerite has slept all afternoon and feels too ill to get up. So I take our water bottles to the mess tent to get filled with hot water and say we won't be up for dinner. Just too tired I say. Back at the tent I struggle to get her to drink. This isn't good and it's not a good place to be ill. Just after 7:00pm, Prem is outside our tent and says, "I have some macaroni and sauce for you if you want?" By now though I'm in my sleeping bag and Marguerite is sleeping so I thank him but decline. Good of him to do that though. I was prepared for a rough night and it was. Marguerite woke a couple of times and needed painkillers and water. She was very restless. And her headache just won't go. She doesn't look well at all and yet I know how strong she is when she's up against it.

Tuesday 5th May – Everest Advanced Base Camp – Tibet.

It's a freezing morning, minus twenty degrees centigrade someone says and again there are snow flurries in the air. Marguerite doesn't feel like getting up or having breakfast so I go up on my own after bed tea. Everyone asks about her and it's evident not everyone is even close to 100% at this height. No one had a great night. So not a cheery mess tent and I think only myself, Grant and Phil are feeling OK. Linda and Meerie are suffering and Diane looks ill this morning. As ever Lawrence says she feels a bit ill but looks really fit and healthy. She's actually the only one who has consistently led the team. I'm sure she was acclimatised before she came. Frank is being examined by Torrey this morning. It appears he has got a retinal haemorrhage and this is not uncommon - the inside of his eye is bleeding. I think this can happen to your brain up here as well. It's his left eye and altitude causes it. He's had it before and it can lead to permanent blindness. He asks about going up the North Col, to which Torrey says, "You can, it's your choice but you're rolling the dice with your sight".

At this low point, Duncan comes in to say we will stay here today as a storm is heading our way and it will hit Everest and the North Col but we might be sheltered a bit where we are. Torrey says it's a good idea to rest today anyway and we should all expect to feel the effect of extreme altitude. Not my best breakfast meeting I'm thinking. I have a quick word with Torrey about Marguerite and she says she'll drop by our tent later. It turns out James - the guy who rowed the Atlantic - is pretty ill with bronchitis and Lobouche is so ill he will have to go back to BC today with suspected pulmonary oedema. Jeez, these are summit climbers! So, after a breakfast of omelette and chapatis, I head back to the tent to tell Marguerite the not so good news. I don't tell her that Torrey has said tonight could be the hardest so far for all of us. She is still in her sleeping bag as I come into the tent. I've brought down some biscuits but she can't eat them.

At just after 10:00am I get into my sleeping bag again to stay warm before giving her a full Diamox and a big 800mg dose of ibuprofen and let her sleep for a while. I'm worried now that everything has taken on a serious turn and all the plans are up in the air. Just before midday, Torrey appears at our tent to reassure us that everyone will feel ill over the next twenty-four hours and gives Marguerite some stronger painkillers to take later. I think it helped Torrey coming in and Marguerite agrees to get up and come up to the mess tent with me to write up her journal if not for lunch. The wind is pretty fierce as we head up and above the wind all you can hear is coughing from other tents. Most of our team is here in the mess tent except for Meerie and Diane. Lunch is bread with chopped tomato and cucumber with salami. I struggle to eat it but Marguerite can't face it at all, but at least is drinking plenty of hot lemon. I have plenty of tea and settle into writing. Only Phil stays on with me into mid-afternoon, reading and sometimes talking. We discuss what might happen if the weather gets worse and how the plans are changing now for the North Col and for Lhakpa Ri. In between this I'm wondering what will happen if Marguerite doesn't get better. I don't feel more acclimatised here at all and at this height if you're ill, you don't get better. I go down to the tent, which has been warmed slightly by the little sunshine we had this afternoon. It feels weird being in this amphitheatre of Himalayan savage beauty not to be in awe of it, rather than wondering how yellow your pee is or how hard you are breathing and is that a sore head beginning? But that was my reality that afternoon - a focus on frailty and of course keeping an eye on my climbing partner.

She can't face dinner and looks no better so I go up to the mess tent on my own. Torrey has joined us tonight and says she is worried about Marguerite. You can't do more than Diamox and painkillers she says. Duncan comes in to say the weather looks no better so no North Col attempt tomorrow but some glacier practice in the morning and maybe some rope work as well. I managed two bowls of vegetable soup and banana and custard but couldn't handle the spag bol. Not much bol, just cold spag really. Marguerite doesn't even wake up as I get into the tent. Maybe sleep is the best thing for her. I don't have a good sleep although I'm warm enough.

Wednesday 6th May – Everest Advanced Base Camp – Tibet.

It was another minus twenty degrees night and a 50mph wind this morning, which makes it really cold. Last night was the worst yet but as the bed tea is being brought to the tents, Marguerite says she feels better but still has a sore head. So it's the routine of Diamox and ibuprofen with tea. She won't come with us today but feels she will be OK by tomorrow for the first attempt at the North Col. Even though I say today will be relatively easy. The revised plan for tomorrow is to have a go at getting up to or close to, our tents on the North Col. These are for the use of the summit guys, leaving time for another attempt or climbing Lhakpa Ri. It's now very weather dependent. I struggle to get my climbing harness on in the confines of the tent ready for our practice day. She comes up with me for breakfast though which is positive and has porridge and tea. Our team is here except Meerie who is too unwell as is Diane. Stefan says he'll only go 'for a bit up the hill'. Frank is also out, not taking a chance with his eye until he has to. The plan is to climb towards the North Col and then divert onto the glacier and make our way back down to Duncan who is fixing some practice ropes. We will be back for a late lunch and Dawa will be leading our group today and will be in radio contact with Duncan.

So we set off at a slow pace - there is no other at this altitude and we have lots of rest stops. We climb up past the derelict broadcasting dish the Chinese used in their Olympic year to film live coverage of their summit team. And we keep on walking until we have reached almost the ice plateau below the North Col. We rest here and Dawa contacts Duncan. It doesn't sound good. We've gone too high. It doesn't get better as we set off across the roof of the glacier. There are seriously real crevasses here. Previously in the Alps with my climbing club mates Tom and Ivan, we practised glacier walking and looking for crevasses on relatively safe parts. This though is too real, especially when Dawa has us jumping across big drops. Although only a couple of feet wide, jumping with crampons on isn't great - and of course we're roped. I also shudder to think halfway across the gap, the rope goes tight. Now, it's fine being roped to someone who has walked roped before, but previous experience in the Himalayas wasn't great with people behind suddenly stopping and not shouting - then you nearly get pulled off your feet. The truth is, we are not where we should be and we end up down climbing on ice and scrambling about trying to get back off the bloody glacier and back to the trail. As we head down I can see ABC now and we are only a few hundred feet from the track back down. This has taken three hours and we are just at the area we should have started in. Torrey asks Dawa for the radio and says to Duncan that we are all exhausted and not in good shape for rope work but he thinks we should take a break then come down to the ropes. It's about going the extra mile he says. It's 4:30pm when I get back so hardly a late lunch and some others won't be back till almost darkness.

As expected, Marguerite is in the mess tent and so is Meerie who looks pretty weak. Diane hasn't appeared at all today. Lobouche has gone with a porter back to BC to recuperate. A few black tea brews and I feel fine and because it's very quiet, I order hot water for a shower. This time I take a jug into the canvas shower tent. I have a great wash at around 21,000 feet - my highest shower and a strange place to be totally naked. In the interests of practicality, I wash my clothes as well, but hesitate to sing. We sit in the mess tent until the others arrive, looking exhausted and cold. We can hear James with his wracking cough in the summit mess tent next door. Duncan comes in to say that tomorrow will be an attempt on the North Col, not next day. And that Diane is ill and will go down to BC with a porter tomorrow morning. I don't think Marguerite is better and I think that Torrey should be doing more for her - I've given her more drugs than the doctor! We head down to our tent at 5:00pm for a lie down and for me to sort out my gear - and particularly my harness and climbing stuff. At dinner, Katy comes into the mess tent to say the weather report for tomorrow is really good so the North Col is on. Fine, but today's 'easy' day wasn't that for most people. So, the day after tomorrow will be a rest day, and then we can do Lhakpa Ri, or some will do the North Col if they don't make it tomorrow. So that gives us all two attempts at the North Col. I seem to detect from Duncan and Katy, a reluctance about Lhakpa Ri. But we still have the chance of doing both.

Dinner starts with chicken soup, which is fine but then the dreaded dal bhat, which I always struggle with, especially when it's hardly warm. This is followed by warm fruit salad, which is good. I also had a sweet and lots of lemon tea. We hear that some tents were wrecked and blown away in last night's storm on the North Col. The plan is to leave around 9:00am tomorrow so not the early start I'm used with during these Himalayan adventures. As we walk carefully through the ice and snow to our tent there are snow flurries in the air. Tonight, Marguerite has two hot water bottles to help her stay warm and sleep, But she says she won't go tomorrow to help build up her strength for a later attempt which is fine though I'd like to do both things.

Thursday 7th May – Everest Advanced Base Camp – Tibet.

Despite having plenty to drink and both Diamox and Ibuprofen, Marguerite has a troubled night. In the morning I don't feel any different, not worse certainly but not better either and I had a really scary nightmare about being halfway down the North Col on a rope and dropping my descender - it seems I'm the only one with an old fashioned figure of eight. So I was stuck there and no one could help me and it was getting dark. I woke up before I died. So, up for breakfast on my own and again it took ages to get my harness on - is this just nervousness? At breakfast, only Meerie, Marguerite and Diane are absent. I have porridge and toast and jam and plenty of lemon tea. It's the best morning yet up here, blue sky and no wind. I think this is the best I've felt at this height. So we are led by both Prem and Dawa and I walk a fair way with Stefan who is really laid back compared with my nervousness. He says he has no interest in climbing up the Col - today's trek is fine - and what a place to be today. He's right of course you are supposed to enjoy some of it. Our crampons are on from our camp. We stretch out on the track and some of the summit team are here too but away ahead of us and Torrey is with them too. Later we have a conversation about Marguerite. Crunch time is coming, she says - if there is no improvement, she might need to go to BC to recover. Her symptoms are not at all good. So it looks like she has been keeping an eye on her all the time, but in the background.

We wait at the high point of yesterday's trek for everyone to catch up. It's so warm, I have just a shirt on but my down jacket is in my rucksack. From here, we follow the marker wands with their wee red flags to guide us on a crevasse free route to the bottom of the Col. It looks quite benign from here until you think of the storm two days ago. I don't know what I expected but there are only two fixed ropes from here. I expected maybe a dozen. Anyway, these lower ropes and this route replace the ropes lost when the two Hungarians fell. The route is now apparently steeper, but away from the towering ice pinnacles. Also, the ropes are a bit inconsistent here as some local teams will have replaced them, not the Chinese Army Team who we know are still on the North Col or higher. However, there is a queue! A big American team was starting up the ropes and then it was our summit team, then us, so we sat on our rucksacks for almost an hour and I pulled a fleece on. Fortunately it isn't cold or windy. I wish though that we were here really early and already well on our way. That wasn't good planning. So, at last we are ready to go but Stefan says he'll stay here and it is amazingly warm. It's a chance and a risk but as with Dawa's suggestion, we could leave our rucksacks with Stefan. I still take mine and my axe although Dawa says I don't need it but I wouldn't feel right without it, fixed ropes or not. It doesn't feel right not having a rucksack either. So with my ice axe slung on my back Alpine style I start to climb Everest. What! I can hardly believe I'm climbing Everest, it doesn't feel like I thought it would, with lovely weather and a light rucksack and a Sherpa leading three of us.

We are slower than the others and I feel slow with my jumar attached to the rope and pulling slowly upwards at about forty degrees. The track is well worn but the snow is surprisingly soft even this early. Every one hundred feet or so the rope ends and another starts. We have to clip another sling on the next rope, clip on the jumar, then unclip off the previous rope. And I'm doing all this wearing just thin gloves as it's warm but it would be a lot slower and harder if conditions were colder or windier. Often Dawa is there to unclip and clip on for us, which helps. I'm still out of breath every ten steps and sometimes gasping and we make slow progress up steeper sections and over crevasses bridged by other ladders but no real exposure. But queues form here too. Just gasping for breath constantly and having to rest every five minutes. Dawa is very patient and is often there to help at rope changes and at one ladder, which does feel quite exposed. It's getting cooler as we get higher and catch the wind coming over the top of the Col.

The plan is to get up and over the Col to our tents and

have a couple of cups of tea and a rest before going back down. The others are well ahead and over the ridge on the Col itself as the three of us are stopped by Dawa, 'Look down' he says. And there away below us, maybe a hundred tiny, dark figures are starting to cross the glacier plateau, which we crossed earlier.

They are high altitude porters with full loads coming up to service the North Col camps, taking advantage of this rare day of settled weather. Dawa says we can go on as the tents are close or down now. If we don't go down now, we will have to descend in the dark as the ropes will be full for hours with the porters coming up. We plod on a bit then I think of my nightmare, look at my altimeter and it says 22,455 feet. We are on the Col itself and we can see some tents, maybe even ours. I got my photograph taken with the far travelled Saltire flying on Everest. This is the best weather so far on the trip and we have been very lucky.

This is also the highest the three of us have been and Simon and Linda have had enough and anyway we can all come back in two day's time so we all decide to go down in the daylight. Dawa is intrigued with my figure of eight descender and shows me a quick and dirty way to descend quickly using two karabiners as a friction brake, and it is I am sure faster, but at nearly 23,000 feet up on Everest, this is not the place to learn a new technique so I persevere with my figure of eight and I'm so careful not to drop the bloody thing as I did in my nightmare. I don't want to be here in darkness. We got down really quickly and just beat the porters who were finishing their brew before getting up the ropes. The last few of the 'replaced' ropes were interesting. One, which we all zoom down almost out of control, must only be about 8mm. About the thickness of my old mum's washing line. The second last rope is so thick I can lean right back fully horizontal and not move. I have to push the rope through the figure of eight to get down. And Dawa was right that I didn't need an ice-axe or a rucksack.

At the bottom of the Col, there must be well over a hundred porters here having a brew. They will carry up their loads before dark, stay up there tonight and come down in the morning. I found it hard going up even with a light rucksack and these guys must be carrying twenty-five kilos at least. So we are down in time and we are soon following the red marker wands back across the glacier plateau. I haven't had a sore head at all today and it feels good going back to camp. Everyone is feeling tired and it's been a hard day but what a feeling doing that today. It will be a much longer day of course for our people up on the Col waiting to get down still. The thought of coming down in the dark doesn't appeal. And, of course, it's getting colder all the time too. So at last, back down and straight into the mess tent to get my harness off and heat up. Marguerite is there and looks a bit better with her hands around a hot water bottle. I go to the tent to drop my climbing harness off then join the rest for more tea and biscuits. A couple of hours later, Duncan arrived from the North Col - he is exceptionally fast. He says we have to decide at dinner tonight whether we want to go back up the North Col - with a very early start or climb Lhakpa Ri with a 3:00am start. Tomorrow will be a rest day.

Marguerite wants to have a go and the North Col is possibly the easier option and a climb I think of around 1,000 feet but still awfully hard at this altitude, but I am keen on climbing a mountain - the North Col was a bit artificial and a bit of a circus. I didn't get a 'mountain' experience. I know that sounds daft because it was Everest after all but Marguerite agrees, so Lhakpa Ri it will be. A possible fourteen-hour day says Duncan. I think secretly he's trying to put us off. Although Marguerite is hesitant, there is a full rest day coming up tomorrow. Most of our guys will be up for it even although only two of our North Col team made it to the North Col camp. We are already in the mess tent at dinner time. Some of the summit guys and Torrey aren't back yet. Duncan comes in before dinner to get the numbers. Meerie says the North Col but only if she has (and will pay for) her own Sherpa who will carry everything. Simon and Linda and Frank are up for that option too. We might consider that to make it easier. Duncan cautions the rest of us on Lhakpa Ri - there will be fresh snow on the glacier so we can't see crevasses - travel will be slow with everyone roped together. That, of course, is a big change from what we heard at Base Camp when we arrived as it had no snow on it then. There is also hardened, blue ice on the summit approach. The forecast isn't great either with winds picking up within forty hours. And he says hurricane force at Everest's summit.

Dinner is soup then pasta and vegetables. As this is served, Torrey bursts into the mess tent as high as a kite. She had tea at the North Col camp, the highest she's ever been in her life and she's letting us all know how good she feels but had to wait hours for the ropes to be free. She looks terrible. Absolutely shattered but in good spirits and she cheers us all up. Despite his bronchitis, James made it too and Richard. These guys will be on the summit, no worries. And eight out of ten of them will be, a few weeks later. Marguerite can't eat but at least is drinking. Torrey gives her a hard time but at least she has had some soup. I have no appetite either but force some pasta down and tinned fruit too. Plenty of time tomorrow to plan the big day so we head off for a ridiculously early night at 8:00pm with snow in the air again tonight. I give Marguerite two hot water bottles and more drugs and we get into our sleeping bags.

Friday 8th May – Everest Advanced Base Camp – Tibet.

Not a good night again. I was up for a pee at 2:00am as quietly as possible but when I turned to see if I'd wakened her, it was that deathly grey-white face again. I couldn't hear her breathing but she woke up and accepted a drink and went back to sleep as if she was in a trance. It didn't help me sleep and I felt a bit helpless. I wake at exactly 5:00am. No wind this morning but overcast. Bed tea arrives at 6:00am and by that time I'm up and dressed, teeth brushed and ready for breakfast. Marguerite has slept on till the bed tea arrives and sits up in her sleeping bag to drink. We go up for breakfast and I struggle with some porridge but like Marguerite, manage some Spam and toast with more tea. Everyone is a bit quiet today, no doubt thinking about the big day tomorrow. Torrey is in our mess tent this morning and looks 100% better than she looked last night. After breakfast she comes over to have a look at Marguerite, checks her oxygen saturation, shakes her head and offers even stronger painkillers and says she is concerned that she is going downhill. Her oxygen saturation - the measurement of how well your body is coping with reduced oxygen - was at '94' on the train. Now it's '60' and that's very, very bad news. If that was the reading at home you would be in intensive care. All of a sudden I'm seeing how serious this is.

There is only Frank and Grant in this big tent now and the two of us and all very quiet. We just sit drinking tea for a while when Torrey reappears with Duncan and they sit across from us looking serious. Now Torrey is saying that Marguerite has Acute Mountain Sickness (AMS) with very low oxygen saturation, probably ataxia. There is only one cure - to go down. Stupidly I ask if that means tomorrow but she says now, this morning and 'before she just keels over and can't get down - she's going to collapse very soon'. It's a shock I suppose. That's it - end of trip and of course Marguerite is insisting I stay to do Lhakpa Ri tomorrow. Until Torrey says to her quite firmly, and to all listening, "do you really think a mere mountain is more important to him than you being safe?" And that for me is the wake-up call and we shake hands with Duncan and Torrey and the other guys and I give her a big hug and we go and pack. We will have porters of course to carry all our gear. We will follow them down to Interim Camp then down to Base Camp next day. I have no problem with the decision.

Duncan has said to take whatever dried food I want and chocolate bars from the summit guys stores in case there is a lack of catering at Intermediate Camp. But he says there will be a couple of tents still there and he will radio ahead to say we are coming. It takes ages to get packed up as we can't move quickly and it ends up a bit fraught between us. However by mid-morning we are all packed up and go up to the mess tents to say goodbye and wish the team's success tomorrow and for the summit. That's when Duncan realises the porters who came up this morning have already left to go down - a ploy he reckons so they have no load going back. However, clearly it gives us a problem. Incredible as it seems, Duncan asks if I can find my way back to Intermediate Camp on my own. I think I can but hey man, this is Everest and the weather is to deteriorate. Duncan says getting Marguerite lower quickly is the priority and I'm fine with that.

Our kit will follow soon he promises with porters expected from the North Col in a couple of hours. They will bring our bags down to us at Intermediate Camp. So here we are, leaving Advanced Base Camp on our own, just with our rucksacks. I am in charge of route finding with a very sick Marguerite, very high in the Tibetan Himalaya. This wasn't in the expedition plans. And I think about the situation - no detailed map, no radio, no GPS. You'd hardly venture out on a Scottish hill in winter conditions like this. So we leave ABC and follow the East Rongbuk Glacier again, following a scratchy path where we can see it, but in reality it would be hard to get too lost with the huge white fins of the glacier on our right.

I reckoned at our slow pace it would take us at least four hours to get to the next camp and we looked out for where we camped on the way up at Changtse Camp. It's hard going as Marguerite is really exhausted and we have lots of stops and I try to make sure she drinks plenty. There are a couple of times I wonder if we'll make it at all and I just have to hold her upright to rest for a few minutes. I know Duncan will have radioed ahead but who would come to look for us if the weather changed? Not the cook in charge of Intermediate Camp. As I think about the gloom and doom, five porters appear behind us walking fast and laughing and talking loudly. They are carrying our big kit bags as well as other stuff. They shout 'Namaste' and say the camp is close and have disappeared in ten minutes. I never imagined being in this situation. It feels a bit serious now. After almost five hours we can see the camp and a few yellow tents but we have a huge ravine to cross. On our way up this was all covered in snow and it's amazing how much it has thawed in a few days. It gives us a problem as there is now a river to cross. Marguerite says we should wave to the camp - there are two people watching us - to see if they know the way across but there's no response.

We just head straight down and I jump across after throwing my rucksack across and then help her across too. Then it's a hard pull back up the slope but eventually we are in the campsite. It took the last of Marguerite's willpower to get up the hill and she almost collapsed in my arms. And I'm thinking that there is no one here to help us if she gets worse. And for a few minutes we just hold each other. Both of us under pressure, hers physical and mine psychological maybe. Anyway Mingma the cook is watching us and when we turn around, he smiles and says 'tea inside - I saw you across the river'. Our sleeping bags and kit bags are in the two yellow tents. Amazingly, it starts to snow, just like last time here. It's almost dark too. After tea and biscuits, Marguerite needs to lie down so we go to the tents and put our gear into one tent.

After getting things sorted I nip down to the mess tent with our dried food - a packet of dried lasagne - how does that work? No one in the mess tent so I go to the cooking tent and there are three of them in here and just laugh at my dried food, 'no, no', they say, 'dinner is already being made'. The porters are here too. And they are cooking just for us as there is no one else here. And I hear him saying on the radio it's snowing heavily at ABC. I hope it isn't coming our way. So I go back to rest for a wee while and then head into the freezing mess tent to have our specially cooked dinner. The soup goes down well but then spaghetti with a sauce of sorts, but too much for both of us - we are asked if we want more of course, no way, but we do have another cup of tea and wait on our water bottles being filled with hot water. Then it's into our tent and the drugstore routine and settled down for, hopefully, a better sleep.

Saturday 9th May – Intermediate Camp – Tibet.

Saturday 9th May – Intermediate Camp – Tibet.

I'm awake at 6:00am. Marguerite too and she stretches for a few minutes and it's a while since I remember her doing that and she says she feels better and I can hear Mingma's stove on the go for breakfast but first we have bed tea as usual. I keep her on a full Diamox but she has no sore head - the first time for days and days. Breakfast is quite relaxed with omelette and chapati and lots of tea. It's an easy walk to BC from here and you couldn't get lost so we're cool about going down on our own. A fine morning too with blue skies and it's amazing the difference in Marguerite - and me. Mingma will radio BC to say we are on our way and we will be there for lunchtime hopefully. So we wave goodbye to Mingma at

9.30am and head down the stone path. The porters are away before us with our kit-bags and as cheery as ever. This is an easy day for them, albeit that they are carrying big loads, not just ours. We pass the odd porter and yak team heading to ABC, and a few breathless climbers too, none of them looking happy and all of them and us wearing face coverings against the dust.

At one point a small group appears heading up past us, but not on our path, and all in expensive looking gear and sunglasses. The last of their group isn't quite so smart looking but is wearing a Scotland bandana around his face and a beard and shades on too. We shout hello and ask if he's Scottish and he shouts back, 'yes, where are you from?' I shout back 'Lanark' and he replies, 'I'm from Law'. What? Then he asks 'are you Marguerite'? 'Are you Jim'? Amazingly it's Mungo Ross, one of Jagged Globe's top guides. He lives about five miles from where I live. The last time I saw him was in a remote village fifty miles well west of Lukla in Nepal although he's been up Tinto, our local hill on some summer Wednesday nights too with our club. He's off up to ABC to climb Lhakpa Ri and maybe the North Col. Amazing, we haven't seen him since two years back in Nepal, now here in this corner of Tibet. You couldn't make that up. We have a blether for about fifteen minutes, all of us smiling after this unusual meeting.

The meeting has cheered us both up and we are now walking in warm sunshine down towards Base Camp. We even have our jackets off because it's so warm. There is a real difference too in the melt water from the glacier. It was pretty much frozen on the way up but now it's flowing amidst the ice and snow. Soon we are heading downhill steeply and are approaching the blue lakes, with the sun now on our backs. We still have an hour and a half to go and Marguerite is really tired but we plod on. We can see our camp in the distance and soon we are passing the Chinese Army Expedition camp and into the sanctuary of our own camp.

Diane is there to meet us and she looks a lot better. Also there is an attractive tall blonde woman who says hello and at first I can't place her accent. Then it dawns on me - South African. She is very extroverted and ushers us into the South African mess tent. Her son is one of their team. Her husband had gone up to ABC to see him. She flew all the way here "to give him a kiss" - honestly!

251

More importantly she is offering us beer and cashew nuts. Yippee!

After my initial suspicion of her, I got to like her - she's really all right and so OTT, but amusing too. When she arrived in Lhasa she went to the Radisson and booked their biggest suite. Her husband has gone to ABC to see their son. She has never camped in her life. So, after a few beers and a few laughs we go to find our tents. A lot less here now as they were all taken down in case of storms while we were away. It is almost idyllic here at Base Camp. Time to text Mags and my sons to say I'm safely back and of course to think about the logistics for the next part of the adventure. Richard is the first to reply and this is the first I hear about the volcanic ash cloud and the havoc to flights. Alastair is stuck in Greece - there are worse places but there are work commitments too. It might give us a problem getting home. I speak to Mags who tells me of the general strike in Kathmandu on the day she landed - so no buses, no taxis at the airport and nothing open. Anyway, she got to her hotel eventually by taking some sort of bus but had no money to pay the fare but got away with it. Jeez, you just focus on your own problems!

I give Marguerite a shout and we head to the big mess tent as the summit team are of course still at ABC - and our team as well. I have lots of journal writing to catch up on and time to recharge everything too. But a problem with my video camera too with the lens protector jamming shut. Not long after we get in and a flask for tea, some of the South African guys come in and they are a good bunch. We discuss whisky and they have Glenfiddich with them. I tell them about Highland Park and offer to educate them more later on. However, dinner is earlier tonight and we never left the mess tent. We have soup - chicken and pasta with vegetables and tinned fruit for a sweet - we both have some of our appetite back. The South Africans are off to join the Seven Summits team about a quarter of a mile away and want us to join them for 'a big party'. This lot have just got some of their guys on the summit so want to celebrate. We decline which is incredibly sensible. As we go to our tents the sky is clear and the stars like crystals and almost a full moon and over Everest in a few hours. Anyway, I have more mundane things to think about - a half tab of Diamox each and off to sleep.

Sunday 10th May – Everest Base Camp – Tibet.

I wake up feeling brilliant and the sun is shining in a clear, blue sky as I stand outside sipping my bed tea at 6:30am, encouraging my climbing partner to join me. Funny to think this is our last night here. A sleepy Marguerite emerges from her tent, hair a mess but hey, she's smiling and feels better so who cares and all the pressure off and no more altitude issues. Teeth brushed and down for breakfast, which is porridge with toast and omelette. No South Africans due to heavy partying last night no doubt. Just Diane in the mess tent, so glad we didn't go - we will plan to party when we get to Kathmandu. That is until Geylu, the cook, tells us about the latest news. The strikes are still on in Nepal and big problems at the border with nothing getting through. There are plans to helicopter us out from the border to Nepal somewhere. No rush today so we order hot water for two showers from Geylu who has no pressure this morning apart from getting a late lunch for the guys coming down from ABC. Still warm and sunny so the shower was actually pleasant rather than just being necessary.

So, clean, ready for the next few days and feeling good, we head back over to the memorials as a wee walk before lunch.

It is really pleasant in the sunshine and no ice smoke from the top of Everest so maybe a summit push for some teams. There was a telescope set up here at Base Camp before we went higher, but it's gone now. So we take our last photographs of Everest. Marguerite is looking a lot better but I can't forget thinking she had died that night at ABC. Makes you wonder why you do all this stuff.

We wander slowly back to the camp and we watch some Tibetan people scouring the moraine we're crossing and picking stuff up. No idea what they are collecting, probably diamonds with my luck but we don't find any. We meet Geylu on the way into camp who says Lhakpa Ri was a disaster for our team as very high winds and snow forced them to abandon the climb and head back from the glacier. And yet today is so calm. Not so calm are Grant and Phil who are first into camp for a delayed lunch. Grant looks shattered and tells us the story. They left at 3.00am and got through the difficult glacier spires and up onto the top of it only to be hit with hurricane winds with snow and spindrift blasting them. After three hours Duncan abandoned the attempt. So, no one made it to Lhakpa Ri and the second attempt on the North Col was also abandoned and when I think about it, only a couple of us actually got to the North Col Camp and only myself and two others to the top of the North Col.

Over lunch we hear more of their tale. No one attempted the North Col again as the forecast was for dangerously high winds. Everyone on the team looked tired and also so glad to be down here in relative comfort. So we are all back at Base Camp, no one injured, no one dead, so not that bad. Everyone now organising showers and getting tents sorted. Most will sleep until dinner. We hear later that Mungo and his Jagged Globe clients didn't manage Lhakpa Ri either due to bad weather but did climb the North Col. The plan tomorrow is to leave at 10:00am and drive overland by Landcruiser - not all on roads - towards Zhangmu and the border with Nepal. It's supposed to be a bit of a dump. We will arrive too late to cross the border so an overnight stay is required before heading into Nepal. The loose plan is to try and meet Margaret here too. It will be her birthday there and I have carried all her birthday cards from Scotland from the boys, her brothers and sisters, her mum and auntie and from me of course. She is only a day behind us in Tibet somewhere. Her Birthday cards have all been up to ABC as well. High altitude birthday cards!

Late this afternoon we get all our climbing gear packed away and pack all the rest. My walking boots I give to Dawa to give to who he wants. We have a discussion about what goes where and get as much done today to save hassle tomorrow. My bottle of Highland Park, untouched so far, will be taken to the dining tent tonight. A very cheerful mess tent at dinner. A few of us have a pre-dinner beer and even the cooking team looks happy and we have chicken tonight, which is great. After dinner, the bottle of Highland Park is passed round. I ask Prem and Dawa carefully, thinking they might refuse for religious reasons. In fact it's only them, Grant and I that have a second drink.

Monday 11th May – Everest Base Camp – Tibet.

I text Mags a Happy Birthday message wherever she is and we were up in plenty of time for bed tea, breakfast and the final packing. Our bags are last down with the others, however and we hang about for another half hour after the arranged departure time. The Land Cruisers are ready to go and we pack our stuff into the nearest one. Originally we would have a guide to get us to the border and probably our cook but Prem and Dawa are going home now to Nepal and will be with us all the way to Kathmandu which is good news as we all trust these guys. We are sharing the vehicle with Simon and Lawrence.

The South Africans have hired another three Land Cruisers and they are going down to Zhangmu to rest for a couple of days at low altitude before coming back to make their summit attempt. So we say our goodbyes to the cooking guys and head off in a big convoy of identical black Land Cruisers. The plan is to follow the dirt track from BC then go across the country, sometimes on tracks, but not on any roads. The route is not possible in bad weather, but OK today in fine weather and no wind and blue sky. I sit beside the driver. Marguerite thinks he's good looking but I think he looks like a sleekit oriental baddie from a James Bond film. But this guy can drive and there is a bit of competition between the drivers and we take some interesting short cuts to stay in front. We get thrown about a bit and it's like a Disney ride at times. It isn't ever a road. We cross the high Tibetan plateau for miles and miles. Like driving on the moon I suppose. We pass horses and carts and go through deserted villages and it's like going back in time. We see no other vehicles, not even tractors. After a couple of hours we can see away ahead down in a valley, a wee township. It is called Tingri and this is where we will have lunch.

At lunch, in a deserted main street restaurant, we sit with the South Africans and they are good craic. One of their team was born in Dumfries but he has no accent at all. Well, except South African. This is a self-funded expedition and they obviously have money and maybe sponsors too. Very laid back but very confident they will get to the summit and I'm quite jealous of these young guys with bags of confidence. The food is fresh and good and Chinese and we have a couple of beers too. Despite the restaurant being fine, the toilets are squat type and filthy. I had to squeeze past a wee black calf to get there. As we hang about in the street there are some people playing pool and all smoking. A monk in a crimson robe walks past, someone says something to him and he turns round and punches the man so hard in the face he knocks him into the road and the monk just turns and walks on. No turning the other cheek for him and quite shocking for us.

After lunch and back into the 4X4's and now driving on tarmac to the border. A new road and we are now on the 'Friendship Highway' built by the Chinese. In the next two hours as we descend into increasing greenery, we are stopped three times by army checkpoints. There are a lot of landslide repairs going on and our progress is slow. The road is also becoming quite busy. It's so nice to see trees and bushes again. As we enter the stretched out hillside town of Zhangmu, we pass lots of ancient Tata trucks struggling uphill past us and lots of parked up trucks waiting to cross the border the next day. Every truck, some Indian, looks dilapidated, albeit incredibly decorated. Ah, civilisation. We passed a police station on the way into the town. The traffic gets so bad we often grind to a halt for a few minutes. It's so narrow and with parked cars and trucks it looks one way but it isn't, so we wait in traffic jams for ages. Needless to say, our hotel is on the other side of this stretched out, twisty town. This is the steepest road descent in the world, dropping from 17,000 feet from the Tibetan plateau to 1,935 feet into Zhangmu.

We get parked at our hotel, but only by stopping all the traffic each way as we quickly unload all the kit bags and rucksacks. The hotel doesn't look great, just a doorway really and we can hardly get in for people trying to get us to exchange our money for Chinese money, which is a bit odd. Ahead, I can see room keys being given out and I'm not at the front of the queue! No Mr Kong to help me out. I shout to Marguerite and grab two keys. It's chaotic and the South Africans are here too trying to get rooms as well. We press through those still waiting. Our stuff is still in the hall but the priority is to get a decent room. Marguerite has a huge room with four beds so I leave her there to find mine. And I can't. Eventually I ask this Tibetan boy I find in a corridor and he takes me along a landing outside the hotel and up another stair and points to the end of the corridor. Room 42 is there all right, a big room with two single beds and an equally large bathroom with a shower and western type toilet. The shower looks as if it's just a fifty-gallon white drum up on the wall with some dodgy wires going into it. No curtains, just a big wet room.

I go to get Marguerite and our bags but she now has Linda and Meerie sharing with her. I keep quiet about seemingly having a room to myself. Especially when they say they have no shower. As we get our bags up to the rooms - no porters here - I say she can use my shower after me. And it worked great and the first real shower in weeks. It felt good being really clean, although there was only a hand towel to dry myself which was a challenge. I'm changed and waiting as Marguerite appears. She says the other two women would like a shower too. Now, never in my life have I had three women wanting to share my shower. Anyway, I go downstairs to look for a beer. Outside I try to phone Mags to see where she is and, unbelievably, she is here too and just arrived. I say I'll call when I know when our dinner will be and we can meet up later. I'm amazed this has worked out so well. Across the road I see Dawa standing at the doorway of a restaurant and go over to enquire about dinner. "It's in here," he says. "Do they sell beer?" I ask. "You would like a beer?" "Yes please".

So I bought a bottle of beer and at the doorway I hung about with Dawa talking about his plan to start his own company offering touring adventures in Tibet and Nepal, travelling on vintage motorbikes - actually Indian copies but it sounds good. He would fly clients to Lhasa and travel back overland to Kathmandu and go over some of the high passes we travelled across. He says he's coming to Scotland next year so I tell him to call me when he gets there. He is close to getting funding from someone in Scotland. My phone rings and it's Marguerite looking for me, so I say just to come to reception. It seems some of our guys have gone for a drink somewhere with the South Africans without knowing the dinner arrangements - I only knew because I met Dawa. Anyway at about 6:30pm, we wander over to the restaurant with Meerie and Linda and Diane. Diane has complained about not having a shower and dirty sheets on the bed and hairs on her pillow. Nothing is done about it of course. Both Prem and Dawa join us and a few others drift in about 7:00pm. I nip back out and call Mags to say we will meet for a birthday drink in two hours, after our meal and Dawa has said it's a half hour walk to the other side of town and uphill all the way.

The meal is the usual Chinese fare but all good and fresh. We all have beer, but no one has the same type of glass I notice. There are really tasty vegetables but apart from one shared plate of chicken, no other meat. Our new 'minder' will pay for it but isn't happy some others have eaten elsewhere - he likes to know where we are, especially at the border. No doubt they will be suitably punished when they come back. It turns out that Prem and Dawa are also going to the hotel where Mags is staying so they will take us, which is brilliant. On our way we get talking about when our hotel might close the doors tonight. That's when we both realise our watches are still on Expedition time, which is Nepalese time. This is Tibet, which makes it well after 10:00pm in reality. No wonder my wife sounded bemused when I said we would be up in a couple of hours!

So better late than never we are soon peering through a wee hotel window to see my wife with white silk kata scarves round her and wearing a paper party hat. So have the others so we go in and get introduced to her party and someone buys the beers. A big hug and kiss then all the birthday cards from home and a wee present from me of course. So despite having special birthdays in New York, Reykjavik and Dubai, here we are in a totally run-down border town in Tibet for this birthday. Ah, the rich tapestry of life.

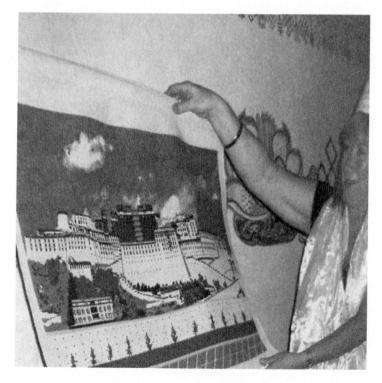

So, after more drinks, kisses and hugs we head back down the dark twisty road back to the hotel. Quite safe here I think. Only after passing window after window of reddish, pink lights do I realise almost every lit up window is a brothel, or a 'club'. Even the real bars look really dodgy, so we forgo a nightcap and get back to the hotel. No bar in the hotel or restaurant, so off to our rooms. My room has a big sliding window that only looks onto a corridor. It doesn't lock, but my kitbag and rucksack are too heavy to steal. I'm probably easier to steal! Without looking into the bed-sheets, I get in and sleep soundly.

Tuesday 12th May – Zhangmu – Tibet.

I am up, packed and showered and downstairs by 7:30am. We are to leave after breakfast at 8.00am. We had breakfast in the same place as last night's meal and I'm glad we are early. We have tea and rolls with boiled eggs. And fortunately we're finished just before our fleet of 4X4's arrive outside and engulf the restaurant in blue diesel fumes and quite funny, if you've already had breakfast. No one moves any of the vehicles or switches them off despite a few requests. The Chinese minder is looking mean this morning, maybe he's trying to gas those who didn't come to dinner last night? All the bags are being loaded yet again for another journey although it can't be far as we walked down and round the corner from our hotel and there was a sign saying passport control. We're in the same teams with the same driver and we set off slowly through heavy traffic for twenty minutes and suddenly, we can go no further. It's chaos with trucks abandoned everywhere.

This is the border. Porters appear and all Nepalese and all women. Dawa says it's OK to hand over our kit bags to them, so we do. The Land Cruisers are already turning to head back into deepest Tibet. Our transport will be Nepalese from here to Kathmandu. We can see the 'Friendship Bridge' and of course take photographs. The middle of the bridge is the official border. We walk in a queue towards immigration control. Staffed by the Chinese Army it looks like and everyone's rucksack is emptied, everything looked at and put back. We get through OK but behind us by a few hours, some of Margaret's party get books confiscated. Meanwhile our Nepalese porters carry on through customs and only get a stamp in their passports, nothing is opened. So if you want to smuggle a kilo of opium from Tibet into Nepal, put it in your kit bag - no one will open it!

We all get cleared through OK. Now we have to cross the bridge and go through it all again to clear Nepalese immigration. The bridge is a big white concrete affair but I can't fathom what actually happens when trucks cross because China and Nepal drive on different sides of the road (arguably, any side), so what happens when they meet in the middle? I don't know either as we never saw a vehicle cross. We walk over the bridge into the border village of Kodari in Nepal. Immigration Control is a big wooden building with lots of official looking men with moustaches. Dawa guides us - there is a queue for people without visas and they have a big form to fill out and of course pay. We already have our visas, all paid for too but it actually takes us longer to get the stamp on our passports than those without visas. Welcome to Nepal. It's almost tropically warm here and we are taken by Prem and Dawa to a restaurant to wait for word of our bus. It will be here soon we are told. Some people order food, but we have just tea. We overlook the river here just down from the border bridge and it should be a pleasant spot to sit but there is an incredible amount of rubbish that has just been chucked down to the river. I've seen this in Kathmandu as well as a truck just drove up to a stream and tipped garbage into it. We decide to go for a walk and buy some coke to drink on the journey. It's getting warmer all the time as we walk down the main street of this border town. There are scores of ancient looking Tata trucks, all elaborately painted, just waiting to cross the border. No sign of our bus so after a quarter of a mile we head back and join the others. There's a really relaxed feeling from everyone as we know that in six hours we will be in comparative luxury in a good quality hotel in Kathmandu.

After fifteen minutes, Prem marches us back down the street we have just come up. Most people try to stay in the shade but we're all sweating and it takes us a good fifteen minutes to reach our bus. I shouldn't be shocked at things with all the travelling in third world countries I've done, but I am. The bus looks like a wreck. I would guess it must be at least forty years old. Another Indian Tata of course but it's nicely decorated if you like flowers and gaudy colours. It looks like it has twenty-two seats. The bags are loaded and as there is limited room under the bus, some bags come inside. We sit as far at the back as we can but there are bags on the back seat. I want to take some film and photographs from the bus so this is a good place to be. So, at 11.30am, Nepalese time we head from the border and into rural

261

Nepal. We have a window that opens which is good because there is no air conditioning of course. The driver is very friendly and smiles a lot, which is reassuring I think.

At first it's just good to be moving again after all the hanging about this morning. I text Mags to tell her to get all the Dalai Lama stuff out of her rucksack - just a joke, but for her to warn the rest of her party. The scenery is wonderful and at first the road isn't too bad. Then it gets worse and worse again. This is the poorest road I have ever been on in a motor vehicle. So bad that we both get our sitting mats out of our rucksacks and me, Finlay's pillow and Marguerite, her fleece to put under our bums to protect them from the constant bumps. At one point as I was about to stand up, the jolt is so severe that I smack my head off the luggage rack. Marguerite will have pain in her backside for weeks to come from this journey. However, the sights are wonderful. I photograph buses with people on the roof and on one occasion, with goats on the roof. We pass through wee crowded villages full of colour. There is talk about stopping for lunch but everyone just wants to get to Kathmandu. So, for hours, we rattle and roll and jolt our way along what is little better than a dirt track in places. At one point we attempt to have a mug of coke. I drink quickly but the jarring is so bad, Marguerite is getting covered in it so she has to hold the cup out of the window where the bumping soon empties it. Quite funny I suppose.

Eventually we are climbing up through terraced fields, actually passing other slower traffic at great risk and usually on blind bends but soon we are heading back down into the big valley where Kathmandu sits. Soon we are going through the congested streets we know but at least now on tarmac and a very, very different city from Beijing but somehow more personal. At least for me it is. We negotiate some tight turns and suddenly the opulent building that is the Shankar Hotel is in front of us. Many Everest expeditions started from here and Dougal Haston stayed here in 1971. The hotel is beautiful with fantastic well-kept grounds. However, we want to be staying at the Shangri La Hotel with Margaret who we think is a few hours behind us. We quickly find out that mobile coverage isn't what it was in China or Tibet. So, it looks like I'm staying here tonight, Marguerite too. I try for ages but the signal is very weak or non-existent. The phone signal in Tibet, at least where we were, was generally better than at home but not good here.

After getting our bags to our rooms, we go down to say goodbye to Dawa and Prem, who have been good guides. At Base Camp, we all put in a big tip for these guys and they will be well off for a while, but they were worth it. We head into the gardens with Diane and sit in lovely surroundings with an expensive beer. Who cares? We've survived it and had some adventures too. So, with no arrangements made, Marguerite and I decide to head into town for a meal. We get reception to call us a cab, which duly arrives. We want to go to, I think, the Third Eye restaurant. It's well known but not apparently to our driver but we only know this when he gets into town. 'Where is it now?" he asks me. I don't know either but after we cruised about a bit, I knew where I was so just said stop. We walked the rest. We walk upstairs to the open rooftop restaurant and it's quite dark but we are shown to a table for two and candles lit.

Amazingly, at the next table, are Margaret and her party, celebrating their last night! Now that is some coincidence! Well, we celebrated with many bottles of Everest beer and a really nice meal and shared a taxi and got back to our respective hotels and planned to meet around lunchtime at the Shangri La where we will stay for a couple of nights of indulgence after the hardships of our treks.

Wednesday 13th May – Kathmandu – Nepal.

After a good night's sleep Marguerite and I have a very quick breakfast and get a taxi to the Shangri-La to check-in. Yes, they have our booking and we have two rooms overlooking the gardens. I saw monkeys here last time. Try to text and call Mags but no luck. It turns out she was on the back of her guide's motorbike doing last minute sightseeing. By this time of course, since it's after 11:00am, we are in the gardens having the first beer of the day and it was very pleasant too. So we had another, and then Mags arrived and we had another. Then John and Karen who only went to ABC, came over for a farewell drink and John said the Everest beer I was drinking was rubbish, we should be drinking Ghorka beer. So we did, and in between it all, we actually did have lunch and I suppose we were quite loud, Two Kiwis and three Jocks. And far too many beers.

The master plan was to meet with John and Karen at the Third Eye restaurant tonight. Mags had contacted some of her trekking people who said they might come along too. So, upstairs for some light unpacking with Mags and a shower and then the three of us meet at reception and get a taxi right away to take us into town. And the same thing happens, the driver doesn't know where it is, so again we get out and walk. En route I buy ten cigarettes and a lighter. Just an old tradition as I don't smoke at all but just here somehow. Anyway, we get a bit lost so we hire a passing rickshaw. They are really two-seaters but our driver has no problem with three up front and with me smoking too.

At what I really thought was our restaurant I shouted for the driver to stop and we dropped quickly into a courtyard and stopped so quickly that Marguerite fell out head first. I spring out to help but fall on my head too and quite a height to fall too. Waiters rush out of the restaurant with cloths as I've cut my nose and eyebrow, which are bleeding. Marguerite has grazed her knees and arm, so we made quite an entrance. Other diners just stare at us but we're here now. Only we aren't. This isn't the Third Eye restaurant. It's actually the restaurant next door. I'm now sitting here with more injuries than I've encountered on the entire expedition. Mags tried to call her pals to no effect. Then Marguerite gets a text from Karen to say John is too ill to come out but it was sent two hours ago. We decide to stay put. Anyway, the meal was great and we laughed all night but got a taxi back. Ach, a blow-out was inevitable after all we had done. We have a couple of gin and tonics back at the hotel. I have never seen Marguerite drinking gin before and she didn't remember it the next day.

Thursday 14th May – Kathmandu – Nepal.

The first things I see out of the window are two big, light brown monkeys in the next garden area. We all have a late breakfast taken outside in the colourful gardens. It's a huge buffet with an amazing selection of food and drink, some traditional, some western. A constant supply of tea as well. Today is to be our shopping day. I know my way about Thamel quite well and have walked from the hotel before although it's quite far. It's a lovely sunny morning. Soon, we are really lost. So lost we have to get a taxi to take us back the way we came and into Thamel. We ended up in some strange places where there were no tourists but I've always felt safer in the backstreets of Kathmandu than Glasgow.

So, lots of haggling but lots of bargains too. Although Marguerite thinks I don't haggle enough. She's really hard on some really poor people for a few rupees, but that's Carnwath for you. The next decision is lunch but an easy one. We have to take Mags to the most famous bar in Kathmandu, The Rum Doodle - named after the book about the spoof expedition to Rum Doodle, the highest mountain known at forty nine and a half thousand feet and a very funny book. And although I have been here three times before I can't find it today. In desperation we stop an old, white-haired rickshaw driver to ask where it is. He says "I know. I know" and signals for us to get on board. At some point he can hardly pedal the thing and has to get off to push us. As we passed western looking people I'm sure they had disgust in their faces seeing three well fed, suntanned, healthy white people making this old guy struggle. Quite embarrassing, but at least we didn't fall off!

All embarrassment fades as we have the first sip of chilled Cobra beer on the balcony of Rum Doodle. We all have spicy chicken and naan breads and side dishes too. It's really good here just chilling out, telling each other stories from our treks and a lot better than two weeks in a tent in the snow and wind. Tonight the hotel has a big buffet dinner in the grounds. Marguerite and I were at it three years ago, Live music too of a sort but very atmospheric with flares and candles providing some of the lighting. We get a good table next to the lawn but on the restaurant patio and our own candles. When the band starts up, they are really good, not like last time. There must be twenty chefs running about getting gas burners turned up and loads of food being brought out and lots of salad stuff and vegetables too. All the chefs have tables in the middle of the huge lawn and have electric lighting. Soon we are asked to come over to choose. At some tables you pick your raw meat and it's cooked in front of you. You then add your sauce, vegetables and salad. The food is excellent and we have some beers to wash it down.

At one point, both girls are away for more food when something catches my eye. Just behind Marguerite's seat is a drainage hole in the block paving. I saw some movement so I watched carefully and out of the drainage hole popped up a really big rat. He has a look at me and goes back in, then out again and has a wee wander for a few feet then back down the hole. He must know it's barbeque night! I mention it to Mags, who says don't tell Marguerite. But I do the next day. I was so tempted to say 'it's behind you'!

Friday 15th May – Kathmandu – Nepal.

We all have breakfast together but today Mags and I will spend some time on our own and I want to take her to Durbar Square, the oldest part of Kathmandu. Again, we get a taxi from reception and this time the driver knows where it is. You have to pay a few rupees to get a ticket to enter the area and we walk about all morning, lots of photographs and some really interesting sights. We decide to walk back into Thamel and don't get lost. Some more shopping and then a taxi back to the hotel for lunch with Marguerite. A bit more sensible this time. Then it's time to think about packing. We get most of it done in the afternoon but our bags are a bit over the limit. Marguerite won't come with us for our final dinner despite us both asking and we go back to the Third Eye and make it to the right place and have a nice quiet dinner together and back for an early night.

Saturday 16th May – Kathmandu – Nepal.

We fly out this morning, which is the first time I've flown out from here in the daylight. Usually the flights back to the UK are in the evening. We have pre-booked seats together with Qatar Airways and I've flown with them before and they're good. We will have a thirty-minute changeover in Doha and then onto Heathrow, arriving late afternoon UK time. That's also very tight for us. From there a BM flight up to Glasgow where Rickie will pick us up. Again, a short flight change-over time. Mixed feelings about it all ending but good to get home too. Now, Kathmandu security is a bit weird. You go through the normal X-ray stuff after check-in then another X-ray before boarding where all hand luggage is inspected. But this only happens when your flight is called. So instead of heading to the gate, everyone has to queue at security again, which sometimes delays flights. We have, of course, used all our left-over Nepalese money to buy beer but there is little else to buy in the duty free. Soon though, our flight is called. There are separate queues for men and women. As there are more men, my queue is huge and I can see both girls away up-front. To make matters worse, there are two queues for women, one for men.

When you get past the X-ray machine you have to empty your rucksack. I've never had a problem here as the security guy asks, "first visit to Nepal'?" And I say that it's my fourth time. "You like our country?" He smiles all the time and I say I like Nepal very much which of course he likes. By this time, he's already putting the things back into the rucksack he's taken out and you're waved on. And this time too and I'm actually through before the girls. Mags is not far behind me. But suddenly there is no sign of Marguerite at all. She's not in the queue and not beside us either. Mags went to look and ask someone but it's all a mystery. The final call for our flight is given and we can only assume she's gone ahead of us so we head to boarding. This is a bit worrying. At the door of the plane Marguerite appears from another door. What happened was that she put all her climbing gear such as harness and karabiners and ascender into her rucksack and that triggered the scanner. The security guy had said her slings and karabiners had to go into the hold, put them in a tray and marched her downstairs, onto the runway, up to the cargo hold and said they had to stay here, and then took her up steps to the plane to meet us. She never saw them again.

So, with all the ridiculous security stuff we end up leaving fifteen minutes late - not like Qatar at all, who are very punctual. This might be a problem for us but the crew say Qatar will delay the Heathrow Airbus at Doha for us, which is amazing. A bit more relaxed, we all enjoy the food and wine. The reality at Doha is quite different as we are rushed through the terminal. The delay affects about thirty people and we are actually running until we meet another X-ray machine but soon we are on the plane and we have pre-booked seats together again. A longer haul this time and we try to get some sleep after another good meal - in fact the same meal as the last flight and some wine too of course. We get into Heathrow bang on time and it's a smooth flight all the way. The theory is that British Midland, as a code-share partner of Qatar we will get our hold luggage transferred up to Glasgow so we get the bus from Terminal Three round to Terminal One, which is strangely empty. Then we remember about the ash cloud. This is brought home to us at security where the guy in front of us is told there are no flights to Dublin tonight and to get a hotel. We are OK and get through. But our worries aren't over as BM has no record of luggage coming from Qatar. And there seems to be a problem with our flights. And, of course, that is the flight that is now showing 'boarding now' on the screen above.

All this bloody way to have this hassle, but now we are on

268

the flight. That's not to say our bags are of course but that can be tomorrow's problem. Right now, we just want to get home. We have a last celebratory glass of wine on board and talk about how weird the time differences are. We left Kathmandu at 9:00am their time and we are now landing at Glasgow at 9:00pm our time. However, the reality is it's still fourteen hours flying time. Reassuringly, it's raining as we land in Glasgow. Something I've not seen really in five weeks. Our bags are all there after all but no sign of Marguerite's climbing stuff. The hassle of claiming insurance for that would last for many weeks and she eventually just gave up. So Rickie drove us home to Lanark and this will be the first night in almost a month and a half I will be in my own bed, in my own house. And it feels good. We read later that Mungo's expedition only put one guy on the North Col and conditions were too severe to attempt Lhakpa Ri due to "unusually crevassed and icy conditions".

Reunited with Mags in Kathmandu

Epilogue

The end of this expedition is like the end of them all or an important friendship or relationship or even retiring from work. You always have the sensations of loss, disappointment, frustration, emptiness and self-questioning, even feelings of selfishness. But life would be a pretty dismal affair if we only measured it by its good times and success but no one plans to fail either. For me, the North Col was a necessary dream. I wanted to be on Everest in my 60th year and I did that. But I am glad too that I didn't want to go back and climb Everest itself, which surprised me. This journey wasn't just about the highest mountain, the highest I've ever been, or the highest train journey in the world, or highest tunnel or the steepest road descent in the world. It wasn't about any one thing. And like the ending of any relationship, or a film or a book, there is re-consideration of everything that's gone before. Before we left, getting to the top of the North Col and Lhakpa Ri was the whole point of being there. Now all these expeditions are over, everything is somehow re-distributed through the whole length of the adventure. It's a feeling realising what an adventure it all was and an appreciation of what happened along the way - and lots did happen along the way. The value of all these adventures is, to me, no longer dwelling on summits but is spread throughout the amazing times and experiences we all had. And it stretches back through previous times in Nepal but also of course, The North Col, Tibet, The Train, China and all the way back to planning this back at home in Lanark. In fact, right back to the original planning for the first trip to the Himalayas. I have said it before but I don't plan to return to the Himalayas, unless there was a big temptation - like an unclimbed mountain. But that's another story…

Don't forget to check out my website for more information:

www.jim-wilson.com

Published by
www.publishandprint.co.uk